Theory Test
for car drivers

All the official DSA Questions and Answers explained for learners

Valid for tests taken from 1st September 2008

Published by BSM in association
with Virgin Books

New edition published in the UK in 2008 by
The British School of Motoring Ltd
8 Surrey Street
Norwich
Norfolk NR1 3NG

ISBN: 978-0-7535-1680-5

Designed by Thalamus Publishing

Printed in Italy

In the quote on the back cover: *A pass every two minutes is calculated using 2007 pass statistics and standard test centre opening hours.

Contents

About BSM

BSM has been in the business of teaching people to drive for nearly a hundred years.

In that time we have acquired a great deal of knowledge and experience about driving, which we'd like to share with you to help you pass your driving and theory tests.

This book has been put together with the aim of making it easier for you to learn what you need to know about the theory test at your own pace, whenever it suits you, so that you can sit the test confidently.

If you like the sound of that, you'll probably like the way we go about teaching people to drive. We have over 3,000 highly trained driving instructors around the country who are ready and waiting to teach you to drive. We'll help you find one close to where you live. So, why not join the millions of others in the UK who have learned to drive with Britain's largest driving school?

Call us today on 08457 276 276
or visit www.bsm.co.uk.

Introduction

This book has been designed specifically for people like you who want to pass the Driving Theory Test. It contains highly valuable information that will help you learn the rules of the road and importantly how to pass the theory test.

On the following pages you will find:

- All the official questions in the theory test as set by the Driving Standards Agency (DSA)

- The correct answers to all these questions with full explanations of the reasons behind the answers

- Useful tips to help you with your study

- Hints to help you remember the right answers

- Plus, a FREE Hazard Perception CD-ROM – a valuable tool to help you get to grips with identifying and understanding road hazards and how to deal with them.

This book together with the CD-ROM provides you with everything you need to be fully prepared for both sections of your theory test.

The sooner you pass your theory test, the sooner you can progress to your practical test. So, get motoring through the pages of this book now and you'll be well on your way to becoming a qualified driver.

Learn to drive successfully – the ten essential stages

The steps are listed in an order that you might choose to follow, especially if you want to get through everything as quickly as possible.

Most people tend to study their theory alongside their practical lessons as it makes the subject matter all the more real. What's important is that you know the requirements of each step and progress in a way that suits your needs.

The ten steps are:
1 Applying for a licence
2 Studying for the theory test
3 Applying for the theory test
4 Taking the theory test
5 Passing the theory test
6 Learning to drive
7 Applying for the test
8 Taking the test
9 Passing the test
10 Post-test training

This book concentrates on the first five stages but on the following pages we give you a brief overview of what's involved in all ten. We also include what you need to do and provide you with some tips to make sure everything runs smoothly as you learn to drive.

1 – Applying for a licence

You must have a provisional driving licence (issued by the Driver and Vehicle Licensing Agency (DVLA)) before you can apply to take your theory test and start learning to drive. So, it's very important that you organise this well in advance of when you plan to start. You can download an application form online from the DVLA's web site at www.dvla.gov.uk or you can pick up a form from a Post Office.

Your eyesight has to be good enough to drive on the road. Your provisional licence application form requires that you must be

5

You can begin learning what you need to ow even before getting your provisional iving licence.

able to read a standard registration plate from a minimum distance of 20.5 metres – that's about 67 feet. This will be checked by the DSA examiner at the start of your test.

When you send in your application you'll need to attach a passport-style photo of yourself for identification purposes, so make sure you get an up-to-date one done. Remember you can't drive until you've received your licence.

2 – Studying for the theory test

You don't have to wait for your provisional driving licence to arrive before you start learning what you need to know for the theory test. Many people start this before they are 17 to get ahead of the game.

There are a variety of ways of studying for the test. Experience tells us that it's best to use a combination of learning methods to give yourself the best chance of passing first time.

Let's take a look of what options are available to you.

This book

There are a number of ways you can use this book to help you learn about the theory of driving. For instance, you can:

- Read and understand the questions, answers and explanations given. Then you can test yourself. You can do this by covering the answers when reading the questions back and try to answer them correctly. You can then reveal the answers to see if you were right. If there are any questions that you can't answer, or aren't completely sure about, remember to check the explanations as these will tell you why the answers are what they are.

- Get a friend, a brother or sister or one of your parents to help you by asking you

■ Get friends or family to test your knowledge of the questions in the book.

questions from the book. Set yourself a target to be asked a certain number of questions and to aim to answer a specific number.

• Set yourself mock tests. Pick 50 questions – 3 or 4 from each section (there are 14 sections in the book) and answer them under test conditions. In the real test you'll need to answer 43 of them correctly to pass the test so you should work to this target.

• And don't forget to use your FREE Hazard Perception CD-ROM to make sure that you are fully prepared for both parts of your test.

Tips

Most people find it easier to study in short bursts. Be realistic. Don't over-burden yourself with unachievable goals. Study little and often.

Find a quiet place where you will be uninterrupted. Tell people what you are doing so that they don't disturb you.

Interactive learning

As well as this book you may find it helpful to use an interactive learning tool. BSM has a number of these available to you:

CD-ROM

This is a completely interactive Theory Test study aid that runs on a Windows-compatible PC. It contains all of the official DSA questions and answers and also includes our Hazard Perception training package.

Online study

If you prefer to log on to study then we have the perfect place for you to go. At BSM's web site – www.bsm.co.uk – we have an online

7

interactive version of the DSA Driving Theory test, which, like this book contains all of the official DSA questions, answers and explanations. It also includes hazard perception training with a tutorial and interactive exercises.

You can purchase all of BSM's Theory Test products at www.bsm.co.uk.

3 – Booking a theory test

You'll need to take your theory test at a DSA test centre. There are over 150 centres in England, Scotland and Wales. You can stipulate which centres you'd prefer to go to.

When you feel you are ready to take the theory test, if you are learning to drive with BSM, you

■ Find a quiet place to study where you will be uninterrupted. Tell people what you are doing so that they don't disturb you.

can pop into your local BSM centre to arrange it or book it with them over the phone. A booking fee will apply.

Alternatively, if you're not learning with BSM, you can call the DSA direct on 0870 0101 372 to book, or go online at www.direct.gov.uk/motoring.

Before you can actually book a theory test you'll have to have received a photo card licence and paper counterpart, or, your provisional driving licence. You'll need to take these with you when you sit your test together with some other form of photo identification and your appointment letter.

Important: If you have special needs, please tell the test centre at the time of your booking as you may well be able to get extra time to complete the multiple choice section of the theory test.

■ You can go online as well...

4 – Taking the theory test

Registering for your test
When you arrive at the test centre to take your theory test you will be asked for your documents, so make sure you have them ready the day before. A member of the test centre staff will then register you for the test. You will be provided with a locker and key. This is a safe place for you to put away any personal possessions that you have with you, such as a bag or mobile phone. At the appointed time that has been booked for you, you will be taken to a touch-screen computer in the test centre where you will take your test.

Tips
Once you know the date of your test, do a 'reccy' to find out exactly where the test centre is so you know how long it'll take you to get there. Make sure you do get there in good time on the day because if you are late you might miss your slot and have to rearrange another date.

If you take someone with you, they will have to wait outside while you take your test.

The documents you'll need to show the test centre staff so that you can sit the theory test are:

• the test appointment letter

• your signed photo card licence and paper counterpart; or

• your signed driving licence and valid passport (your passport does not have to be British). No other identification is acceptable.

Important: All these documents must be originals. The test centre will not accept photocopies. If you don't have all your documents with you your test will be cancelled and you will lose your fee.

The test itself
There are two sections to the test:

• The multiple choice theory test

• The hazard perception test.

Each section has a separate pass mark. You need to pass both sections in the same test in order to pass the overall theory test.

Multiple choice questions
You will be asked 50 multiple choice questions and allowed a maximum of 57 minutes to answer them. The questions appear on a computer touch-screen. You simply select the answer for each question by touching the

screen. You need to answer at least 43 correctly in order to pass the multiple choice section of the theory test.

Most of the questions in the test require you to select one correct answer from four possible options. On occasions, you may be asked for two or more correct answers from a selection of between four and six options. If this is the case, it will be stated clearly next to the question.

Important: Extra time can be provided if you have special needs, but you need to notify the test centre at the time you booked your test.

Tips

Read the questions carefully. When reading multiple choice questions, avoid 'recognising' the question or the answer as this often stops you from reading the whole question which can, in turn, lead to mistakes being made. You should read the question carefully all the way through, together with each choice of answer.

If you have no idea what the correct answer is, you should at least have a guess. You can always pass over a question if you're unsure of the correct answer, and 'flag' it so that you can return to it later when you have had time to think about it.

■ Turn up in good time and make sure you have all the correct documentation ready.

Example test questions

The following four examples provide you with some hints on how you should approach each question and the possible answers. Some of the points made may seem obvious, but many people have got questions wrong by making basic mistakes such as these.

Example 1

Which FOUR of these MUST be in good working order for your car to be roadworthy?

- ❑ Speedometer
- ❑ Oil warning light
- ❑ Windscreen washers
- ❑ Temperature gauge
- ❑ Horn
- ❑ Windscreen wipers

Hint

Here you are being asked to identify the legal requirements, which MUST be adhered to. MUST is the key word.

You are also being asked to identify FOUR correct answers so if you only mark one, two or three answers, you will not score a point for this question.

If you do only select one answer initially, don't worry. The test programme software will remind you that more answers are required.

The correct answers to this question are 'Speedometer', 'Windscreen washers', 'Horn' and Windscreen wipers'.

■ It's easy when you know all the answers...

Example 2

When should you NOT use your horn in a built-up area?

- ❑ Between 8pm and 8am
- ❑ Between 11.30pm and 7am
- ❑ Between 9pm and dawn
- ❑ Between dusk and 8pm

Hint

The key word here is NOT. If you didn't take enough time to read this question carefully, you might have misread it and answered it incorrectly. Always take your time to read both the question and the answers thoroughly.

The correct answer to this question is 'Between 11.30pm and 7am'.

Example 3

You are driving on an icy road. How can you avoid wheel spin?

- ❑ Drive at a slow speed in as high a gear as possible
- ❑ Use the handbrake if the wheels start to slip
- ❑ Brake gently and repeatedly
- ❑ Drive in a low gear at all times

Hint

In this question, the key word is 'icy'. You need to think about how the condition of the road can affect the performance of the car and select the appropriate answer.

The correct answer to the question is 'Drive at a slow speed in as high a gear as possible'.

Example 4

Where may you overtake on a one-way street?

- ❑ Only on the left-hand side
- ❑ Overtaking is not allowed
- ❑ Only on the right-hand side
- ❑ Either on the right or the left

Hint

The key phrase here is 'one-way street'. You need to be aware of the special rules that apply to one-way streets that are different to two-way streets to be able to answer this question correctly. There will be times when you are driving, when you will need to use this knowledge.

The correct answer to this question is 'Either on the right or the left' whereas on a two-way street the correct answer would be 'Only on the right-hand side'.

Tip

When you actually sit the test you will have plenty of time to read the questions thoroughly. Make sure you understand what is being asked. Don't rush or panic. Think carefully about each option before selecting your answer.

Hazard perception

Once you have completed the multiple choice section of the test you can take a break of up to three minutes before starting the second part of the test – the hazard perception test. The aim of this section is to test your hazard perception awareness skills.

You'll be shown 14 video clips of 'real-life' road situations as though you were driving. You're required to identify developing hazards which may require you, the driver, to take some form of action, such as changing speed or direction. This section lasts about 20 minutes.

It's important to be aware that:

- No extra time is allowed.

- You cannot replay any of the clips, nor are you allowed a second chance to see a developing hazard.

- You have to click on the mouse as soon as you see a potential hazard developing.

- The earlier you spot a hazard developing and click the mouse the higher the marks you'll earn.

- You can score up to five marks for each hazard.

- One clip contains two developing hazards.

- The test contains a total of 15 developing hazards.

- To pass this part of the test, you need to score 44 out of a possible 75.

Remember, you need to pass the hazard perception section in the same test that you pass the multiple choice section, to pass the theory test overall. If you fail one of the sections you'll need to take the whole theory test again.

Tip
Use your FREE Hazard Perception CD-ROM to fully prepare for your test.

Preferred language
If you are not a fluent English speaker, you may listen to the test questions through a headset in one of twenty languages. In alphabetical order these are:

Albanian	Arabic	Bengali	Cantonese
Dari	Farsi	Gujarati	Hindi
Kasmiri	Kurdish	Mirpuri	Polish
Portuguese	Punjabi	Pushto	Spanish
Tamil	Turkish	Urdu	Welsh.

Theory test centres in Wales and on the Welsh border can also provide the test in Welsh text on the screen.

Translation
You may also take your test in languages other than those listed above with the aid of a translator. Your translator must be approved by the DSA and you will have to pay the costs

for the translator's assistance. Any other special needs must be booked well in advance with your test centre.

Tests with translators can only be taken at test centres in:

Aldershot	Birkenhead	Birmingham
Cardiff	Derby	Edinburgh
Glasgow	Ipswich	Leeds
Milton Keynes	Preston	Southgate

5 – Passing the theory test

If everything has gone to plan, you'll only need to wait ten minutes or so, to find out whether you've passed. If you have passed, you'll be given a certificate that is valid for two years. This means that you have to pass the driving test within the next two years otherwise you'll have to re-take and pass the theory test all over again.

If you have failed either or both sections of the test, you'll need to re-apply for, and re-take the test. Please note you cannot re-take the test within three working days.

Tip
If you fail, it is important to understand where you went wrong. Don't do it there and then. Take the information home with you and when you are ready, study the information supplied and work out where you need to improve. Next, draw up a study plan that will concentrate on the areas that need improvement.

If you have difficulties analysing your results or you would just like some help, you can always talk to a good driving instructor, who will be able to explain the results to you.

6 – Learning to drive

The good thing is you don't have to wait until you have passed your theory test to start learning to drive. In fact, most people find that it really helps to learn the theory while they learn to drive. It means you can put into practice the knowledge you have acquired on the road. Similarly, your experiences of driving will help you to visualise the exercises you'll come across when you learn the theory and take the theory test.

The DSA recommends that 'The best way to learn is by having, regular planned lessons with a good professional instructor, (and) as much practice as possible'*. Anyone who gives driving lessons for payment or reward must be registered with the DSA and they are required to display an Approved Driving Instructor (ADI) identification certificate on the windscreen of the tuition car. The ADI qualification is earned by individuals who have to pass an examination following a programme of intensive training.

With BSM you'll receive expert tuition from one of our 3,000 plus driving instructors. You'll also get great value for money and the opportunity to drive either the latest Vauxhall Corsa or Astra. All you need to do to book your lessons is call us on 08457 276 276 and we'll tell you everything you need to know to get you on the road.

Tip

It's important not to underestimate the amount of driving lessons you'll need to take in order to pass your driving test. To get a good idea of how many you'll need, ask some of your friends or family who have passed their test recently.

* Source: The Official DSA Guide to Driving – the Essential Skills

15

It's a good idea to practise what you have learned by driving with someone like your parents, elder brother or sister or family friend. They need to have passed their test of course, have three years' driving experience and be at least 21 years old. It's also vital for you that you get on well with them and that they are happy about accompanying you. And don't forget, you'll need to have 'L' plates on the car along with adequate insurance!

7 – Applying for the driving test

While you don't need to apply for your test the moment you start driving, it's a good idea to try and plan well ahead. There are times when demand is high for tests and you could find yourself on a waiting list. The best thing to do is to ring the DSA to find out what the situation is. If you are learning to drive with BSM your instructor will be able to advise you about when is the right time to apply for your test. And, if they think you are ready your local BSM Centre will be able to book it for you. Alternatively, you can book it yourself by phone on 0870 0101 372, or online at www.direct.gov.uk/motoring.

Tip
Once you have booked your test, make sure that you plan a series of lessons and practice sessions so that you arrive on the day in the best shape possible. You'll find that having a date booked will provide you with focus and motivation.

If you're learning to drive with BSM, we can arrange for you to take a mock test, which will allow you to practise in test conditions so that you're fully prepared and know what to expect on the day.

If, for whatever reason, you feel under-prepared as your test approaches, don't worry. You can always change the date, as long as you give the DSA relevant notice.

8 – Taking the driving test

Make sure that you have all the essential documents with you when you set off for the test centre. You'll need:

- the test appointment letter

- your signed photo card licence and paper counterpart; or

- your signed driving licence and valid passport (your passport does not have to be British) No other identification is acceptable

- your theory test pass certificate

Important: All these documents must be the originals; the test centre will not accept photocopies.

Be warned! If you don't have all your documents with you, your test will be cancelled. It's a good idea to do a reccy in the weeks leading up to your test of where the test centre is and what the roads around it are like. You'll feel more comfortable knowing how long it'll take you to get there and it'll give you the chance to familiarise yourself with some of the roads you will be driving on in your test. If you're learning to drive with BSM, your instructor will suggest that you do this either as part of a lesson or one of your practice sessions. On the day, get there with plenty of time to spare so that there is no danger of you missing your slot.

Tip
The examiner will make a visual inspection of the vehicle that you're going to take your test in. It must be legally roadworthy and mechanically sound. If it is three or more years old it will need a current MOT test certificate. As well as a valid tax disc, L-plates and working seat belts, there are a number of other additional requirements, including an extra interior rear mirror for the examiner's use and

properly fitted head restraints. When taking your driving lessons and test with a BSM instructor all this will be taken care of for you.

9 – Passing the test

If everything has gone to plan, you'll only have to wait a few minutes for the examiner to give you your test result...and hopefully a pass certificate! If you do fail, don't get too downhearted. You'll feel disappointed but lots of people fail first time. It's important that you listen to the feedback the examiner will give you about why you failed. When you're ready, discuss this with your instructor and work out a plan for improving the areas that you weren't up to scratch on.

Tip

If you feel comfortable with the idea, let your instructor sit in the back of the car on your test. They will be able to provide you with a valuable debrief once your test is over.

10 – Post-test training

Once you have passed your driving test you are legally entitled to drive unaccompanied. But, it's a really good idea to get some help and advice on those driving situations or conditions that were not a mandatory part of the test. Things like motorway driving, night driving or driving in extreme conditions can be daunting the first time you have to do them.

You'll come across a question (number 40 in fact) in section 12 of this book, about the need for post-test training. The explanation states, 'It is strongly recommended that all newly qualified drivers take post-test tuition, to improve on their basic skills and cover gaps in their knowledge or experience, for example motorway driving.'

At BSM, you can get expert coaching and tuition from one of our instructors on a specific skill or set of road conditions. You can do this when it suits you but most people find that it's best to do it soon after they have passed their test. If you think you would like to arrange some post-test training all you need to do is call us on 08457 276 276.

Tip

Most accidents occur within the first few years of a new driver taking to the road. Make sure you reduce the risk of it happening to you by building your driving skills sooner rather than later. It's also great fun!

The question sections

The theory test was developed to satisfy EU regulations. It has a specific syllabus, which covers a wide range of topics relating to road safety. It is split into 14 topics or sections, with a varying number of questions in each section. The following is a list of the fourteen topics covered in the complete DSA question bank.

		Questions
1	Alertness	37
2	Attitude	50
3	Safety and your vehicle	112
4	Safety margins	59
5	Hazard awareness	96
6	Vulnerable road users	81
7	Other types of vehicle	27
8	Vehicle handling	62
9	Motorway rules	67
10	Rules of the road	75
11	Road and traffic signs	156
12	Documents	47
13	Accidents	79
14	Vehicle loading	15

At this point, with over 950 questions ahead of you, it may seem a little daunting, but don't worry. You already know – or partly know – the answers to a lot of the questions you will be asked and many others concern sound

■ Despite all the questions, it's not really as daunting as you might think...

judgement. Some questions may appear to be repeated but no two questions are exactly the same so make sure you read each question thoroughly.

We have included all the questions, all the answers and all the explanations, regardless of how easy or complex the question is, so that you can leave no stone unturned in your quest for knowledge and test success.

You must work out the best way to study. Be realistic, don't set unachievable goals; try different methods of study, take regular breaks and give yourself a small reward every time you reach a goal.

Good luck!

Section 1
Alertness

There are 37 questions in this section, covering the following subjects:

- ❑ Observation
- ❑ Anticipation
- ❑ Concentration
- ❑ Awareness
- ❑ Distraction
- ❑ Boredom

You will need to think about:

- ❑ How you see
- ❑ How you interpret what you see
- ❑ What to expect
- ❑ How easy it is to become distracted for a variety of reasons while driving.

Tip

A large number of questions in this section just require you to think 'What would be the safest thing to do?' If you're not sure of the answer, it might help by asking yourself this question.

mark one answer

Before you make a U-turn in the road, you should

☐ give an arm signal as well as using your indicators
☐ signal so that other drivers can slow down for you
☐ look over your shoulder for a final check
☐ select a higher gear than normal

☐ **look over your shoulder for a final check**

You should always check your blind spot just before moving off or starting a manoeuvre.

mark three answers

As you approach this bridge you should

☐ Move into the middle of the road to get a better view
☐ slow down
☐ get over the bridge as quickly as possible
☐ consider using your horn
☐ find another route
☐ beware of pedestrians

☐ **slow down**

☐ **consider using your horn**

☐ **beware of pedestrians**

All these actions will enable you to deal with the hazard in the safest way possible.

mark one answer

In which of these situations should you avoid overtaking?

☐ Just after a bend
☐ In a one-way street
☐ On a 30 mph road
☐ Approaching a dip in the road

☐ **Approaching a dip in the road**

The dip in the road may hide an approaching vehicle.

1.4   mark **one** answer

This road marking warns

❑ drivers to use the hard shoulder
❑ overtaking drivers there is a bend to the left
❑ overtaking drivers to move back to the left
❑ drivers that it is safe to overtake

❑ **overtaking drivers to move back to the left**

To begin overtaking where you see this 'throw back' road marking would be unsafe.

1.5   mark **one** answer

Your mobile phone rings while you are travelling. You should

❑ stop immediately
❑ answer it immediately
❑ pull up in a suitable place
❑ pull up at the nearest kerb

❑ **pull up in a suitable place**

Answering a hands-free mobile phone while driving might distract your attention. You should pull up first in a safe and convenient place.

1.6   mark **one** answer

Why are these yellow lines painted across the road?

❑ To help you choose the correct lane
❑ To help you keep the correct separation distance
❑ To make you aware of your speed
❑ To tell you the distance to the roundabout

❑ **To make you aware of your speed**

The spacing between these yellow lines increases a driver's perception of road speed.

mark one answer

You are approaching traffic lights that have been on green for some time. You should

❑ accelerate hard
❑ maintain your speed
❑ be ready to stop
❑ brake hard

❑ **be ready to stop**

Be ready to stop because the traffic lights may change colour before you pass them.

mark one answer

Which of the following should you do before stopping?

❑ Sound the horn
❑ Use the mirrors
❑ Select a higher gear
❑ Flash your headlights

❑ **Use the mirrors**

You need to know what is behind you, before you slow down or stop. If something is close behind you might choose to show your brake lights earlier and slow down over a longer period.

mark one answer

When following a large vehicle you should keep well back because this

❑ allows you to corner more quickly
❑ helps the large vehicle to stop more easily
❑ allows the driver to see you in the mirrors
❑ helps you to keep out of the wind

❑ **allows the driver to see you in the mirrors**

If you can see the driver's mirrors then they can see you, and therefore know that you are there.

mark one answer

When you see a hazard ahead you should use the mirrors. Why is this?

❑ Because you will need to accelerate out of danger
❑ To assess how your actions will affect following traffic
❑ Because you will need to brake sharply to a stop
❑ To check what is happening on the road ahead

❑ **To assess how your actions will affect following traffic**

The hazard might make you slow down or stop. You need to know what is behind you, before you slow down or stop. If something is close behind you might choose to show your brake lights earlier to warn any following drivers of the hazard ahead.

1.11   mark **one** answer

You are waiting to turn right at the end of a road. Your view is obstructed by parked vehicles. What should you do?

❏ Stop and then move forward slowly and carefully for a proper view
❏ Move quickly to where you can see so you only block traffic from one direction
❏ Wait for a pedestrian to let you know when it is safe for you to emerge
❏ Turn your vehicle around immediately and find another junction to use

❏ **Stop and then move forward slowly and carefully for a proper view**

Use clutch control to edge the car forwards until you can see clearly. Keeping your speed right down will prevent you from being involved in a collision with any traffic you cannot see.

1.12   mark **two** answers

Objects hanging from your interior mirror may

❏ restrict your view
❏ improve your driving
❏ distract your attention
❏ help your concentration

❏ **restrict your view**

❏ **distract your attention**

Either of these increases the risk of you being involved in a collision.

1.13   mark **four** answers

Which of the following may cause loss of concentration on a long journey?

❏ Loud music
❏ Arguing with a passenger
❏ Using a mobile phone
❏ Putting in a cassette tape
❏ Stopping regularly to rest
❏ Pulling up to tune the radio

❏ **Loud music**

❏ **Arguing with a passenger**

❏ **Using a mobile phone**

❏ **Putting in a cassette tape**

Driving requires your full attention. It can be easy to lose concentration on a long journey. You need to avoid anything that can cause your concentration to lapse while driving.

mark two answers

On a long motorway journey boredom can cause you to feel sleepy. You should

- leave the motorway and find a safe place to stop
- keep looking around at the surrounding landscape
- drive faster to complete your journey sooner
- ensure a supply of fresh air into your vehicle
- stop on the hard shoulder for a rest

- **leave the motorway and find a safe place to stop**
- **ensure a supply of fresh air into your vehicle**

Falling asleep at the wheel is a significant cause of motorway collisions. Never drive while sleepy; if you become sleepy between exits, opening a window will lower the temperature and increase the fresh air in the car, which will help to keep you awake for a short while.

mark two answers

You are driving at dusk. You should switch your lights on

- even when street lights are not lit
- so others can see you
- only when others have done so
- only when street lights are lit

- **even when street lights are not lit**
- **so others can see you**

See and be seen. As soon as you think it might be time to switch your lights on, do so.

mark two answers

You are most likely to lose concentration when driving if you

- use a mobile phone
- listen to very loud music
- switch on the heated rear window
- look at the door mirrors

- **use a mobile phone**
- **listen to very loud music**

Distractions which cause you to remove either of your hands off the steering wheel or take your eyes off the road are potentially dangerous. The law requires that you must retain full control of your vehicle at all times.

1.17   mark **four** answers

Which FOUR are most likely to cause you to lose concentration while you are driving?

❑ Using a mobile phone
❑ Talking into a microphone
❑ Tuning your car radio
❑ Looking at a map
❑ Checking the mirrors
❑ Using the demisters

❑ **Using a mobile phone**

❑ **Talking into a microphone**

❑ **Tuning your car radio**

❑ **Looking at a map**

Driving requires your full attention. It can be easy to lose concentration while driving. You should avoid anything that can cause your concentration to lapse while driving.

1.18   mark **one** answer

You should ONLY use a mobile phone when

❑ receiving a call
❑ suitably parked
❑ driving at less than 30 mph
❑ driving an automatic vehicle

❑ **suitably parked**

Even using a hands-free mobile phone will take some of your attention away from driving; the correct option is to park in a safe and convenient place.

1.19   mark **one** answer

You are driving on a wet road. You have to stop your vehicle in an emergency. You should

❑ apply the handbrake and footbrake together
❑ keep both hands on the wheel
❑ select reverse gear
❑ give an arm signal

❑ **keep both hands on the wheel**

This helps you maintain control of your car.

When you are moving off from behind a parked car you should

- ❏ look round before you move off
- ❏ use all the mirrors on the vehicle
- ❏ look round after moving off
- ❏ use the exterior mirrors only
- ❏ give a signal if necessary
- ❏ give a signal after moving off

❏ **look round before you move off**

❏ **use all the mirrors on the vehicle**

❏ **give a signal if necessary**

Before moving off from any position, you need to know if it is safe to do so by looking around and in all the mirrors. Then signal if necessary to warn other road users of your intentions.

You are travelling along this narrow country road. When passing the cyclist you should go

- ❏ slowly, sounding the horn as you pass
- ❏ quickly, leaving plenty of room
- ❏ slowly, leaving plenty of room
- ❏ quickly, sounding the horn as you pass

❏ **slowly, leaving plenty of room**

Because by doing so you will give time and space for the cyclist should they wobble as you pass.

Your vehicle is fitted with a hand-held telephone. To use the telephone you should

- ❏ reduce your speed
- ❏ find a safe place to stop
- ❏ steer the vehicle with one hand
- ❏ be particularly careful at junctions

❏ **find a safe place to stop**

You must not use a hand-held telephone while you are driving.

1.23   mark **one** answer

To answer a call on your mobile phone while travelling you should

❑ reduce your speed wherever you are
❑ stop in a proper and convenient place
❑ keep the call time to a minimum
❑ slow down and allow others to overtake

❑ **stop in a proper and convenient place**

If it's a hand-held phone you must pull up before answering. If it's hands-free it is still advisable to stop.

1.24   mark **one** answer

You lose your way on a busy road. What is the best action to take?

❑ Stop at traffic lights and ask pedestrians
❑ Shout to other drivers to ask them the way
❑ Turn into a side road, stop and check a map
❑ Check a map, and keep going with the traffic flow

❑ **Turn into a side road, stop and check a map**

Because the road is busy it would be better to turn off the main road before stopping to check the map.

1.25   mark **one** answer

Windscreen pillars can obstruct your view. You should take particular care when

❑ driving on a motorway
❑ driving on a dual carriageway
❑ approaching a one-way street
❑ approaching bends and junctions

❑ **approaching bends and junctions**

The pillars can obstruct your view of a cyclist or motorcyclist. Move your head to get the full picture.

1.26   mark **one** answer

You cannot see clearly behind when reversing. What should you do?

❑ Open your window to look behind
❑ Open the door and look behind
❑ Look in the nearside mirror
❑ Ask someone to guide you

❑ **Ask someone to guide you**

If you cannot see properly, you need to get someone to help.

1.27   mark **one** answer

What does the term 'blind spot' mean for a driver?

❏ An area covered by your right-hand mirror
❏ An area not covered by your headlights
❏ An area covered by your left-hand mirror
❏ An area not covered by your mirrors

❏ **An area not covered by your mirrors**

There is a gap between your peripheral vision – between your immediate right and the start of the view in the side door mirrors. These blindspots could easily hide other road users.

1.28   mark **one** answer

Your vehicle is fitted with a hands-free phone system. Using this equipment whilst driving

❏ is quite safe as long as you slow down
❏ could distract your attention from the road
❏ is recommended by The Highway Code
❏ could be very good for road safety

❏ **could distract your attention from the road**

Even using a hands-free mobile phone will take some of your attention away from driving. Be safe and switch your phone off when driving. Collect any messages when you pull up for a break.

1.29   mark **one** answer

Using a hands-free phone is likely to

❏ improve your safety
❏ increase your concentration
❏ reduce your view
❏ divert your attention

❏ **divert your attention**

You are not allowed to use a hand-held mobile phone while driving. Even a hands-free system can distract your attention from the road.

1.30   mark **one** answer

What is the safest way to use a mobile phone in your vehicle?

❏ Use hands-free equipment
❏ Find a suitable place to stop
❏ Drive slowly on a quiet road
❏ Direct your call through the operator

❏ **Find a suitable place to stop**

Where using a mobile phone causes careless or dangerous driving, drivers are liable for prosecution. The penalties include an unlimited fine, possible disqualification and imprisonment.

1.31   mark **one** answer

Your mobile phone rings while you are on the motorway. Before answering you should

❏ reduce your speed to 30 mph
❏ pull up on the hard shoulder
❏ move into the left-hand lane
❏ stop in a safe place

❏ **stop in a safe place**

Even using a hands-free mobile phone will take some of your attention away from driving, a task which requires your full attention.

1.32   mark **one** answer

You are turning right onto a dual carriageway. What should you do before emerging?

❏ Stop, apply the handbrake and then select a low gear
❏ Position your vehicle well to the left of the side road
❏ Check that the central reservation is wide enough for your vehicle
❏ Make sure that you leave enough room for a vehicle behind

❏ **Check that the central reservation is wide enough for your vehicle**

This is because if there is no traffic coming from the right, but there is traffic coming from the left, you may wait in the central reservation provided that it's wide enough for your vehicle.

1.33   mark **one** answer

You are waiting to emerge from a junction. The windscreen pillar is restricting your view. What should you be particularly aware of?

❏ Lorries
❏ Buses
❏ Motorcyclists
❏ Coaches

❏ **Motorcyclists**

This is because they are small enough to be hidden by the pillar.

When emerging from junctions, which is most likely to obstruct your view?

❑ Windscreen pillars
❑ Steering wheel
❑ Interior mirror
❑ Windscreen wipers

❑ **Windscreen pillars**

The pillars could obstruct your view of a cyclist or motorcyclist. Move your head to get the full picture.

Your vehicle is fitted with a navigation system. How should you avoid letting this distract you while driving?

❑ Keep going and input your destination into the system
❑ Keep going as the system will adjust to your route
❑ Stop immediately to view and use the system
❑ Stop in a safe place before using the system

❑ **Stop in a safe place before using the system**

Driving requires your full attention. Road and traffic conditions can change quickly, so you will need to pull up in a safe and convenient place before using or adjusting your navigation system.

You are driving on a motorway and want to use your mobile phone. What should you do?

❑ Try to find a safe place on the hard shoulder
❑ Leave the motorway and stop in a safe place
❑ Use the next exit and pull up on the slip road
❑ Move to the left lane and reduce your speed

❑ **Leave the motorway and stop in a safe place**

If you need to use the mobile phone, leave the motorway and find a suitable place to stop. Use your voicemail to receive calls. Your driving requires your full attention, not the phone.

1.37   mark **one** answer

You must not use a hand-held phone while driving. Using a hands-free system

❏ is acceptable in a vehicle with power steering
❏ will significantly reduce your field of vision
❏ will affect your vehicle's electronic systems
❏ is still likely to distract your attention from the road

❏ **is still likely to distract your attention from the road**

Evidence from research shows that drivers using a hands-free phone kits are not able to concentrate properly on their driving, so the risk of an incident or collision is increased.

Section 2
Attitude

There are 50 questions in this section, covering the following subjects:

- ❑ Consideration
- ❑ Close following
- ❑ Courtesy
- ❑ Priority

You will need to think about:

- ❑ The effect that considerate and courteous driving will have on other drivers

- ❑ Interacting with pedestrians crossing the road

- ❑ Dealing with emergency vehicles, buses, and trams

- ❑ Keeping space around your vehicle.

Tips

There are quite a few questions in this section that can be answered, if you think about being patient or driving patiently: questions about, 'How you would react if...', or 'What you would do in...' a certain situation. Quite often the most 'patient' answer is the correct one.

Some of the questions in this section require you to know facts, like the colour of a beacon on a doctor's car, or the shape of a sign for tram drivers. Sorry, but there is no substitute for simply learning the facts.

mark **one** answer

At a pelican crossing the flashing amber light means you MUST

❏ stop and wait for the green light
❏ stop and wait for the red light
❏ give way to pedestrians waiting to cross
❏ give way to pedestrians already on the crossing

❏ **give way to pedestrians already on the crossing**

The flashing amber light is there to protect any pedestrians who have started to cross. You may move off when the light is green or the crossing is clear.

mark **one** answer

You should never wave people across at pedestrian crossings because

❏ there may be another vehicle coming
❏ they may not be looking
❏ it is safer for you to carry on
❏ they may not be ready to cross

❏ **there may be another vehicle coming**

You decide when and where to stop – the pedestrian decides when and where to cross.

mark **one** answer

'Tailgating' means

❏ using the rear door of a hatchback car
❏ reversing into a parking space
❏ following another vehicle too closely
❏ driving with rear fog lights on

❏ **following another vehicle too closely**

Originally an American term meaning that you're driving too close to the tailgate (boot) of the vehicle in front.

mark **one** answer

You are following a vehicle on a wet road. You should leave a time gap of at least

❏ one second
❏ two seconds
❏ three seconds
❏ four seconds

❏ **four seconds**

In good conditions you should allow two seconds but on a wet road you should double this to four.

2.5 mark **one** answer

Following this vehicle too closely is unwise because

- ❏ your brakes will overheat
- ❏ your view ahead is increased
- ❏ your engine will overheat
- ❏ your view ahead is reduced

❏ **your view ahead is reduced**

If you hang back you will have a much better view of the road ahead. This will help you to see any hazards that might occur and allow you time to react.

2.6 mark **one** answer

A long, heavily-laden lorry is taking a long time to overtake you. What should you do?

- ❏ Speed up
- ❏ Slow down
- ❏ Hold your speed
- ❏ Change direction

❏ **Slow down**

A long lorry with a heavy load will need more time to pass you than a car, especially on an uphill section of road. By slowing down, you allow the lorry to get past, which is the only safe option.

2.7 mark **three** answers

Which of the following vehicles will use blue flashing beacons?

- ❏ Motorway maintenance
- ❏ Bomb disposal
- ❏ Blood transfusion
- ❏ Police patrol
- ❏ Breakdown recovery

❏ **Bomb disposal**

❏ **Blood transfusion**

❏ **Police patrol**

Not only police, fire and ambulance use blue flashing lights. Other emergency vehicles include bomb disposal and the blood transfusion service.

mark three answers

Which THREE of these emergency services might have blue flashing beacons?

❑ Coastguard
❑ Bomb disposal
❑ Gritting lorries
❑ Animal ambulances
❑ Mountain rescue
❑ Doctors' cars

❑ **Coastguard**

❑ **Bomb disposal**

❑ **Mountain rescue**

Blue flashing lights are used by emergency vehicles travelling at speed. Assist their progress by moving over and allowing them to pass. Do not stop suddenly or in a dangerous road position.

mark one answer

When being followed by an ambulance showing a flashing blue beacon you should

❑ pull over as soon as safely possible to let it pass
❑ accelerate hard to get away from it
❑ maintain your speed and course
❑ brake harshly and immediately stop in the road

❑ **pull over as soon as safely possible to let it pass**

Don't just stop straight away. Look for a place where the ambulance can pass safely.

mark one answer

What type of emergency vehicle is fitted with a green flashing beacon?

❑ Fire engine
❑ Road gritter
❑ Ambulance
❑ Doctor's car

❑ **Doctor's car**

Doctors on emergency call may display a flashing green beacon. Slow-moving vehicles have amber flashing beacons. Police, fire and ambulance service vehicles have blue flashing beacons.

mark one answer

A flashing green beacon on a vehicle means

❑ police on non-urgent duties
❑ doctor on an emergency call
❑ road safety patrol operating
❑ gritting in progress

❑ **doctor on an emergency call**

Green flashing lights are for vehicles used by, or carrying, a doctor on an emergency call. Allow the vehicle to pass when you can do so safely.

2.12   mark **one** answer

Diamond-shaped signs give instructions to

- ❑ tram drivers
- ❑ bus drivers
- ❑ lorry drivers
- ❑ taxi drivers

❑ **tram drivers**

Signs are shaped differently to tell us what type of sign it is. Circles give instructions to drivers, triangles warn drivers, rectangles inform drivers, and diamond shaped signs advise tram drivers.

2.13   mark **one** answer

On a road where trams operate, which of these vehicles will be most at risk from the tram rails?

- ❑ Cars
- ❑ Cycles
- ❑ Buses
- ❑ Lorries

❑ **Cycles**

Cyclists are most at risk because their narrow wheels could slip into the rail lines.

2.14   mark **one** answer

What should you use your horn for?

- ❑ To alert others to your presence
- ❑ To allow you right of way
- ❑ To greet other road users
- ❑ To signal your annoyance

❑ **To alert others to your presence**

It is illegal to use the horn for any other purpose than that for which it was designed: 'To alert others of your presence'.

2.15   mark **one** answer

You are in a one-way street and want to turn right. You should position yourself

- ❑ in the right-hand lane
- ❑ in the left-hand lane
- ❑ in either lane, depending on the traffic
- ❑ just left of the centre line

❑ **in the right-hand lane**

Remember you are in a one-way street. So to turn right you would normally position in the right-hand lane.

mark **one** answer

You wish to turn right ahead. Why should you take up the correct position in good time?

❑ To allow other drivers to pull out in front of you
❑ To give a better view into the road that you're joining
❑ To help other road users know what you intend to do
❑ To allow drivers to pass you on the right

❑ **To help other road users know what you intend to do**

The position of your car helps signal your intentions to other road users

---

mark **one** answer

At which type of crossing are cyclists allowed to ride across with pedestrians?

❑ Toucan
❑ Puffin
❑ Pelican
❑ Zebra

❑ **Toucan**

This is the only crossing that cyclists may ride across. There will be a cycle lane as well as a pavement on either side of the road. On all other types of crossing cyclists should dismount before joining pedestrians.

---

mark **one** answer

You are travelling at the legal speed limit. A vehicle comes up quickly behind, flashing its headlights. You should

❑ accelerate to make a gap behind you
❑ touch the brakes sharply to show your brake lights
❑ maintain your speed to prevent the vehicle from overtaking
❑ allow the vehicle to overtake

❑ **allow the vehicle to overtake**

This is your only safe option.

---

mark **one** answer

You should ONLY flash your headlights to other road users

❑ to show that you are giving way
❑ to show that you are about to turn
❑ to tell them that you have right of way
❑ to let them know that you are there

❑ **to let them know that you are there**

This is the only correct and unambiguous meaning of this signal.

2.20   mark **one** answer

You are approaching unmarked crossroads. How should you deal with this type of junction?

❑ Accelerate and keep to the middle
❑ Slow down and keep to the right
❑ Accelerate looking to the left
❑ Slow down and look both ways

❑ **Slow down and look both ways**

Because no one has priority and caution is required.

2.21   mark **one** answer

You are approaching a pelican crossing. The amber light is flashing. You must

❑ give way to pedestrians who are crossing
❑ encourage pedestrians to cross
❑ not move until the green light appears
❑ stop even if the crossing is clear

❑ **give way to pedestrians who are crossing**

You must give way to pedestrians already on the crossing but may proceed if the crossing is clear.

2.22   mark **one** answer

The conditions are good and dry. You could use the 'two-second rule'

❑ before restarting the engine after it has stalled
❑ to keep a safe gap from the vehicle in front
❑ before using the 'Mirror-Signal-Manoeuvre' routine
❑ when emerging on wet roads

❑ **to keep a safe gap from the vehicle in front**

A two-second time gap from the vehicle in front provides a safe gap in good conditions.

2.23   mark **one** answer

At a puffin crossing, which colour follows the green signal?

❑ Steady red
❑ Flashing amber
❑ Steady amber
❑ Flashing green

❑ **Steady amber**

The sequence of lights at a Pelican Crossing beginning with the green signal is – Green – Steady Amber – Red – Red and Amber together – Green; exactly the same as at ordinary traffic lights.

mark one answer

You are in a line of traffic. The driver behind you is following very closely. What action should you take?

❏ Ignore the following driver and continue to travel within the speed limit
❏ Slow down, gradually increasing the gap between you and the vehicle in front
❏ Signal left and wave the following driver past
❏ Move over to a position just left of the centre line of the road

❏ **Slow down, gradually increasing the gap between you and the vehicle in front**

By increasing the gap between you and the vehicle in front, you give yourself and the driver behind more room to stop should you need it.

mark one answer

A vehicle has a flashing green beacon. What does this mean?

❏ A doctor is answering an emergency call
❏ The vehicle is slow-moving
❏ It is a motorway police patrol vehicle
❏ The vehicle is carrying hazardous chemicals

❏ **A doctor is answering an emergency call**

Green flashing lights are for vehicles used by a doctor on an emergency call. Blue flashing lights are used by emergency vehicles. Orange flashing lights are used by large or potentially slow-moving vehicles.

mark one answer

A bus has stopped at a bus stop ahead of you. Its right-hand indicator is flashing. You should

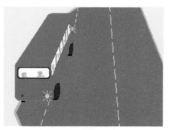

❏ flash your headlights and slow down
❏ slow down and give way if it is safe to do so
❏ sound your horn and keep going
❏ slow down and then sound your horn

❏ **slow down and give way if it is safe to do so**

The Highway Code advises drivers to give priority to buses waiting to pull out from a bus stop. Drivers need to demonstrate courtesy and consideration by giving way to buses where it is safe to do so.

2.27   mark **one** answer

You are driving on a clear night. There is a steady stream of oncoming traffic. The national speed limit applies. Which lights should you use?

❏ Full beam headlights
❏ Sidelights
❏ Dipped headlights
❏ Fog lights

❏ **Dipped headlights**

Only use full beam headlights when you are sure that you won't dazzle others. If you are likely to dazzle, use the dipped beam.

2.28   mark **one** answer

You are driving behind a large goods vehicle. It signals left but steers to the right. You should

❏ slow down and let the vehicle turn
❏ drive on, keeping to the left
❏ overtake on the right of it
❏ hold your speed and sound your horn

❏ **slow down and let the vehicle turn**

The vehicle may do this because, as a large vehicle, it may need to swing out to make the turn. Keep well back and do not try to pass

2.29   mark **one** answer

You are driving along this road. The red van cuts in close in front of you. What should you do?

❏ Accelerate to get closer to the red van
❏ Give a long blast on the horn
❏ Drop back to leave the correct separation distance
❏ Flash your headlights several times

❏ **Drop back to leave the correct separation distance**

Keep calm and don't retaliate in response to other drivers' errors. Maintain the safety zone around your car.

You are waiting in a traffic queue at night. To avoid dazzling following drivers you should

❏ apply the handbrake only
❏ apply the footbrake only
❏ switch off your headlights
❏ use both the handbrake and footbrake

❏ **apply the handbrake only**

Using the footbrake would activate your brake lights and might dazzle following drivers.

You are driving in traffic at the speed limit for the road. The driver behind is trying to overtake. You should

❏ move closer to the car ahead, so the driver behind has no room to overtake
❏ wave the driver behind to overtake when it is safe
❏ keep a steady course and allow the driver behind to overtake
❏ accelerate to get away from the driver behind

❏ **keep a steady course and allow the driver behind to overtake**

Do not react negatively to other drivers' behaviour. Keep yourself, your passengers and your car safe.

A bus lane on your left shows no times of operation. This means it is

❏ not in operation at all
❏ only in operation at peak times
❏ in operation 24 hours a day
❏ only in operation in daylight hours

❏ **in operation 24 hours a day**

A blue rectangular sign will often tell you when the bus lane is in operation. If there are no times of operation this means it is in use 24 hours a day.

2.33   mark **two** answers

You are driving along a country road. A horse and rider are approaching. What should you do?

❑ Increase your speed
❑ Sound your horn
❑ Flash your headlights
❑ Drive slowly past
❑ Give plenty of room
❑ Rev your engine

❑ **Drive slowly past**

❑ **Give plenty of room**

You can avoid startling horses by taking these actions.

2.34   mark **one** answer

A person herding sheep asks you to stop. You should

❑ ignore them as they have no authority
❑ stop and switch off your engine
❑ continue on but drive slowly
❑ try and get past quickly

❑ **stop and switch off your engine**

Animals are unpredictable. This is the safest option. Stay calm and be patient.

2.35   mark **one** answer

When overtaking a horse and rider you should

❑ sound your horn as a warning
❑ go past as quickly as possible
❑ flash your headlights as a warning
❑ go past slowly and carefully

❑ **go past slowly and carefully**

This will enable you to deal with the hazard in the safest manner possible and avoid startling the horse.

2.36   mark **one** answer

You are approaching a zebra crossing. Pedestrians are waiting to cross. You should

❑ give way to the elderly and infirm only
❑ slow down and prepare to stop
❑ use your headlights to indicate they can cross
❑ wave at them to cross the road

❑ **slow down and prepare to stop**

The pedestrians may want to cross. Doing this will enable you to deal with the crossing in the safest manner possible.

43

mark **one** answer

A vehicle pulls out in front of you at a junction. What should you do?

❏ Swerve past it and sound your horn
❏ Flash your headlights and drive up close behind
❏ Slow down and be ready to stop
❏ Accelerate past it immediately

❏ **Slow down and be ready to stop**

Be tolerant and do not react to other drivers' errors. Keep calm, keep yourself, your passengers and your car safe.

mark **one** answer

You stop for pedestrians waiting to cross at a zebra crossing. They do not start to cross. What should you do?

❏ Be patient and wait
❏ Sound your horn
❏ Carry on
❏ Wave them to cross

❏ **Be patient and wait**

The pedestrians may want to cross. Doing this will enable you to deal with the pedestrians in the safest manner possible.

mark **one** answer

You are following this lorry. You should keep well back from it to

❏ give you a good view of the road ahead
❏ stop following traffic from rushing through the junction
❏ prevent traffic behind you from overtaking
❏ allow you to hurry through the traffic lights if they change

❏ **give you a good view of the road ahead**

Never follow too closely. Keeping well back opens up your vision and increases your time to react.

2.40   mark **one** answer

You are approaching a red light at a puffin crossing. Pedestrians are on the crossing. The red light will stay on until

- ❑ you start to edge forward on to the crossing
- ❑ the pedestrians have reached a safe position
- ❑ the pedestrians are clear of the front of your vehicle
- ❑ a driver from the opposite direction reaches the crossing

- ❑ **the pedestrians have reached a safe position**

Puffin crossing lights are controlled by sensors that detect pedestrians using the crossing. Wait for the green light and make sure it is otherwise safe to move off.

2.41   mark **one** answer

Which instrument panel warning light would show that headlights are on full beam ?

❑   ❑

❑   ❑

❑

You must be alert to any light that appears on your dashboard. This blue light shows that you are on main beam. Take care not to dazzle approaching traffic or vehicles that you might be following.

2.42   mark **one** answer

At puffin crossings, which light will not show to a driver?

- ❑ Flashing amber
- ❑ Red
- ❑ Steady amber
- ❑ Green

- ❑ **Flashing amber**

The sequence is Red – Red and Amber together – Green – steady Amber – Red; exactly the same as an ordinary traffic light. A flashing amber light shows on pelican crossings.

2.43
mark **one** answer

You should leave at least a two-second gap between your vehicle and the one in front when conditions are

- ❏ wet
- ❏ good
- ❏ damp
- ❏ foggy

❏ **good**

This gap should leave sufficient space for you to stop in an emergency in good weather conditions.

2.44
mark **one** answer

You are driving at night on an unlit road behind another vehicle. You should

- ❏ flash your headlights
- ❏ use dipped beam headlights
- ❏ switch off your headlights
- ❏ use full beam headlights

❏ **use dipped beam headlights**

Full beam will dazzle the driver ahead, so use dipped beam.

2.45
mark **one** answer

You are driving a slow-moving vehicle on a narrow winding road. You should

- ❏ keep well out to stop vehicles overtaking dangerously
- ❏ wave following vehicles past you if you think they can overtake quickly
- ❏ pull in safely when you can, to let following vehicles overtake
- ❏ give a left signal when it is safe for vehicles to overtake you

❏ **pull in safely when you can, to let following vehicles overtake**

The first and second answers are dangerous and the last is confusing. Other drivers might think you are stopping or turning left.

2.46   mark **two** answers

You have a loose filler cap on your diesel fuel tank. This will

- ❏ waste fuel and money
- ❏ make roads slippery for other road users
- ❏ improve your vehicle's fuel consumption
- ❏ increase the level of exhaust emissions

❏ **waste fuel and money**

❏ **make roads slippery for other road users**

The rubber of tyres will not grip the road through the diesel, making the road more slippery than ice.

2.47   mark **one** answer

To avoid spillage after refuelling, you should make sure that

- ❏ your tank is only three quarters full
- ❏ you have used a locking filler cap
- ❏ you check your fuel gauge is working
- ❏ your filler cap is securely fastened

❏ **your filler cap is securely fastened**

A properly secured filler cap will stop any fuel spillage through the tank neck.

2.48   mark **one** answer

If your vehicle uses diesel fuel, take extra care when refuelling. Diesel fuel when spilt is

- ❏ sticky
- ❏ odourless
- ❏ clear
- ❏ slippery

❏ **slippery**

Spilt fuel is very slippery. If you get it on the soles of your shoes your feet are likely to slip off the pedals.

2.49   mark **one** answer

What style of driving causes increased risk to everyone?

- ❏ Considerate
- ❏ Defensive
- ❏ Competitive
- ❏ Responsible

❏ **Competitive**

Competitive driving puts you at greater risk of losing control of the vehicle and colliding with another road user, even a pedestrian.

mark one answer

Young, inexperienced and newly qualified drivers can often be involved in crashes. This is due to

❑ being too cautious at junctions
❑ driving in the middle of their lane
❑ showing off and being competitive
❑ staying within the speed limit

❑ **showing off and being competitive**

Showing off might seem like fun at the time, however, evidence shows that the risk of a serious collision becomes high. You need to adopt a positive, but defensive driving style to keep out of collisions.

Section 3

Safety and your

There are 112 questions in this section, covering the following subjects:

❏ Fault detection and its effect on your vehicle's safety
❏ Vehicle defects and their effects on your safety
❏ Use of safety equipment
❏ Emissions
❏ Pollution
❏ Noise

You will need to think about:

❏ Vehicle maintenance with regard to safety

❏ Passenger safety

❏ Pedestrian safety

❏ Vehicle safety

❏ Environmental issues.

Tips

If vehicle maintenance isn't one of your strengths, logic will help you find the answer.

For example, an over-inflated tyre would not sit flat on the road, the profile would be more rounded. So if you were asked how it would wear, the answer would be along the centre of the tread. As less tread would be touching the road, the tyre would grip the road less and the steering would feel lighter. Logical thinking. Remember these types of question focus on the safety aspects.

If you can't think of an answer, guess it, but make a note of your guesses, and check out the explanations even if you got them right. You need to know why, you may not guess correctly next time.

mark **two** answers

Which TWO are badly affected if the tyres are under-inflated

❑ Braking
❑ Steering
❑ Changing gear
❑ Parking

❑ **Braking**

❑ **Steering**

Under-inflated tyres will drag. This affects their grip on the road reducing braking and steering efficiency.

3.2   mark **one** answer

You must NOT sound your horn

❑ between 10 pm and 6 am in a built-up area
❑ at any time in a built-up area
❑ between 11.30 pm and 7 am in a built-up area
❑ between 11.30 pm and 6 am on any road

❑ **between 11.30 pm and 7 am in a built-up area**

The regulation applies in a built-up area only.

3.3   mark **three** answers

The pictured vehicle is 'environmentally friendly' because it

❑ reduces noise pollution
❑ uses diesel fuel
❑ uses electricity
❑ uses unleaded fuel
❑ reduces parking spaces
❑ reduces town traffic

❑ **reduces noise pollution**

❑ **uses electricity**

❑ **reduces town traffic**

Electric trams make less noise and electricity is regarded as cleaner energy than petrol or diesel. More people will travel per vehicle, taking up less road space per person.

3.4   mark **one** answer

Supertrams or Light Rapid Transit (LRT) systems are environmentally friendly because

❏ they use diesel power
❏ they use quieter roads
❏ they use electric power
❏ they do not operate during rush hour

❏ **they use electric power**

Electricity is regarded as cleaner energy than petrol or diesel because it doesn't emit toxic fumes into the atmosphere.

3.5   mark **one** answer

'Red routes' in major cities have been introduced to

❏ raise the speed limits
❏ help the traffic flow
❏ provide better parking
❏ allow lorries to load more freely

❏ **help the traffic flow**

Parking is strictly limited and rigorously policed, both of which ensure a better traffic flow.

3.6   mark **one** answer

Road humps, chicanes, and narrowings are

❏ always at major road works
❏ used to increase traffic speed
❏ at toll-bridge approaches only
❏ traffic calming measures

❏ **traffic calming measures**

Traffic has to slow to navigate these obstacles – thus it is calmed.

3.7   mark **one** answer

The purpose of a catalytic converter is to reduce

❏ fuel consumption
❏ the risk of fire
❏ toxic exhaust gases
❏ engine wear

❏ **toxic exhaust gases**

Catalytic converters are fitted to vehicles to reduce harmful exhaust emissions. They specifically reduce carbon monoxide (CO), hydrocarbons (HC) and oxides of nitrogen by up to 90%.

3.8

mark **one** answer

Catalytic converters are fitted to make the

❏ engine produce more power
❏ exhaust system easier to replace
❏ engine run quietly
❏ exhaust fumes cleaner

❏ **exhaust fumes cleaner**

The harmful gases from the engine that pollute the atmosphere are reduced by up to 90%.

3.9

mark **one** answer

It is essential that tyre pressures are checked regularly. When should this be done?

❏ After any lengthy journey
❏ After travelling at high speed
❏ When tyres are hot
❏ When tyres are cold

❏ **When tyres are cold**

When a tyre is hot the pressure is higher. Manufacturers' guidelines for tyre pressures are written to be used when the tyres are cold.

3.10

mark **one** answer

When should you NOT use your horn in a built-up area?

❏ Between 8 pm and 8 am
❏ Between 9 pm and dawn
❏ Between dusk and 8 am
❏ Between 11.30 pm and 7 am

❏ **Between 11.30 pm and 7 am**

Because this would cause annoyance for the residents. Flash your headlights instead.

3.11

mark **one** answer

You will use more fuel if your tyres are

❏ under-inflated
❏ of different makes
❏ over-inflated
❏ new and hardly used

❏ **under-inflated**

If the tyre is under-inflated the rolling resistance is increased. This will cause the engine to work harder causing more fuel consumption.

3.12   mark **two** answers

How should you dispose of a used battery?

- ❑ Take it to a local authority site
- ❑ Put it in the dustbin
- ❑ Break it up into pieces
- ❑ Leave it on waste land
- ❑ Take it to a garage
- ❑ Burn it on a fire

❑ **Take it to a local authority site**

❑ **Take it to a garage**

Batteries contain acid. Both these locations will be able to dispose of or recycle the battery in an environmentally friendly way.

3.13   mark **one** answer

What is most likely to cause high fuel consumption?

- ❑ Poor steering control
- ❑ Accelerating around bends
- ❑ Staying in high gears
- ❑ Harsh braking and accelerating

❑ **Harsh braking and accelerating**

Harsh braking and accelerating is one of the major causes of high fuel consumption.

3.14   mark **one** answer

The fluid level in your battery is low. What should you top it up with?

- ❑ Battery acid
- ❑ Distilled water
- ❑ Engine oil
- ❑ Engine coolant

❑ **Distilled water**

This is the manufacturers' recommendation. Non-distilled water may contain harmful minerals which will have a cumulative adverse effect on battery performance.

3.15   mark **one** answer

You are parked on the road at night. Where must you use parking lights?

- ❑ Where there are continuous white lines in the middle of the road
- ❑ Where the speed limit exceeds 30 mph
- ❑ Where you are facing oncoming traffic
- ❑ Where you are near a bus stop

❑ **Where the speed limit exceeds 30 mph**

When parking at night, legally you must park in the direction of travel and use your parking lights where the speed limit for the road is more than 30 mph.

53

3.16   mark **three** answers

Motor vehicles can harm the environment.
This has resulted in

- ❏ air pollution
- ❏ damage to buildings
- ❏ less risk to health
- ❏ improved public transport
- ❏ less use of electrical vehicles
- ❏ using up of natural resources

❏ **air pollution**

❏ **damage to buildings**

❏ **using up of natural resources**

Exhaust emissions are harmful to our health.
Vibration from traffic can damage buildings
and fossil fuels are a finite resource.
Reducing vehicle use will help the
environment.

3.17   mark **three** answers

Excessive or uneven tyre wear can be caused
by faults in which THREE of the following?

- ❏ The gearbox
- ❏ The braking system
- ❏ The accelerator
- ❏ The exhaust system
- ❏ Wheel alignment
- ❏ The suspension

❏ **The braking system**

❏ **Wheel alignment**

❏ **The suspension**

Tyres need to be checked regularly and the
vehicle serviced properly to minimise the risk
of serious faults developing.

3.18   mark **one** answer

You need to top up your battery. What level
should you fill to?

- ❏ The top of the battery
- ❏ Half-way up the battery
- ❏ Just below the cell plates
- ❏ Just above the cell plates

❏ **Just above the cell plates**

The 'topping up' level will normally be
marked on the battery and is above the cell
plates.

3.19   mark **one** answer

You are parking on a two-way road at night. The speed limit is 40 mph. You should park on the

❑ left with parking lights on
❑ left with no lights on
❑ right with parking lights on
❑ right with dipped headlights on

❑ **left with parking lights on**

On a two-way road, to be lawful you MUST park facing the direction of traffic, with your parking lights on.

3.20   mark **one** answer

Before starting a journey it is wise to plan your route. How can you do this?

❑ Look at a map
❑ Contact your local garage
❑ Look in your vehicle handbook
❑ Check your vehicle registration document

❑ **Look at a map**

To plan a route before starting your journey, you could also use an internet route planner like the one to be found on the RAC website or a satellite navigation system.

3.21   mark **one** answer

It can help to plan your route before starting a journey. You can do this by contacting

❑ your local filling station
❑ a motoring organisation
❑ the Driver Vehicle Licensing Agency
❑ your vehicle manufacturer

❑ **a motoring organisation**

Planning your route before starting a journey saves time, fuel and stress. Motoring organisations such as the RAC are a great source of information.

3.22   mark **one** answer

How can you plan your route before starting a long journey?

❑ Check your vehicle's workshop manual
❑ Ask your local garage
❑ Use a route planner on the internet
❑ Consult your travel agents

❑ **Use a route planner on the internet**

Use an internet route planner like the one to be found on the RAC website, or a satellite navigation system, or a map.

mark one answer

Planning your route before setting out can be helpful. How can you do this?

❑ Look in a motoring magazine
❑ Only visit places you know
❑ Try to travel at busy times
❑ Print or write down the route

❑ **Print or write down the route**

This will help to reduce journey time, fuel costs, and stress.

mark one answer

Why is it a good idea to plan your journey to avoid busy times?

❑ You will have an easier journey
❑ You will have a more stressful journey
❑ Your journey time will be longer
❑ It will cause more traffic congestion

❑ **You will have an easier journey**

It will help to reduce journey time, fuel costs, and stress, because there will be less traffic.

mark one answer

Planning your journey to avoid busy times has a number of advantages. One of these is

❑ your journey will take longer
❑ you will have a more pleasant journey
❑ you will cause more pollution
❑ your stress level will be greater

❑ **you will have a more pleasant journey**

Having a pleasant journey can have safety benefits. You will be less tired and stressed, so you will be able to conventrate better on your driving.

mark one answer

It is a good idea to plan your journey to avoid busy times. This is because

❑ your vehicle will use more fuel
❑ you will see less road works
❑ it will help to ease congestion
❑ you will travel a much shorter distance

❑ **it will help to ease congestion**

If you can avoid travelling in busy times your journey will be easier and you will help to ease congestion.

3.27   mark **one** answer

By avoiding busy times when travelling

❏ you are more likely to be held up
❏ your journey time will be longer
❏ you will travel a much shorter distance
❏ you are less likely to be delayed

❏ **you are less likely to be delayed**

If you can avoid busy times there will be one less driver on the road, which helps to ease congestion. Plan your route before you start the journey to save time, fuel and stress.

3.28   mark **one** answer

It can help to plan your route before starting a journey. Why should you also plan an alternative route?

❏ Your original route may be blocked
❏ Your maps may have different scales
❏ You may find you have to pay a congestion charge
❏ Because you may get held up by a tractor

❏ **Your original route may be blocked**

Planning an alternative will help reduce stress and will help to reduce journey time and fuel costs.

3.29   mark **one** answer

As well as planning your route before starting a journey, you should also plan an alternative route. Why is this?

❏ To let another driver overtake
❏ Your first route may be blocked
❏ To avoid a railway level crossing
❏ In case you have to avoid emergency vehicles

❏ **Your first route may be blocked**

It is always a good idea to plan an alternative route, in case your original route is blocked for any reason.

3.30   mark **one** answer

You are making an appointment and will have to travel a long distance. You should

❏ allow plenty of time for your journey
❏ plan to go at busy times
❏ avoid all national speed limit roads
❏ prevent other drivers from overtaking

❏ **allow plenty of time for your journey**

If you allow time for unexpected delays and hold-ups, it will help reduce stress.

mark **one** answer

Rapid acceleration and heavy braking can lead to

❏ reduced pollution
❏ increased fuel consumption
❏ reduced exhaust emissions
❏ increased road safety

❏ **increased fuel consumption**

Looking well ahead and planning your driving allows you to accelerate and brake smoothly, which will improve your fuel consumption as well as keeping you safer.

mark **one** answer

What percentage of all emissions does road transport account for?

❏ 10%
❏ 20%
❏ 30%
❏ 40%

❏ **20%**

By improving your car's fuel consumption, you will reduce exhaust emissions.

mark **one** answer

New petrol-engined cars must be fitted with catalytic converters. The reason for this is to

❏ control exhaust noise levels
❏ prolong the life of the exhaust system
❏ allow the exhaust system to be recycled
❏ reduce harmful exhaust emissions

❏ **reduce harmful exhaust emissions**

This helps the car operate more efficiently and causes less air pollution.

mark **one** answer

Which of these, if allowed to get low, could cause you to crash?

❏ Anti-freeze level
❏ Brake fluid level
❏ Battery water level
❏ Radiator coolant level

❏ **Brake fluid level**

It is important that you regularly make regular engine checks. Open your bonnet and check all fluid levels, particularly the brake fluid. As the brake pads and shoes wear, the fluid level will fall and air can enter the hydraulic system. This will reduce braking efficiency, meaning longer stopping distances and therefore an increased risk of a crash happening.

3.35   mark **one** answer

What can cause heavy steering?

- ❏ Driving on ice
- ❏ Badly worn brakes
- ❏ Over-inflated tyres
- ❏ Under-inflated tyres

❏ **Under-inflated tyres**

If the tyre is under-inflated the contact patch between the tyre and the road will be altered and the stiffness of the tyre will be reduced, which will make the steering heavier.

3.36   mark **two** answers

Driving with under-inflated tyres can affect

- ❏ engine temperature
- ❏ fuel consumption
- ❏ braking
- ❏ oil pressure

❏ **fuel consumption**

❏ **braking**

The law requires that you must keep your tyres correctly inflated. Driving with correctly inflated tyres will reduce fuel consumption and your vehicle will brake more safely.

3.37   mark **two** answers

Excessive or uneven tyre wear can be caused by faults in the

- ❏ gearbox
- ❏ braking system
- ❏ suspension
- ❏ exhaust system

❏ **braking system**

❏ **suspension**

Either of these may cause the tyre to sit or turn incorrectly on the road surface affecting tyre wear.

3.38   mark **one** answer

The main cause of brake fade is

- ❏ the brakes overheating
- ❏ air in the brake fluid
- ❏ oil on the brakes
- ❏ the brakes out of adjustment

❏ **the brakes overheating**

Metal expands when it is hot. When brake systems overheat in some circumstances metal parts within the system can expand causing the brake shoe or pad to be less efficient and not have the normal braking effect.

mark one answer

Your anti-lock brakes warning light stays on. You should

❏ check the brake fluid level
❏ check the footbrake free play
❏ check that the handbrake is released
❏ have the brakes checked immediately

❏ **have the brakes checked immediately**

The braking system has a fault. For safety reasons this needs to be checked out immediately by a qualified professional.

mark one answer

While driving, this warning light on your dashboard comes on. It means

❏ a fault in the braking system
❏ the engine oil is low
❏ a rear light has failed
❏ your seat belt is not fastened

❏ **a fault in the braking system**

This is a standard panel light. The design and colour mean there is a fault in the braking system.

mark one answer

It is important to wear suitable shoes when you are driving. Why is this?

❏ To prevent wear on the pedals
❏ To maintain control of the pedals
❏ To enable you to adjust your seat
❏ To enable you to walk for assistance if you break down

❏ **To maintain control of the pedals**

It is important that you can reach, feel and operate all the controls comfortably.

3.42   mark **one** answer

What will reduce the risk of neck injury resulting from a collision?

❑ An air-sprung seat
❑ Anti-lock brakes
❑ A collapsible steering wheel
❑ A properly adjusted head restraint

❑ **A properly adjusted head restraint**

If you are involved in an accident, the head restraint helps protect your neck from whiplash.

3.43   mark **one** answer

You are testing your suspension. You notice that your vehicle keeps bouncing when you press down on the front wing. What does this mean?

❑ Worn tyres
❑ Tyres under-inflated
❑ Steering wheel not located centrally
❑ Worn shock absorbers

❑ **Worn shock absorbers**

Shock absorbers have a major influence on road handling and braking. Worn shock absorbers can be dangerous.

3.44   mark **one** answer

A roof rack fitted to your car will

❑ reduce fuel consumption
❑ improve the road handling
❑ make your car go faster
❑ increase fuel consumption

❑ **increase fuel consumption**

Because of increased wind resistance, this makes the engine work harder, therefore using more fuel.

3.45   mark **one** answer

It is illegal to drive with tyres that

❑ have been bought second-hand
❑ have a large deep cut in the side wall
❑ are of different makes
❑ are of different tread patterns

❑ **have a large deep cut in the side wall**

This is dangerous because the tyre could 'blow-out' at any time

3.46   mark **one** answer

The legal minimum depth of tread for car tyres over three quarters of the breadth is

❏ 1 mm
❏ 1.6 mm
❏ 2.5 mm
❏ 4 mm

❏ **1.6 mm**

Tyre tread determines grip on wet or greasy surfaces. This is an important safety issue.

3.47   mark **one** answer

You are carrying two 13 year old children and their parents in your car. Who is responsible for seeing that the children wear seat belts?

❏ The children's parents
❏ You, the driver
❏ The front-seat passenger
❏ The children

❏ **You, the driver**

All children under the age of 14 are the driver's responsibility.

3.48   mark **one** answer

When a roof rack is not in use it should be removed. Why is this?

❏ It will affect the suspension
❏ It is illegal
❏ It will affect your braking
❏ It will waste fuel

❏ **It will waste fuel**

Using a roof rack increases wind resistance, making it harder for the car to move through the air and therefore causing the car to use more fuel.

3.49   mark **three** answers

How can you, as a driver, help the environment?

❏ By reducing your speed
❏ By gentle acceleration
❏ By using leaded fuel
❏ By driving faster
❏ By harsh acceleration
❏ By servicing your vehicle properly

❏ **By reducing your speed**

❏ **By gentle acceleration**

❏ **By servicing your vehicle properly**

All the above will help reduce exhaust emissions.

3.50   mark **three** answers

To help the environment, you can avoid wasting fuel by

❑ having your vehicle properly serviced
❑ making sure your tyres are correctly inflated
❑ not over-revving in the lower gears
❑ driving at higher speeds where possible
❑ keeping an empty roof rack properly fitted
❑ servicing your vehicle less regularly

❑ **having your vehicle properly serviced**

❑ **making sure your tyres are correctly inflated**

❑ **not over-revving in the lower gears**

Any of the above will help reduce exhaust emissions.

3.51   mark **three** answers

To reduce the volume of traffic on the roads you could

❑ use public transport more often
❑ share a car when possible
❑ walk or cycle on short journeys
❑ travel by car at all times
❑ use a car with a smaller engine
❑ drive in a bus lane

❑ **use public transport more often**

❑ **share a car when possible**

❑ **walk or cycle on short journeys**

These options will help reduce traffic volume and pollution.

3.52   mark **three** answers

Which THREE of the following are most likely to waste fuel?

❑ Reducing your speed
❑ Carrying unnecessary weight
❑ Using the wrong grade of fuel
❑ Under-inflated tyres
❑ Using different brands of fuel
❑ A fitted, empty roof rack

❑ **Carrying unnecessary weight**

❑ **Under-inflated tyres**

❑ **A fitted, empty roof rack**

Any of these options will make the engine work harder and use more fuel.

Which THREE things can you, as a road user, do to help the environment?

❑ Cycle when possible
❑ Drive on under-inflated tyres
❑ Use the choke for as long as possible on a cold engine
❑ Have your vehicle properly tuned and serviced
❑ Watch the traffic and plan ahead
❑ Brake as late as possible without skidding

❑ **Cycle when possible**

❑ **Have your vehicle properly tuned and serviced**

❑ **Watch the traffic and plan ahead**

These options will help reduce exhaust emissions.

To help protect the environment you should NOT

❑ remove your roof rack when unloaded
❑ use your car for very short journeys
❑ walk, cycle, or use public transport
❑ empty the boot of unnecessary weight

❑ **use your car for very short journeys**

Cars are at their least efficient when their engines are cold.

Which THREE does the law require you to keep in good condition?

❑ Gears
❑ Transmission
❑ Headlights
❑ Windscreen
❑ Seat belts

❑ **Headlights**

❑ **Windscreen**

❑ **Seat belts**

These are all vehicle safety issues for which a driver has full responsibility.

Driving at 70 mph uses more fuel than driving at 50 mph by up to

❑ 10%
❑ 30%
❑ 75%
❑ 100%

❑ **30%**

This is based on aerodynamic efficiency and engine power requirements.

3.57   mark **one** answer

Your vehicle pulls to one side when braking.
You should

❑ change the tyres around
❑ consult your garage as soon as possible
❑ pump the pedal when braking
❑ use your handbrake at the same time

❑ **consult your garage as soon as possible**

Take the vehicle to be inspected
professionally by a qualified mechanic.

3.58   mark **one** answer

Unbalanced wheels on a car may cause

❑ the steering to pull to one side
❑ the steering to vibrate
❑ the brakes to fail
❑ the tyres to deflate

❑ **the steering to vibrate**

The wheel will rotate unevenly at certain
speeds causing a vibration on the steering.

3.59   mark **two** answers

Turning the steering wheel while your car is
stationary can cause damage to the

❑ gearbox
❑ engine
❑ brakes
❑ steering
❑ tyres

❑ **steering**

❑ **tyres**

'Dry steering' will damage the mechanism
and put needless wear on the tyres.

3.60   mark **one** answer

You have to leave valuables in your car.
It would be safer to

❑ put them in a carrier bag
❑ park near a school entrance
❑ lock them out of sight
❑ park near a bus stop

❑ **lock them out of sight**

If belongings can't be seen, a thief may
assume the vehicle is empty.

3.61   mark **one** answer

How could you deter theft from your car when leaving it unattended?

❏ Leave valuables in a carrier bag
❏ Lock valuables out of sight
❏ Put valuables on the seats
❏ Leave valuables on the floor

❏ **Lock valuables out of sight**

If no valuables can be seen, a thief may assume the vehicle is empty.

3.62   mark **one** answer

Which of the following may help to deter a thief from stealing your car?

❏ Always keeping the headlights on
❏ Fitting reflective glass windows
❏ Always keeping the interior light on
❏ Etching the car number on the windows

❏ **Etching the car number on the windows**

Would-be thieves may well be able to steal any vehicle but the fact that the number is etched on the windows may deter them.

3.63   mark **one** answer

Which of the following should not be kept in your vehicle?

❏ A first aid kit
❏ A road atlas
❏ The tax disc
❏ The vehicle documents

❏ **The vehicle documents**

If the car was stolen containing its documents, ownership could be transferred.

3.64   mark **one** answer

What should you do when leaving your vehicle?

❏ Put valuable documents under the seats
❏ Remove all valuables
❏ Cover valuables with a blanket
❏ Leave the interior light on

❏ **Remove all valuables**

This is the safest option, especially if you're unable to lock them in the boot.

3.65   mark **one** answer

Which of these is most likely to deter the theft of your vehicle?

❑ An immobiliser
❑ Tinted windows
❑ Locking wheel nuts
❑ A sun screen

❑ **An immobiliser**

An anti-theft device like an immobiliser makes it more difficult for a thief to steal your car.

3.66   mark **one** answer

When parking and leaving your car you should

❑ park under a shady tree
❑ remove the tax disc
❑ park in a quiet road
❑ engage the steering lock

❑ **engage the steering lock**

This increases the security of your vehicle and will reduce the risk of your car being stolen.

3.67   mark **one** answer

When leaving your vehicle parked and unattended you should

❑ park near a busy junction
❑ park in a housing estate
❑ remove the key and lock it
❑ leave the left indicator on

❑ **remove the key and lock it**

Never leave the keys in the ignition – it creates too good an opportunity for a thief to miss.

3.68   mark **two** answers

Which TWO of the following will improve fuel consumption?

❑ Reducing your road speed
❑ Planning well ahead
❑ Late and harsh braking
❑ Driving in lower gears
❑ Short journeys with a cold engine
❑ Rapid acceleration

❑ **Reducing your road speed**

❑ **Planning well ahead**

These options will improve fuel consumption by increasing engine and driver efficiency.

mark **one** answer

You service your own vehicle. How should you get rid of the old engine oil?

❑ Take it to a local authority site
❑ Pour it down a drain
❑ Tip it into a hole in the ground
❑ Put it into your dustbin

❑ **Take it to a local authority site**

They will be able to dispose of it in an environmentally friendly way.

mark **one** answer

Why do MOT tests include a strict exhaust emission test?

❑ To recover the cost of expensive garage equipment
❑ To help protect the environment against pollution
❑ To discover which fuel supplier is used the most
❑ To make sure diesel and petrol engines emit the same fumes

❑ **To help protect the environment against pollution**

The MOT tests your vehicle's safety and emission efficiency.

mark **three** answers

To reduce the damage your vehicle causes to the environment you should

❑ use narrow side streets
❑ avoid harsh acceleration
❑ brake in good time
❑ anticipate well ahead
❑ use busy routes

❑ **avoid harsh acceleration**

❑ **brake in good time**

❑ **anticipate well ahead**

These make for smoother driving, which uses less fuel and so cuts down on pollution.

mark **one** answer

Your vehicle has a catalytic converter. Its purpose is to reduce

❑ exhaust noise
❑ fuel consumption
❑ exhaust emissions
❑ engine noise

❑ **exhaust emissions**

Catalytic converters are fitted to vehicles to reduce harmful exhaust emissions. The gases are changed by a chemical process as they pass through the converter.

3.73   mark **two** answers

A properly serviced vehicle will give

❏ lower insurance premiums
❏ you a refund on your road tax
❏ better fuel economy
❏ cleaner exhaust emissions

❏ **better fuel economy**

❏ **cleaner exhaust emissions**

A properly serviced engine works at peak efficiency.

3.74   mark **one** answer

You enter a road where there are road humps. What should you do?

❏ Maintain a reduced speed throughout
❏ Accelerate quickly between each one
❏ Always keep to the maximum legal speed
❏ Drive slowly at school times only

❏ **Maintain a reduced speed throughout**

Road humps are there to slow the traffic in residential areas.

3.75   mark **one** answer

When should you especially check the engine oil level?

❏ Before a long journey
❏ When the engine is hot
❏ Early in the morning
❏ Every 6000 miles

❏ **Before a long journey**

This will help reduce the chances of a breakdown or engine damage.

3.76 mark **one** answer

You are having difficulty finding a parking space in a busy town. You can see there is space on the zigzag lines of a zebra crossing. Can you park there?

❏ No, unless you stay with your car
❏ Yes, in order to drop off a passenger
❏ Yes, if you do not block people from crossing
❏ No, not in any circumstances

❏ **No, not in any circumstances**

Parking on a zigzag line will dangerously reduce both pedestrians' view of the traffic, and the driver's view of the crossing.

3.77 mark **one** answer

When leaving your car unattended for a few minutes you should

❏ leave the engine running
❏ switch the engine off but leave the key in
❏ lock it and remove the key
❏ park near a traffic warden

❏ **lock it and remove the key**

It will reduce the risk of your car being stolen.

3.78 mark **one** answer

When parking and leaving your car for a few minutes you should

❏ leave it unlocked
❏ lock it and remove the key
❏ leave the hazard warning lights on
❏ leave the interior light on

❏ **lock it and remove the key**

An unlocked car is an open invitation to a car thief. When you get out of your car, always take your key out of the ignition.

3.79 mark **one** answer

When leaving your vehicle where should you park if possible?

❏ Opposite a traffic island
❏ In a secure car park
❏ On a bend
❏ At or near a taxi rank

❏ **In a secure car park**

This is the only option that will reduce the risk of your car being stolen.

3.80   mark **three** answers

In which THREE places would parking your vehicle cause danger or obstruction to other road users?

❑ In front of a property entrance
❑ At or near a bus stop
❑ On your driveway
❑ In a marked parking space
❑ On the approach to a level crossing

❑ **In front of a property entrance**

❑ **At or near a bus stop**

❑ **On the approach to a level crossing**

Parking in any of these locations prevents access to, or visibility of something.

3.81   mark **three** answers

In which THREE places would parking cause an obstruction to others?

❑ Near the brow of a hill
❑ In a lay-by
❑ Where the kerb is raised
❑ Where the kerb has been lowered for wheelchairs
❑ At or near a bus stop

❑ **Near the brow of a hill**

❑ **Where the kerb has been lowered for wheelchairs**

❑ **At or near a bus stop**

Parking here will prevent access to, or visibility of something.

3.82   mark **one** answer

You are away from home and have to park your vehicle overnight. Where should you leave it?

❑ Opposite another parked vehicle
❑ In a quiet road
❑ Opposite a traffic island
❑ In a secure car park

❑ **In a secure car park**

This is the only option that will reduce the risk of your car being stolen.

3.83   mark **one** answer

The most important reason for having a properly adjusted head restraint is to

❏ make you more comfortable
❏ help you to avoid neck injury
❏ help you to relax
❏ help you to maintain your driving position

❏ **help you to avoid neck injury**

In the event of an accident the head restraint is designed to help reduce whiplash.

3.84   mark **two** answers

As a driver you can cause more damage to the environment by

❏ choosing a fuel-efficient vehicle
❏ making a lot of short journeys
❏ driving in as high a gear as possible
❏ accelerating as quickly as possible
❏ having your vehicle regularly serviced

❏ **making a lot of short journeys**

❏ **accelerating as quickly as possible**

A lot of short journeys use up a lot of petrol and pollute the atmosphere with exhaust fumes

3.85   mark **one** answer

As a driver, you can help reduce pollution levels in town centres by

❏ driving more quickly
❏ over-revving in a low gear
❏ walking or cycling
❏ driving short journeys

❏ **walking or cycling**

Only these options will reduce vehicle emissions; the other answers increase them.

3.86   mark **one** answer

How can you reduce the chances of your car being broken into when leaving it unattended?

❏ Take all valuables with you
❏ Park near a taxi rank
❏ Place any valuables on the floor
❏ Park near a fire station

❏ **Take all valuables with you**

Your car is more likely to be broken into if valuables are visible through the windows.

3.87   mark **one** answer

How can you help to prevent your car radio being stolen?

❑ Park in an unlit area
❑ Hide the radio with a blanket
❑ Park near a busy junction
❑ Install a security-coded radio

❑ **Install a security-coded radio**

Having a security-coded radio makes your vehicle less desirable to a thief.

3.88   mark **one** answer

You are parking your car. You have some valuables which you are unable to take with you. What should you do?

❑ Park near a police station
❑ Put them under the driver's seat
❑ Lock them out of sight
❑ Park in an unlit side road

❑ **Lock them out of sight**

If no valuables can be seen a thief may assume the vehicle is empty.

3.89   mark **one** answer

Wherever possible, which one of the following should you do when parking at night?

❑ Park in a quiet car park
❑ Park in a well-lit area
❑ Park facing against the flow of traffic
❑ Park next to a busy junction

❑ **Park in a well-lit area**

It will reduce the risk of your car being stolen or broken into.

3.90   mark **one** answer

How can you lessen the risk of your vehicle being broken into at night?

❑ Leave it in a well-lit area
❑ Park in a quiet side road
❑ Don't engage the steering lock
❑ Park in a poorly-lit area

❑ **Leave it in a well-lit area**

Avoid leaving your car unattended in poorly-lit areas, especially if they are known to be high risk.

mark one answer

To help keep your car secure you could join a

☐ vehicle breakdown organisation
☐ vehicle watch scheme
☐ advanced driver's scheme
☐ car maintenance class

☐ **vehicle watch scheme**

This is the only option that relates to vehicle theft.

mark one answer

On a vehicle, where would you find a catalytic converter?

☐ In the fuel tank
☐ In the air filter
☐ On the cooling system
☐ On the exhaust system

☐ **On the exhaust system**

They are fitted to vehicles to reduce harmful exhaust emissions.

mark one answer

When leaving your car to help keep it secure you should

☐ leave the hazard warning lights on
☐ lock it and remove the key
☐ park on a one-way street
☐ park in a residential area

☐ **lock it and remove the key**

This is the only option that relates to vehicle theft.

mark one answer

You will find that driving smoothly can

☐ reduce journey times by about 15%
☐ increase fuel consumption by about 15%
☐ reduce fuel consumption by about 15%
☐ increase journey times by about 15%

☐ **reduce fuel consumption by about 15%**

Gentle use of the major controls increases driver and passenger comfort, reduces wear and tear on the vehicle and decreases fuel consumption.

3.95   mark **one** answer

You can save fuel when conditions allow by

❑ using lower gears as often as possible
❑ accelerating sharply in each gear
❑ using each gear in turn
❑ missing out some gears

❑ **missing out some gears**

It is not necessary to use all of the gears all of the time. Block changing is a fuel-efficient, relaxed and effective technique when used appropriately.

3.96   mark **one** answer

How can driving in an Eco-safe manner help protect the environment?

❑ Through the legal enforcement of speed regulations
❑ By increasing the number of cars on the road
❑ Through increased fuel bills
❑ By reducing exhaust emissions

❑ **By reducing exhaust emissions**

Emissions cause pollution. Motor vehicles emit harmful exhaust gasses which damage the environment. They also use up valuable natural resources by requiring energy to build, maintain and run them.

3.97   mark **one** answer

What does Eco-safe driving achieve?
❑ Increased fuel consumption
❑ Improved road safety
❑ Damage to the environment
❑ Increased exhaust emissions

❑ **Improved road safety**

Eco-safe driving is about adopting a style of driving which reduces emissions that damage the environment.

3.98   mark **one** answer

How can missing out some gear changes save fuel?

❑ By reducing the amount of time you are accelerating
❑ Because there is less need to use the footbrake
❑ By controlling the amount of steering
❑ Because coasting is kept to a minimum

❑ **By reducing the amount of time you are accelerating**

Every time you change up through the gears you come off the accelerator and then reapply it. This uses more fuel than maintaining a constant pressure on the accelerator. Missing out gears reduces the need to come off and back on the accelerator.

mark one answer

Missing out some gears saves fuel by reducing the amount of time you spend

❑ braking
❑ coasting
❑ steering
❑ accelerating

❑ **accelerating**

When you change up a gear, you come off the accelerator then reapply it. This uses more fuel than maintaining a constant pressure on the accelerator. Missing out gears reduces the need to reapply the accelerator constantly.

mark one answer

You are checking your trailer tyres. What is the legal minimum tread depth over the central three quarters of its breadth?

❑ 1 mm
❑ 1.6 mm
❑ 2 mm
❑ 2.6 mm

❑ **1.6 mm**

Tyre regulations also cover tyres on your trailer or caravan.

mark one answer

Fuel consumption is at its highest when you are

❑ braking
❑ coasting
❑ accelerating
❑ steering

❑ **accelerating**

Because the others do not require the engine to work harder.

mark one answer

Car passengers MUST wear a seat belt/restraint if one is available, unless they are

❑ under 14 years old
❑ under 1.5 metres (5 feet) in height
❑ sitting in the rear seat
❑ exempt for medical reasons

❑ **exempt for medical reasons**

The law requires that all passengers, front and rear, must were seat belts, if fitted, unless exempt for medical reasons.

3.103   mark **one** answer

Car passengers MUST wear a seat belt if one is available, unless they are

❏ in a vehicle fitted with air bags
❏ travelling within a congestion charging zone
❏ sitting in the rear seat
❏ exempt for medical reasons

❏ **exempt for medical reasons**

All passengers – front and rear – must wear safety belts; this is a safety issue.

3.104   mark **one** answer

You are driving the children of a friend home from school. They are both under 14 years old. Who is responsible for making sure they wear a seat belt or approved child restraint where required?

❏ An adult passenger
❏ The children
❏ You, the driver
❏ Your friend

❏ **You, the driver**

All children under the age of 14 are the driver's responsibility.

3.105   mark **one** answer

You have too much oil in your engine. What could this cause?

❏ Low oil pressure
❏ Engine overheating
❏ Chain wear
❏ Oil leaks

❏ **Oil leaks**

As the oil and engine heat up, the oil will expand causing it to blow out of a breather or expansion pipe.

3.106   mark **one** answer

You are carrying a 5-year-old child in the back seat of your car. They are under 1.35 metres (4 feet 5 inches). A correct child restraint is NOT available. They MUST

❏ sit behind the passenger seat
❏ use an adult seat belt
❏ share a belt with an adult
❏ sit between two other children

❏ **use an adult seat belt**

This is the only safe option.

mark **one** answer

You are carrying a child using a rear-facing baby seat. You want to put it on the front passenger seat. What MUST you do before setting off?

❑ Deactivate all front and rear airbags
❑ Make sure any front passenger airbag is deactivated
❑ Make sure all the child safety locks are off
❑ Recline the front passenger seat

❑ **Make sure any front passenger airbag is deactivated**

Rear-facing baby seats are not designed to be used in conjunction with an airbag. If one went off in an accident the child could be more severely injured.

mark **one** answer

You are carrying an 11-year-old child in the back seat of your car. They are under 1.35 metres (4 feet 5 inches) in height. You MUST make sure that

❑ they sit between two belted people
❑ they can fasten their own seat belt
❑ a suitable child restraint is available
❑ they can see clearly out of the front window

❑ **a suitable child restraint is available**

This is the only safe option.

mark **one** answer

You are parked at the side of the road. You will be waiting for some time for a passenger. What should you do?

❑ Switch off the engine
❑ Apply the steering lock
❑ Switch off the radio
❑ Use your headlights

❑ **Switch off the engine**

It is more environmentally friendly, cheaper, and more considerate.

3.110   mark **one** answer

You are using a rear-facing baby seat. You want to put it on the front passenger seat which is protected by a frontal airbag. What MUST you do before setting off?

❑ Deactivate the airbag
❑ Turn the seat to face sideways
❑ Ask a passenger to hold the baby
❑ Put the child in an adult seat belt

❑ **Deactivate the airbag**

Modern cars have airbags fitted to reduce injury when a crash occurs. There is however a risk of injury to the baby, where a rear-facing baby seat is used on the front passenger seat. If you do wish to fit a rear-facing baby seat, you must have the airbag deactivated. It is illegal if you don't. The manufacturer's instructions must be followed correctly to do this correctly.

3.111   mark one answer

You are carrying a 5-year-old child in the back seat of your car. They are under 1.35 metres (4 feet 5 inches) in height. They MUST use an adult seat belt ONLY if

❑ a correct child restraint is not available
❑ it is a lap type belt
❑ they sit between two adults
❑ it can be shared with another adult

❑ **a correct child restraint is not available**

This is the safest option.

3.112   mark one answer

You are leaving your vehicle parked on a road unattended. When may you leave the engine running?

❑ If you will be parking for less than five minutes
❑ If the battery keeps going flat
❑ When parked in a 20 mph zone
❑ Never if you are away from the vehicle

❑ **Never if you are away from the vehicle**

It is an offence to leave your vehicle unattended with the engine running. For safety and security, always switch the engine off and remove the keys from the ignition when you leave your vehicle parked.

Section 4
Safety margins

There are 59 questions in this section covering the following subjects:

- ❑ Stopping distances
- ❑ Road surfaces
- ❑ Skidding
- ❑ Weather conditions

You will need to think about:

- ❑ Keeping a safe space around your car
- ❑ Stopping and steering around problems
- ❑ The contact between the road and your car, and how it is affected.

Tip

Watch out for the questions about stopping distances. Are they asking you for the braking distance, which does not include reaction time (or thinking distance)? Or are they asking for the overall stopping distance, which does?

Braking distances on ice can be

- ❏ twice the normal distance
- ❏ five times the normal distance
- ❏ seven times the normal distance
- ❏ ten times the normal distance

❏ **ten times the normal distance**

When the grip between the tyres and the road is lost, in this case by ice, the braking distances are greatly increased.

Freezing conditions will affect the distance it takes you to come to a stop. You should expect stopping distances to increase by up to

- ❏ two times
- ❏ three times
- ❏ five times
- ❏ ten times

❏ **ten times**

Your tyre grip is significantly reduced on icy roads meaning that you need to allow much longer stopping distances.

In windy conditions you need to take extra care when

- ❏ using the brakes
- ❏ making a hill start
- ❏ turning into a narrow road
- ❏ passing pedal cyclists

❏ **passing pedal cyclists**

In windy conditions cyclists are all too easily blown about and may wobble or steer off course.

4.4   mark **one** answer

When approaching a right-hand bend you should keep well to the left. Why is this?

❏ To improve your view of the road
❏ To overcome the effect of the road's slope
❏ To let faster traffic from behind overtake
❏ To be positioned safely if you skid

❏ **To improve your view of the road**

You can see further round the bend earlier if you keep to the left.

4.5   mark **one** answer

You have just gone through deep water. To dry off the brakes you should

❏ accelerate and keep to a high speed for a short time
❏ go slowly while gently applying the brakes
❏ avoid using the brakes at all for a few miles
❏ stop for at least an hour to allow them time to dry

❏ **go slowly while gently applying the brakes**

Drive slowly in case the brakes are flooded, and gently brake to dry them off.

4.6   mark **two** answers

In very hot weather the road surface can become soft. Which TWO of the following will be most affected?

❏ The suspension
❏ The grip of the tyres
❏ The braking
❏ The exhaust

❏ **The grip of the tyres**

❏ **The braking**

If the grip of the tyres is poor, your braking distance will be increased.

mark one answer

Where are you most likely to be affected by a side wind?

❑ On a narrow country lane
❑ On an open stretch of road
❑ On a busy stretch of road
❑ On a long, straight road

❑ **On an open stretch of road**

The wind could catch the side of your vehicle on an open road, and blow you off course.

---

mark one answer

In good conditions, what is the typical stopping distance at 70 mph?

❑ 53 metres (175 feet)
❑ 60 metres (197 feet)
❑ 73 metres (240 feet)
❑ 96 metres (315 feet)

❑ **96 metres (315 feet)**

Stopping distances are calculated to include the time you take to react, and the time it takes to brake to a stop. Despite advances in technology this is the shortest distance you should expect to stop in, at this speed, assuming a dry road in good condition, and a healthy alert driver in a well-maintained car.

---

mark one answer

What is the shortest overall stopping distance on a dry road at 60 mph?

❑ 53 metres (175 feet)
❑ 58 metres (190 feet)
❑ 73 metres (240 feet)
❑ 96 metres (315 feet)

❑ **73 metres (240 feet)**

This is the typical stopping distance. If the road conditions are poor and the driver is not alert, the distance will be longer.

---

mark one answer

You are following a vehicle at a safe distance on a wet road. Another driver overtakes you and pulls into the gap you have left. What should you do?

❑ Flash your headlights as a warning
❑ Try to overtake safely as soon as you can
❑ Drop back to regain a safe distance
❑ Stay close to the other vehicle until it moves on

❑ **Drop back to regain a safe distance**

Keep calm and make the situation safe, widening the gap with the vehicle in front.

4.11   mark **one** answer

You are travelling at 50 mph on a good, dry road. What is your typical overall stopping distance?

- ❏ 36 metres (118 feet)
- ❏ 53 metres (175 feet)
- ❏ 75 metres (245 feet)
- ❏ 96 metres (315 feet)

❏ **53 metres (175 feet)**

You must know the shortest distances that it is possible to stop your car. At fifty mph you need at least 53 metres, providing the road surface is good and dry.

4.12   mark **one** answer

You are on a good, dry, road surface. Your brakes and tyres are good. What is the typical overall stopping distance at 40 mph?

- ❏ 23 metres (75 feet)
- ❏ 36 metres (118 feet)
- ❏ 53 metres (175 feet)
- ❏ 96 metres (315 feet)

❏ **36 metres (118 feet)**

At 40 mph you will need at least 36 metres, providing your brakes and tyres are good. Remember, this is shortest distance that it is possible to stop your car at this speed.

4.13   mark **one** answer

What should you do when overtaking a motorcyclist in strong winds?

- ❏ Pass close
- ❏ Pass quickly
- ❏ Pass wide
- ❏ Pass immediately

❏ **Pass wide**

Wind is a hazard that will particularly affect motorcycle riders. Always give them plenty of room by passing wide when you overtake.

4.14   mark **one** answer

You are overtaking a motorcyclist in strong winds? What should you do?

- ❏ Allow extra room
- ❏ Give a thank you wave
- ❏ Move back early
- ❏ Sound your horn

❏ **Allow extra room**

Think about how the different weather conditions can affect more vulnerable road users. Give extra room when passing motorcyclists in strong winds.

mark **one** answer

Overall stopping distance is made up of thinking and braking distance. You are on a good, dry road surface with good brakes and tyres. What is the typical BRAKING distance from 50 mph?

❏ 14 metres (46 feet)
❏ 24 metres (80 feet)
❏ 38 metres (125 feet)
❏ 55 metres (180 feet)

❏ **38 metres (125 feet)**

The thinking distance is the time it takes you to respond. The braking distance is the time it physically takes your brakes to bring the car to a stop. At 50 mph this is 38 metres.

mark **one** answer

In heavy motorway traffic the vehicle behind you is following too closely. How can you lower the risk of a collision?

❏ Increase your distance from the vehicle in front
❏ Operate the brakes sharply
❏ Switch on your hazard lights
❏ Move onto the hard shoulder and stop

❏ **Increase your distance from the vehicle in front**

It may not feel like the easiest thing to do, but to lower the risk of a collision you do need to open up the distance between your vehicle and the one in front.

mark **one** answer

You are following other vehicles in fog. You have your lights on. What else can you do to reduce the chances of being in a collision?

❏ Keep close to the vehicle in front
❏ Use your main beam instead of dipped headlights
❏ Keep up with the faster vehicles
❏ Reduce your speed and increase the gap in front

❏ **Reduce your speed and increase the gap in front**

Your visibility will be reduced in fog. To reduce the chances of a collision you do need to increase the distance between your vehicle and the one in front.

4.18   mark **three** answers

To avoid a collision when entering a contraflow system, you should

❏ reduce speed in good time
❏ switch lanes at any time to make progress
❏ choose an appropriate lane in good time
❏ keep the correct separation distance
❏ increase speed to pass through quickly
❏ follow other motorists closely to avoid long queues

❏ **reduce speed in good time**
❏ **choose an appropriate lane in good time**
❏ **keep the correct separation distance**

Contraflow systems occur where there are roadworks. To avoid having a collision you do need to check and reduce speed early, be sure to adopt a correct road position early and keep the correct separation ditance.

4.19   mark **one** answer

What is the most common cause of skidding?

❏ Worn tyres
❏ Driver error
❏ Other vehicles
❏ Pedestrians

❏ **Driver error**

Either through inexperience or lack of ability, the driver loses control of the vehicle. This is the most common cause of a skid.

4.20   mark **one** answer

You are driving on an icy road. How can you avoid wheel spin?

❏ Drive at a slow speed in as high a gear as possible
❏ Use the handbrake if the wheels start to slip
❏ Brake gently and repeatedly
❏ Drive in a low gear at all times

❏ **Drive at a slow speed in as high a gear as possible**

Keep the speed down, and keep the engine revs down by being in a higher gear. This will make the car easier to manage in the slippery conditions.

4.21   mark **one** answer

Skidding is mainly caused by

❏ the weather
❏ the driver
❏ the vehicle
❏ the road

❏ **the driver**

Skidding is usually caused by harsh braking, harsh acceleration or steering – all actions of the driver. You are, however, more likely to cause a skid in a poorly-maintained car, in bad weather, or on a poor road surface.

4.22   mark **two** answers

You are driving in freezing conditions. What should you do when approaching a sharp bend?

❏ Slow down before you reach the bend
❏ Gently apply your handbrake
❏ Firmly use your footbrake
❏ Coast into the bend
❏ Avoid sudden steering movements

❏ **Slow down before you reach the bend**

❏ **Avoid sudden steering movements**

Braking on an icy bend is extremely dangerous. It could cause your vehicle to spin.

4.23   mark **one** answer

You are turning left on a slippery road. The back of your vehicle slides to the right. You should

❏ brake firmly and not turn the steering wheel
❏ steer carefully to the left
❏ steer carefully to the right
❏ brake firmly and steer to the left

❏ **steer carefully to the right**

Where the back wheels slide in this manner, to regain control you need to steer into the skid.

4.24   mark **four** answers

Before starting a journey in freezing weather you should clear ice and snow from your vehicle's

❏ aerial
❏ windows
❏ bumper
❏ lights
❏ mirrors
❏ number plates

❏ **windows**

❏ **lights**

❏ **mirrors**

❏ **number plates**

This is so that you can see and be seen. The number plates are a legal requirement.

4.25
mark one answer

You are trying to move off on snow.
You should use

❏ the lowest gear you can
❏ the highest gear you can
❏ a high engine speed
❏ the handbrake and foot brake together

❏ **the highest gear you can**

This will keep the engine revs low and help maintain some grip in these slippery conditions.

4.26
mark one answer

When driving in falling snow you should

❏ brake firmly and quickly
❏ be ready to steer sharply
❏ use sidelights only
❏ brake gently in plenty of time

❏ **brake gently in plenty of time**

Sudden or harsh braking could cause a skid. Be smooth and controlled.

4.27
mark one answer

The MAIN benefit of having four-wheel drive is to improve

❏ road holding
❏ fuel consumption
❏ stopping distances
❏ passenger comfort

❏ **road holding**

Because all four wheels are driven, only road holding is improved.

4.28
mark one answer

You are about to go down a steep hill. To control the speed of your vehicle you should

❏ select a high gear and use the brakes carefully
❏ select a high gear and use the brakes firmly
❏ select a low gear and use the brakes carefully
❏ select a low gear and avoid using the brakes

❏ **select a low gear and use the brakes carefully**

A low gear will help control your speed, but on a steep hill you will also need your brakes.

mark **two** answers

You wish to park facing DOWNHILL. Which TWO of the following should you do?

- ❏ Turn the steering wheel towards the kerb
- ❏ Park close to the bumper of another car
- ❏ Park with two wheels on the kerb
- ❏ Put the handbrake on firmly
- ❏ Turn the steering wheel away from the kerb

❏ **Turn the steering wheel towards the kerb**

❏ **Put the handbrake on firmly**

If the handbrake should fail, the car will roll into the kerb and not down the road.

4.30 mark **one** answer

You are driving in a built-up area. You approach a speed hump. You should

- ❏ move across to the left-hand side of the road
- ❏ wait for any pedestrians to cross
- ❏ slow your vehicle right down
- ❏ stop and check both pavements

❏ **slow your vehicle right down**

They are traffic calming measures designed to slow traffic in a potentially dangerous area, for example outside a school.

4.31 mark **one** answer

You are on a long, downhill slope. What should you do to help control the speed of your vehicle?

- ❏ Select neutral
- ❏ Select a lower gear
- ❏ Grip the handbrake firmly
- ❏ Apply the parking brake gently

❏ **Select a lower gear**

You should ideally have selected the lower gear before starting down the slope. Selecting neutral would be likely to make your car go faster as you would no longer be in any gear at all.

4.32   mark **one** answer

Anti-lock brakes prevent wheels from locking. This means the tyres are less likely to

❏ aquaplane
❏ skid
❏ puncture
❏ wear

❏ **skid**

ABS activates when the system senses hard braking. It prevents the wheels locking so that you can steer while braking.

4.33   mark **one** answer

Anti-lock brakes reduce the chances of a skid occurring particularly when

❏ driving down steep hills
❏ braking during normal driving
❏ braking in an emergency
❏ driving on good road surfaces

❏ **braking in an emergency**

You should brake rapidly and firmly.

4.34   mark **one** answer

Vehicles fitted with anti-lock brakes

❏ are impossible to skid
❏ can be steered while you are braking
❏ accelerate much faster
❏ are not fitted with a handbrake

❏ **can be steered while you are braking**

A vehicle fitted with anti-lock brakes is difficult, but not impossible, to skid. Take care if the road surface is loose or wet.

4.35   mark **two** answers

Anti-lock brakes may not work as effectively if the road surface is

❏ dry
❏ loose
❏ wet
❏ good
❏ firm

❏ **loose**

❏ **wet**

The ABS system allows a driver to brake hard while the car adjusts the braking automatically to the optimum for normal conditions. Hence it is possible to skid a car with ABS fitted in wet conditions or on a loose road surface.

4.36   mark **one** answer

Anti-lock brakes are of most use when you are

- ❑ braking gently
- ❑ driving on worn tyres
- ❑ braking excessively
- ❑ driving normally

❑ **braking excessively**

ABS has a road safety benefit if you have to brake very hard.

4.37   mark **one** answer

Driving a vehicle fitted with anti-lock brakes allows you to

- ❑ brake harder because it is impossible to skid
- ❑ drive at higher speeds
- ❑ steer and brake at the same time
- ❑ pay less attention to the road ahead

❑ **steer and brake at the same time**

Because ABS is designed to stop the vehicle from skidding, it allows the driver to steer at the same time without losing control.

4.38   mark **one** answer

Anti-lock brakes can greatly assist with

- ❑ a higher cruising speed
- ❑ steering control when braking
- ❑ control when accelerating
- ❑ motorway driving

❑ **steering control when braking**

ABS prevents the wheels from locking, allowing drivers to steer at the same time without losing control.

4.39   mark **one** answer

You are driving a vehicle fitted with anti-lock brakes. You need to stop in an emergency. You should apply the foot brake

- ❑ slowly and gently
- ❑ slowly but firmly
- ❑ rapidly and gently
- ❑ rapidly and firmly

❑ **rapidly and firmly**

ABS or anti-lock brakes allow a driver to brake hard while the car adjusts the braking automatically to the optimum for normal conditions. It is difficult but not impossible to skid a car with ABS fitted.

4.40   mark **two** answers

Your vehicle has anti-lock brakes, but they may not always prevent skidding. This is most likely to happen when driving

❑ in foggy conditions
❑ on surface water
❑ on loose road surfaces
❑ on dry tarmac
❑ at night on unlit roads

❑ **on surface water**

❑ **on loose road surfaces**

Sometimes known as ABS, the system allows a driver to brake hard while the car adjusts the braking automatically to the optimum for normal conditions. Hence it is possible to skid a car with ABS fitted in wet conditions or on a loose road surface.

4.41   mark **one** answer

You are driving along a country road. You see this sign. AFTER dealing safely with the hazard you should always

❑ check your tyre pressures
❑ switch on your hazard warning lights
❑ accelerate briskly
❑ test your brakes

❑ **test your brakes**

Drive slowly forwards with your left foot gently on the footbrake. This helps dry out the brakes.

4.42   mark **one** answer

You are driving in heavy rain. Your steering suddenly becomes very light. You should

❑ steer towards the side of the road
❑ apply gentle acceleration
❑ brake firmly to reduce speed
❑ ease off the accelerator

❑ **ease off the accelerator**

This is the only safe option. The tyres have lost contact with the road, because of a thin film of water, and you are now aquaplaning. By gently easing off you should regain control.

mark **one** answer

The roads are icy. You should drive slowly

❑ in the highest gear possible
❑ in the lowest gear possible
❑ with the handbrake partly on
❑ with your left foot on the brake

❑ **in the highest gear possible**

This will keep the engine revs low and easier to manage in the slippery conditions.

mark **one** answer

You are driving along a wet road. How can you tell if your vehicle is aquaplaning?

❑ The engine will stall
❑ The engine noise will increase
❑ The steering will feel very heavy
❑ The steering will feel very light

❑ **The steering will feel very light**

When the tyres lose contact with the road because of a thin film of water, you are aquaplaning and the steering feels very light.

mark **two** answers

How can you tell if you are driving on ice?

❑ The tyres make a rumbling noise
❑ The tyres make hardly any noise
❑ The steering becomes heavier
❑ The steering becomes lighter

❑ **The tyres make hardly any noise**

❑ **The steering becomes lighter**

This is because they are separated and cushioned from the road.

mark **one** answer

You are driving along a wet road. How can you tell if your vehicle's tyres are losing their grip on the surface?

❑ The engine will stall
❑ The steering will feel very heavy
❑ The engine noise will increase
❑ The steering will feel very light

❑ **The steering will feel very light**

This problem is called aquaplaning. Your tyres build up a thin film of water between them and the road and lose all grip. The steering suddenly feels light and uncontrollable. The solution is to ease off the accelerator until you feel the tyres grip the road again.

4.47   mark **one** answer

Your overall stopping distance will be much longer when driving

- ❏ in the rain
- ❏ in fog
- ❏ at night
- ❏ in strong winds

❏ **in the rain**

When the grip between the tyres and the road is reduced, in this case by rain, the braking distances are increased.

4.48   mark **one** answer

You have driven through a flood. What is the first thing you should do?

- ❏ Stop and check the tyres
- ❏ Stop and dry the brakes
- ❏ Check your exhaust
- ❏ Test your brakes

❏ **Test your brakes**

Your brakes may be wet. The first thing you should do is check them and then dry them.

4.49   mark **one** answer

You are on a fast, open road in good conditions. For safety, the distance between you and the vehicle in front should be

- ❏ a two-second time gap
- ❏ one car length
- ❏ 2 metres (6 feet 6 inches)
- ❏ two car lengths

❏ **a two-second time gap**

This gap should leave sufficient space for you to stop in an emergency, in good conditions.

4.50   mark **one** answer

How can you use your vehicle's engine as a brake?

- ❏ By changing to a lower gear
- ❏ By selecting reverse gear
- ❏ By changing to a higher gear
- ❏ By selecting neutral gear

❏ **By changing to a lower gear**

Providing you don't touch the accelerator, doing this will allow you to slow your vehicle with the engine. You might choose to do this on a long descent, where the brakes could overheat.

mark **one** answer

Anti-lock brakes are most effective when you

❑ keep pumping the foot brake to prevent
   skidding
❑ brake normally, but grip the steering wheel
   tightly
❑ brake promptly and firmly until you have
   slowed down
❑ apply the handbrake to reduce the
   stopping distance

❑ **brake promptly and firmly until you
   have slowed down**

The ABS system allows a driver to brake
firmly while the car adjusts the braking
automatically to the optimum for normal
conditions.

mark **one** answer

Your car is fitted with anti-lock brakes. You
need to stop in an emergency. You should

❑ brake normally and avoid turning the
   steering wheel
❑ press the brake pedal promptly and firmly
   until you have stopped
❑ keep pushing and releasing the foot brake
   quickly to prevent skidding
❑ apply the handbrake to reduce the
   stopping distance

❑ **press the brake pedal promptly and
   firmly until you have stopped**

ABS automatically senses that the wheels
are about to lock.

mark **one** answer

When would an anti-lock braking system start
to work?

❑ After the parking brake has been applied
❑ Whenever pressure on the brake pedal is
   applied
❑ Just as the wheels are about to lock
❑ When the normal braking system fails to
   operate

❑ **Just as the wheels are about to lock**

This system allows a driver to brake hard
while the car adjusts the braking
automatically to the optimum (just as the
wheels are about to lock) for normal
conditions.

4.54   mark **one** answer

Anti-lock brakes will take effect when

❑ you do not brake quickly enough
❑ maximum brake pressure has been applied
❑ you have not seen a hazard ahead
❑ speeding on slippery road surfaces

❑ **maximum brake pressure has been applied**

Anti-lock brakes allow a driver to brake hard while the car adjusts the braking automatically to the optimum for normal conditions.

4.55   mark **one** answer

You are on a wet motorway with surface spray. You should use

❑ hazard flashers
❑ dipped headlights
❑ rear fog lights
❑ sidelights

❑ **dipped headlights**

You should always put these on when visibility is reduced, in this case by spray.

4.56   mark **one** answer

Your vehicle is fitted with anti-lock brakes. To stop quickly in an emergency you should

❑ brake firmly and pump the brake pedal on and off
❑ brake rapidly and firmly without releasing the brake pedal
❑ brake gently and pump the brake pedal on and off
❑ brake rapidly once, and immediately release the brake pedal

❑ **brake rapidly and firmly without releasing the brake pedal**

ABS systems allow the driver to brake and steer together in an emergency situation.

4.57   mark **one** answer

Travelling for long distances in neutral (known as coasting)

❑ improves the driver's control
❑ makes steering easier
❑ reduces the driver's control
❑ uses more fuel

❑ **reduces the driver's control**

You cannot accelerate until you have reselected a gear, and your chances of skidding are increased because the engine is no longer connected to the drive wheels.

mark **one** answer

How can you tell when you are driving over black ice?

❑ It is easier to brake
❑ The noise from your tyres sounds louder
❑ You will see tyre tracks on the road
❑ Your steering feels light

❑ **Your steering feels light**

Black ice is normally invisible when you are driving. The tyres will lose grip with the road, which will make the steering feel light.

mark **three** answers

When driving in fog, which THREE of these are correct?

❑ Use dipped headlights
❑ Position close to the centre line
❑ Allow more time for your journey
❑ Keep close to the car in front
❑ Slow down
❑ Use side lights only

❑ **Use dipped headlights**

❑ **Allow more time for your journey**

❑ **Slow down**

To ensure that you arrive at your destination safely where your visibility is affected by fog, you must use dipped headlights, keep your speed in check and allow more time for your journey.

Section 5
Hazard awareness

There are 96 questions in this section covering the following subjects:

- ❑ Anticipation
- ❑ Hazard awareness
- ❑ Attention
- ❑ Speed and distance
- ❑ Reaction time
- ❑ The effects of alcohol and drugs
- ❑ Tiredness

You will need to think about:

- ❑ How you will deal with potential problems on the road

- ❑ Forward planning

- ❑ How easy it is to become distracted for a variety of reasons

- ❑ Managing your speed and space around problems

- ❑ How quickly you will respond to problems

- ❑ How easy it is to be affected by drink, drugs, or drowsiness.

Tips

There are a lot of photographs in this section which pose questions about hazards on the road. Don't just study a picture – try to imagine yourself as the driver and think of the picture as your windscreen. It might bring the hazards into sharper focus.

There are some old fashioned 'learning by rote' parts to this section. Like the signs on a builder's skip, or the signals a police officer might give, they are because they are, and you will just have to learn the ones you don't already know.

Where would you expect to see these markers?

❏ On a motorway sign
❏ At the entrance to a narrow bridge
❏ On a large goods vehicle
❏ On a builder's skip placed on the road

❏ **On a large goods vehicle**

❏ **On a builder's skip placed on the road**

These are the only places where this colour and shape of markings will appear.

What is the main hazard shown in this picture?

❏ Vehicles turning right
❏ Vehicles doing U-turns
❏ The cyclist crossing the road
❏ Parked cars around the corner

❏ **The cyclist crossing the road**

This is a very fast moving, busy junction. The cyclist is crossing in an unexpected place, and will be slow by comparison.

5.3   mark **one** answer

Which road user has caused a hazard?

- ❏ The parked car (arrowed A)
- ❏ The pedestrian waiting to cross (arrowed B)
- ❏ The moving car (arrowed C)
- ❏ The car turning (arrowed D)

❏ **The parked car (arrowed A)**

It will force oncoming vehicles onto this side of the road.

5.4   mark **one** answer

What should the driver of the car approaching the crossing do?

- ❏ Continue at the same speed
- ❏ Sound the horn
- ❏ Drive through quickly
- ❏ Slow down and get ready to stop

❏ **Slow down and get ready to stop**

The pedestrian may want to cross. Doing this will enable the driver to deal with the crossing in the safest manner possible.

What THREE things should the driver of the grey car (arrowed) be especially aware of?

- ❏ Pedestrians stepping out between cars
- ❏ Other cars behind the grey car
- ❏ Doors opening on parked cars
- ❏ The bumpy road surface
- ❏ Cars leaving parking spaces
- ❏ Empty parking spaces

❏ **Pedestrians stepping out between cars**

❏ **Doors opening on parked cars**

❏ **Cars leaving parking spaces**

The road is very narrow and things will happen quickly, even at a slow speed. These are the most likely hazards.

You see this sign ahead. You should expect the road to

- ❏ go steeply uphill
- ❏ go steeply downhill
- ❏ bend sharply to the left
- ❏ bend sharply to the right

❏ **bend sharply to the left**

Officially a 'sharp deviation to the left' (or right when reversed); you will find this at bends and roundabouts.

5.7   mark **one** answer

You are approaching this cyclist. You should

- ❑ overtake before the cyclist gets to the junction
- ❑ flash your headlights at the cyclist
- ❑ slow down and allow the cyclist to turn
- ❑ overtake the cyclist on the left-hand side

❑ **slow down and allow the cyclist to turn**

Trying to force your way past will only add danger. Always give cyclists space and time.

5.8   mark **one** answer

Why must you take extra care when turning right at this junction?

- ❑ Road surface is poor
- ❑ Footpaths are narrow
- ❑ Road markings are faint
- ❑ There is reduced visibility

❑ **There is reduced visibility**

The building on your right is restricting your view of the road. Traffic could be hidden from you.

mark **one** answer

When approaching this bridge you should give way to

❏ bicycles
❏ buses
❏ motorcycles
❏ cars

❏ **buses**

Because of the height of the bridge buses will be forced into the middle of the road.

mark **one** answer

What type of vehicle could you expect to meet in the middle of the road?

❏ Lorry
❏ Bicycle
❏ Car
❏ Motorcycle

❏ **Lorry**

Lorries will have to use the highest point of the bridge by driving in the middle of the road.

5.11   mark **one** answer

At this blind junction you must stop

❏ behind the line, then edge forward to see clearly
❏ beyond the line at a point where you can see clearly
❏ only if there is traffic on the main road
❏ only if you are turning to the right

❏ **behind the line, then edge forward to see clearly**

Your view of the main road is restricted. You must always stop at a stop line and, in this case, then edge forward to see if it's safe to emerge.

5.12   mark **one** answer

A driver pulls out of a side road in front of you. You have to brake hard. You should

❏ ignore the error and stay calm
❏ flash your lights to show your annoyance
❏ sound your horn to show your annoyance
❏ overtake as soon as possible

❏ **ignore the error and stay calm**

Do not react to other drivers' errors or behaviour; keep calm, and keep yourself, your passengers and your car safe.

5.13   mark **one** answer

An elderly person's driving ability could be affected because they may be unable to

❏ obtain car insurance
❏ understand road signs
❏ react very quickly
❏ give signals correctly

❏ **react very quickly**

Everybody's reaction time increases as they get older.

mark one answer

You have just passed these warning lights. What hazard would you expect to see next?

- ❏ A level crossing with no barrier
- ❏ An ambulance station
- ❏ A school crossing patrol
- ❏ An opening bridge

❏ **A school crossing patrol**

All the others have three flashing lights, two red ones in a horizontal line at the top and one amber one below.

mark one answer

You are planning a long journey. Do you need to plan rest stops?

- ❏ Yes, you should plan to stop every half an hour
- ❏ Yes, regular stops help concentration
- ❏ No, you will be less tired if you get there as soon as possible
- ❏ No, only fuel stops will be needed

❏ **Yes, regular stops help concentration**

Driving requires your full attention. It can be easy to lose concentration on a long journey. Worse still falling asleep at the wheel is a significant cause of accidents on long journeys.

mark one answer

A driver does something that upsets you. You should

- ❏ try not to react
- ❏ let them know how you feel
- ❏ flash your headlights several times
- ❏ sound your horn

❏ **try not to react**

Do not react to other drivers' behaviour, keep calm, and keep yourself, your passengers and your car safe.

5.17   mark **one** answer

The red lights are flashing. What should you do when approaching this level crossing?

- ❏ Go through quickly
- ❏ Go through carefully
- ❏ Stop before the barrier
- ❏ Switch on hazard warning lights

❏ **Stop before the barrier**

Red lights mean the same, flashing or not: stop.

5.18   mark **one** answer

You are approaching crossroads. The traffic lights have failed. What should you do?

- ❏ Brake and stop only for large vehicles
- ❏ Brake sharply to a stop before looking
- ❏ Be prepared to brake sharply to a stop
- ❏ Be prepared to stop for any traffic.

❏ **Be prepared to stop for any traffic.**

In this situation treat the junction as a give way, where you do not have priority.

What should the driver of the red car (arrowed) do?

❏ Wave the pedestrians who are waiting to cross
❏ Wait for the pedestrian in the road to cross
❏ Quickly drive behind the pedestrian in the road
❏ Tell the pedestrian in the road she should not have crossed

❏ **Wait for the pedestrian in the road to cross**

This is the safest option. It is the same as at a junction: 'give way to pedestrians already crossing the road'.

You are following a slower-moving vehicle on a narrow country road. There is a junction just ahead on the right. What should you do?

❏ Overtake after checking your mirrors and signalling
❏ Stay behind until you are past the junction
❏ Accelerate quickly to pass before the junction
❏ Slow down and prepare to overtake on the left

❏ **Stay behind until you are past the junction**

Never overtake on an approach to a junction; vehicles may want to turn into the junction, or emerge from it as you pass.

5.21   mark **one** answer

What should you do as you approach this overhead bridge?

❏ Move out to the centre of the road before going through
❏ Find another route, this is only for high vehicles
❏ Be prepared to give way to large vehicles in the middle of the road
❏ Move across to the right hand side before going through

❏ **Be prepared to give way to large vehicles in the middle of the road**

Because of the height of the bridge, large vehicles will be forced into the middle of the road.

5.22   mark **one** answer

Why are mirrors often slightly curved (convex)?

❏ They give a wider field of vision
❏ They totally cover blind spots
❏ They make it easier to judge the speed of following traffic
❏ They make following traffic look bigger

❏ **They give a wider field of vision**

To enable the driver to see more of what is behind, and to reduce blindspots.

mark **one** answer

You see this sign on the rear of a slow-moving lorry that you want to pass. It is travelling in the middle lane of a three-lane motorway. You should

❑ cautiously approach the lorry then pass on either side
❑ follow the lorry until you can leave the motorway
❑ wait on the hard shoulder until the lorry has stopped
❑ approach with care and keep to the left of the lorry

❑ **approach with care and keep to the left of the lorry**

Even though the sign is attached to a lorry – in this case a motorway service vehicle – it is still a keep-left sign.

mark **one** answer

You think the driver of the vehicle in front has forgotten to cancel their right indicator. You should

❑ flash your lights to alert the driver
❑ sound your horn before overtaking
❑ overtake on the left if there is room
❑ stay behind and not overtake

❑ **stay behind and not overtake**

This is only what you think, not what you know.

5.25   mark **one** answer

What is the main hazard the driver of the red car (arrowed) should be aware of?

❏ Glare from the sun may affect the driver's vision
❏ The black car may stop suddenly
❏ The bus may move out into the road
❏ Oncoming vehicles will assume the driver is turning right

❏ **The bus may move out into the road**

The bus will move out at some point. The question for the driver is will it do it now?

5.26   mark **one** answer

This yellow sign on a vehicle indicates this is

❏ a broken-down vehicle
❏ a school bus
❏ an ice cream van
❏ a private ambulance

❏ **a school bus**

You will need to take care – children can be erratic pedestrians.

What TWO main hazards should you be aware of when going along this street?

- ❏ Glare from the sun
- ❏ Car doors opening suddenly
- ❏ Lack of road markings
- ❏ The headlights on parked cars being switched on
- ❏ Large goods vehicles
- ❏ Children running out from between vehicles

❏ **Car doors opening suddenly**

❏ **Children running out from between vehicles**

Because of the parked cars the road is very narrow, things will happen quickly, even at a slow speed. These are the most likely hazards.

What is the main hazard you should be aware of when following this cyclist?

- ❏ The cyclist may move to the left and dismount
- ❏ The cyclist may swerve out into the road
- ❏ The contents of the cyclist's carrier may fall onto the road
- ❏ The cyclist may wish to turn right at the end of the road

❏ **The cyclist may swerve out into the road**

Sometimes cyclists need to swerve round things that would not trouble a driver, a drain for example. Always give cyclists space and time.

5.29   mark **one** answer

A driver's behaviour has upset you. It may help if you

❑ stop and take a break
❑ shout abusive language
❑ gesture to them with your hand
❑ follow their car, flashing your headlights

❑ **stop and take a break**

Driving while stressed can lead to mistakes and a lack of concentration.

5.30   mark **one** answer

In areas where there are 'traffic calming' measures you should

❑ travel at a reduced speed
❑ always travel at the speed limit
❑ position in the centre of the road
❑ only slow down if pedestrians are near

❑ **travel at a reduced speed**

Road humps and rumble strips are examples of traffic calming measures. They are often found in residential areas and have been introduced to reduce the overall speed of traffic.

5.31   mark **two** answers

When approaching this hazard why should you slow down?

❑ Because of the bend
❑ Because it's hard to see to the right
❑ Because of approaching traffic
❑ Because of animals crossing
❑ Because of the level crossing

❑ **Because of the bend**

❑ **Because of the level crossing**

Slowing down gives you more time and space to react to what is ahead. The signs have warned you of potential danger.

mark **one** answer

Why are place names painted on the road surface?

❏ To restrict the flow of traffic
❏ To warn you of oncoming traffic
❏ To enable you to change lanes early
❏ To prevent you changing lanes

❏ **To enable you to change lanes early**

They reinforce the rectangular information signs on the road side.

mark **one** answer

Some two-way roads are divided into three lanes. Why are these particularly dangerous?

❏ Traffic in both directions can use the middle lane to overtake
❏ Traffic can travel faster in poor weather conditions
❏ Traffic can overtake on the left
❏ Traffic uses the middle lane for emergencies only

❏ **Traffic in both directions can use the middle lane to overtake**

Take extra care on these roads. Always ensure it will be safe to complete an overtaking manoeuvre before starting one.

mark **one** answer

You are on a dual carriageway. Ahead you see a vehicle with an amber flashing light. What could this be?

❏ An ambulance
❏ A fire engine
❏ A doctor on call
❏ A disabled person's vehicle

❏ **A disabled person's vehicle**

Orange flashing lights or beacons are fitted to large and/or slow-moving vehicles, milk floats, gritter lorries, disabled persons' vehicles, etc.

5.35   mark **one** answer

What does this signal from a police officer mean to oncoming traffic?

- ☐ Go ahead
- ☐ Stop
- ☐ Turn left
- ☐ Turn right

☐ **Stop**

The officer's raised right arm is for you, and the extended left arm is for the oncoming traffic (behind her). Both mean stop.

5.36   mark **two** answers

Why should you be especially cautious when going past this stationary bus?

- ☐ There is traffic approaching in the distance
- ☐ The driver may open the door
- ☐ It may suddenly move off
- ☐ People may cross the road in front of it
- ☐ There are bicycles parked on the pavement

☐ **It may suddenly move off**

☐ **People may cross the road in front of it**

The Highway Code advises drivers to 'give priority to buses waiting to pull out from a bus stop'. Apart from being courteous it will speed up the general traffic flow. Exiting passengers are not always concentrating on their safety.

5.37   mark **three** answers

Overtaking is a major cause of collisions. In which THREE of these situations should you NOT overtake?

- ☐ If you are turning left shortly afterwards
- ☐ When you are in a one-way street
- ☐ When you are approaching a junction
- ☐ If you are travelling up a long hill
- ☐ When your view ahead is blocked

☐ **If you are turning left shortly afterwards**

☐ **When you are approaching a junction**

☐ **When your view ahead is blocked**

All three are either unnecessary, unwise or both.

Which THREE result from drinking alcohol?

- Less control
- A false sense of confidence
- Faster reactions
- Poor judgement of speed
- Greater awareness of danger

☐ **Less control**

☐ **A false sense of confidence**

☐ **Poor judgement of speed**

Drinking alcohol might well cause 'out of character' behaviour. The result – a drink-driver is likely to take risks that will considerably increase the danger of a collision.

What does the solid white line at the side of the road indicate?

- Traffic lights ahead
- Edge of the carriageway
- Footpath on the left
- Cycle path

☐ **Edge of the carriageway**

It is an unbroken line and should not be crossed, for example to park. The line will be broken where there is a driveway or lay-by, etc.

5.40   mark **one** answer

You are driving towards this level crossing. What would be the first warning of an approaching train?

❏ Both half barriers down
❏ A steady amber light
❏ One half barrier down
❏ Twin flashing red lights

❏ **A steady amber light**

The first warning is a steady amber light as this appears first. This is then followed by twin flashing lights.

5.41   mark **one** answer

You are behind this cyclist. When the traffic lights change, what should you do?

❏ Try to move off before the cyclist
❏ Allow the cyclist time and room
❏ Turn right but give the cyclist room
❏ Tap your horn and drive through first

❏ **Allow the cyclist time and room**

Cyclists can be unpredictable – always give them time and space.

mark one answer

While driving, you see this sign ahead. You should

❏ stop at the sign
❏ slow, but continue around the bend
❏ slow to a crawl and continue
❏ stop and look for open farm gates

❏ **slow, but continue around the bend**

Slowing down gives you more time and space to react to what is ahead. The signs have warned you of potential danger.

mark one answer

When the traffic lights change to green the white car should

❏ wait for the cyclist to pull away
❏ move off quickly and turn in front of the cyclist
❏ move close up to the cyclist to beat the lights
❏ sound the horn to warn the cyclist

❏ **wait for the cyclist to pull away**

Cyclists can be unpredictable – always give them time and space.

5.44   mark **one** answer

You intend to turn left at the traffic lights. Just before turning you should

❑ check your right mirror
❑ move close up to the white car
❑ straddle the lanes
❑ check for bicycles on your left

❑ **check for bicycles on your left**

Cyclists will filter through stationary traffic.

5.45   mark **one** answer

You should reduce your speed when driving along this road because

❑ there is a staggered junction ahead
❑ there is a low bridge ahead
❑ there is a change in the road surface
❑ the road ahead narrows

❑ **there is a staggered junction ahead**

Road signs like this are there to give you advanced warning of danger ahead.

You are driving at 60 mph. As you approach this hazard you should

❑ maintain your speed
❑ reduce your speed
❑ take the next right turn
❑ take the next left turn

❑ **reduce your speed**

This will give you more time and space to deal with the potential danger ahead.

What might you expect to happen in this situation?

❑ Traffic will move into the right-hand lane
❑ Traffic speed will increase
❑ Traffic will move into the left-hand lane
❑ Traffic will not need to change position

❑ **Traffic will move into the left-hand lane**

Road signs like this are there to give you advanced warning of danger ahead.

5.48   mark **one** answer

You are driving on a road with several lanes. You see these signs above the lanes. What do they mean?

❏ The two right lanes are open
❏ The two left lanes are open
❏ Traffic in the left lanes should stop
❏ Traffic in the right lanes should stop

❏ **The two left lanes are open**

If you see a red cross above your lane it means that there is an obstruction ahead. You will need to move into one of the lanes which is showing a green light, in this case, the two left lanes are open.

5.49   mark **one** answer

You are invited to a pub lunch. You know that you will have to drive in the evening. What is your best course of action?

❏ Avoid mixing your alcoholic drinks
❏ Not drink any alcohol at all
❏ Have some milk before drinking alcohol
❏ Eat a hot meal with your alcoholic drinks

❏ **Not drink any alcohol at all**

Alcohol affects perception; not drinking at all is clearly the best option.

5.50   mark **one** answer

You have been convicted of driving while unfit through drink or drugs. You will find this is likely to cause the cost of one of the following to rise considerably. Which one?

❏ Road fund licence
❏ Insurance premiums
❏ Vehicle test certificate
❏ Driving licence

❏ **Insurance premiums**

The cost of your insurance is partly based on the chances of your being involved in an accident. People who drink and drive have significantly more accidents.

What advice should you give to a driver who has had a few alcoholic drinks at a party?

❏ Have a strong cup of coffee and then drive home
❏ Drive home carefully and slowly
❏ Go home by public transport
❏ Wait a short while and then drive home

❏ **Go home by public transport**

The only sensible answer is don't drink and drive.

You have been taking medicine for a few days which made you feel drowsy. Today you feel better but still need to take the medicine. You should only drive

❏ if your journey is necessary
❏ at night on quiet roads
❏ if someone goes with you
❏ after checking with your doctor

❏ **after checking with your doctor**

Don't underestimate the effect of drugs on your system.

You are about to return home from holiday when you become ill. A doctor prescribes drugs which are likely to affect your driving. You should

❏ drive only if someone is with you
❏ avoid driving on motorways
❏ not drive yourself
❏ never drive at more than 30 mph

❏ **not drive yourself**

Although it may be inconvenient, find another way to get home.

5.54   mark **two** answers

During periods of illness your ability to drive may be impaired. You MUST

❏ see your doctor each time before you drive
❏ only take smaller doses of any medicines
❏ be medically fit to drive
❏ not drive after taking certain medicines
❏ take all your medicines with you when you drive

❏ **be medically fit to drive**

❏ **not drive after taking certain medicines**

You mustn't drive if you are unfit. Driving while taking some medications is unsafe.

5.55   mark **two** answers

You feel drowsy when driving. You should

❏ stop and rest as soon as possible
❏ turn the heater up to keep you warm and comfortable
❏ make sure you have a good supply of fresh air
❏ continue with your journey but drive more slowly
❏ close the car windows to help you concentrate

❏ **stop and rest as soon as possible**

❏ **make sure you have a good supply of fresh air**

Do not put other road users at risk. Plan your journey so that you have scheduled rest breaks and while driving make sure that you have a supply of fresh air.

5.56   mark **two** answers

You are driving along a motorway and become tired. You should

❏ stop at the next service area and rest
❏ leave the motorway at the next exit and rest
❏ increase your speed and turn up the radio volume
❏ close all your windows and set heating to warm
❏ pull up on the hard shoulder and change drivers

❏ **stop at the next service area and rest**

❏ **leave the motorway at the next exit and rest**

Driving requires your full attention. It can be easy to lose concentration and – if you are drowsy – to fall asleep at the wheel. Open a window: it will generally lower the temperature and increase the oxygen in the car, which will help until you can leave the motorway and find a safe place to stop.

mark **one** answer

You are taking drugs that are likely to affect your driving. What should you do?

❏ Seek medical advice before driving
❏ Limit your driving to essential journeys
❏ Only drive if accompanied by a full licence-holder
❏ Drive only for short distances

❏ **Seek medical advice before driving**

A substantial number of drugs, even those you can buy in the chemist, can affect your ability to drive. Sometimes a warning is given on the packet, but if in any doubt seek medical advice.

mark **one** answer

You are about to drive home. You feel very tired and have a severe headache. You should

❏ wait until you are fit and well before driving
❏ drive home, but take a tablet for headaches
❏ drive home if you can stay awake for the journey
❏ wait for a short time, then drive home slowly

❏ **wait until you are fit and well before driving**

It is easy to underestimate the effect of illness on your ability to drive.

mark **one** answer

If you are feeling tired it is best to stop as soon as you can. Until then you should

❏ increase your speed to find a stopping place quickly
❏ ensure a supply of fresh air
❏ gently tap the steering wheel
❏ keep changing speed to improve concentration

❏ **ensure a supply of fresh air**

Opening a window generally lowers the temperature and increases the oxygen in the car; this will help until you can find a safe place to stop.

5.60   mark **three** answers

Driving long distances can be tiring. You can prevent this by

- ❑ stopping every so often for a walk
- ❑ opening a window for some fresh air
- ❑ ensuring plenty of refreshment breaks
- ❑ completing the journey without stopping
- ❑ eating a large meal before driving

❑ **stopping every so often for a walk**

❑ **opening a window for some fresh air**

❑ **ensuring plenty of refreshment breaks**

Driving requires your full attention. It can be easy to lose concentration on a long journey; worse still falling asleep at the wheel is a significant cause of accidents on long journeys. Opening a window will generally lower the temperature and increase the oxygen in the car; this will help until you can find a safe place to stop. Plan your breaks to ease the journey.

5.61   mark **one** answer

You go to a social event and need to drive a short time after. What precaution should you take?

- ❑ Avoid drinking alcohol on an empty stomach
- ❑ Drink plenty of coffee after drinking alcohol
- ❑ Avoid drinking alcohol completely
- ❑ Drink plenty of milk before drinking alcohol

❑ **Avoid drinking alcohol completely**

This is clearly the best option. Alcohol affects perception.

5.62   mark **one** answer

You take some cough medicine given to you by a friend. What should you do before driving?

- ❑ Ask your friend if taking the medicine affected their driving
- ❑ Drink some strong coffee one hour before driving
- ❑ Check the label to see if the medicine will affect your driving
- ❑ Drive a short distance to see if the medicine is affecting your driving

❑ **Check the label to see if the medicine will affect your driving**

It is easy to underestimate the effect of drugs on your system.

mark **one** answer

You take the wrong route and find you are on a one-way street. You should

❑ reverse out of the road
❑ turn round in a side road
❑ continue to the end of the road
❑ reverse into a driveway

❑ **continue to the end of the road**

This is the only safe option. It is a one-way street.

mark **three** answers

Which THREE are likely to make you lose concentration while driving?

❑ Looking at road maps
❑ Listening to loud music
❑ Using your windscreen washers
❑ Looking in your wing mirror
❑ Using a mobile phone

❑ **Looking at road maps**

❑ **Listening to loud music**

❑ **Using a mobile phone**

The two other choices are normal parts of the driving task.

mark **one** answer

You are driving along this road. The driver on the left is reversing from a driveway. You should

❑ move to the opposite side of the road
❑ drive through as you have priority
❑ sound your horn and be prepared to stop
❑ speed up and drive through quickly

❑ **sound your horn and be prepared to stop**

Warn the driver of your presence and slow down in case he or she doesn't respond.

5.66   mark **one** answer

You have been involved in an argument before starting your journey. This has made you feel angry. You should

❑ start to drive, but open a window
❑ drive slower than normal and turn your radio on
❑ have an alcoholic drink to help you relax before driving
❑ calm down before you start to drive

❑ **calm down before you start to drive**

Driving while stressed can lead to potentially dangerous mistakes and errors.

5.67   mark **one** answer

You start to feel tired while driving. What should you do?

❑ Increase your speed slightly
❑ Decrease your speed slightly
❑ Find a less busy route
❑ Pull over at a safe place to rest

❑ **Pull over at a safe place to rest**

It is easy to underestimate the effect of tiredness on your driving. Opening a window will generally lower the temperature and increase the oxygen in the car; this will help until you can find a safe place to stop.

5.68   mark **one** answer

You are driving on this dual carriageway. Why may you need to slow down?

❑ There is a broken white line in the centre
❑ There are solid white lines either side
❑ There are roadworks ahead of you
❑ There are no footpaths

❑ **There are roadworks ahead of you**

Road signs like this are there to give you advanced warning of danger ahead.

mark **one** answer

You have just been overtaken by this motorcyclist who is cutting in sharply. You should

❏ sound the horn
❏ brake firmly
❏ keep a safe gap
❏ flash your lights

❏ **keep a safe gap**

Do not react to other road users' actions; keep calm and regain the safety zone around your car.

mark **one** answer

You are about to drive home. You cannot find the glasses you need to wear. You should

❏ drive home slowly, keeping to quiet roads
❏ borrow a friend's glasses and use those
❏ drive home at night, so that the lights will help you
❏ find a way of getting home without driving

❏ **find a way of getting home without driving**

If you couldn't pass the eye test requirement of an 'L' test then it is not safe for you to drive.

mark **three** answers

Which THREE of these are likely effects of drinking alcohol?

❏ Reduced co-ordination
❏ Increased confidence
❏ Poor judgement
❏ Increased concentration
❏ Faster reactions
❏ Colour blindness

❏ **Reduced co-ordination**

❏ **Increased confidence**

❏ **Poor judgement**

Alcohol seriously impairs your ability to drive. Don't drink and drive.

5.72   mark **one** answer

How does alcohol affect you?

❏ It speeds up your reactions
❏ It increases your awareness
❏ It improves your co-ordination
❏ It reduces your concentration

❏ **It reduces your concentration**

You may well feel, after drinking, that the first three choices are true. However, this is never correct and makes you dangerous.

5.73   mark **one** answer

Your doctor has given you a course of medicine. Why should you ask how it will affect you?

❏ Drugs make you a better driver by quickening your reactions
❏ You will have to let your insurance company know about the medicine
❏ Some types of medicine can cause your reactions to slow down
❏ The medicine you take may affect your hearing

❏ **Some types of medicine can cause your reactions to slow down**

It is easy to underestimate the effect of drugs on your system.

5.74   mark **one** answer

You are on a motorway. You feel tired. You should

❏ carry on but go slowly
❏ leave the motorway at the next exit
❏ complete your journey as quickly as possible
❏ stop on the hard shoulder

❏ **leave the motorway at the next exit**

If you feel tired you greatly increase your chances of having an accident. You must stop, but as you are on a motorway you cannot do this unless you leave at the next exit or find a service station before it.

5.75 — mark **one** answer

You find that you need glasses to read vehicle number plates at the required distance. When MUST you wear them?

- ❏ Only in bad weather conditions
- ❏ At all times when driving
- ❏ Only when you think it necessary
- ❏ Only in bad light or at night time

❏ At all times when driving

If you need glasses to drive, you must wear them whenever you are driving.

5.76 — mark **two** answers

Which TWO things would help to keep you alert during a long journey?

- ❏ Finishing your journey as fast as you can
- ❏ Keeping off the motorways and using country roads
- ❏ Making sure that you get plenty of fresh air
- ❏ Making regular stops for refreshments

❏ Making sure that you get plenty of fresh air

❏ Making regular stops for refreshments

Opening a window generally lowers the temperature and increases the oxygen in the car. Get plenty of fresh air, and plan your breaks to ease the journey.

5.77 — mark **one** answer

Which of the following types of glasses should NOT be worn when driving at night?

- ❏ Half-moon
- ❏ Round
- ❏ Bi-focal
- ❏ Tinted

❏ Tinted

This is because they would reduce your vision, not improve it.

5.78 — mark **three** answers

Drinking any amount of alcohol is likely to

- ❏ slow down your reactions to hazards
- ❏ increase the speed of your reactions
- ❏ worsen your judgement of speed
- ❏ improve your awareness of danger
- ❏ give a false sense of confidence

❏ slow down your reactions to hazards

❏ worsen your judgement of speed

❏ give a false sense of confidence

Alcohol seriously impairs your ability to drive. Don't drink and drive.

5.79   mark **three** answers

What else can seriously affect your concentration, other than alcoholic drinks?

- ❑ Drugs
- ❑ Tiredness
- ❑ Tinted windows
- ❑ Contact lenses
- ❑ Loud music

- ❑ **Drugs**
- ❑ **Tiredness**
- ❑ **Loud music**

All can affect your ability to concentrate on the task of driving, which requires your full attention.

5.80   mark **one** answer

As a driver you find that your eyesight has become very poor. Your optician says they cannot help you. The law says that you should tell

- ❑ the licensing authority
- ❑ your own doctor
- ❑ the local police station
- ❑ another optician

- ❑ **the licensing authority**

You must not drive if your eyesight becomes so poor that you can no longer meet the minimum legal requirements, even when wearing glasses or contact lenses if necessary.

5.81   mark **one** answer

When should you use hazard warning lights?

- ❑ When you are double-parked on a two way road
- ❑ When your direction indicators are not working
- ❑ When warning oncoming traffic that you intend to stop
- ❑ When your vehicle has broken down and is causing an obstruction

- ❑ **When your vehicle has broken down and is causing an obstruction**

All the other options are either illegal, irrelevant or ambiguous.

5.82 mark **one** answer

You want to turn left at this junction.
The view of the main road is restricted.
What should you do?

❑ Stay well back and wait to see if something comes
❑ Build up your speed so that you can emerge quickly
❑ Stop and apply the handbrake even if the road is clear
❑ Approach slowly and edge out until you can see more clearly

❑ **Approach slowly and edge out until you can see more clearly**

This is the best option. Never emerge into a new road unless you are sure it is safe to do so.

5.83 mark **one** answer

When may you use hazard warning lights?

❑ To park alongside another car
❑ To park on double yellow lines
❑ When you are being towed
❑ When you have broken down

❑ **When you have broken down**

All the other options are either illegal or irrelevant.

5.84 mark **one** answer

Hazard warning lights should be used when vehicles are

❑ broken down and causing an obstruction
❑ faulty and moving slowly
❑ being towed along a road
❑ reversing into a side road

❑ **broken down and causing an obstruction**

All the other options are either illegal, irrelevant or ambiguous.

5.85 — mark **one** answer

When driving a car fitted with automatic transmission what would you use 'kick down' for?

❏ Cruise control
❏ Quick acceleration
❏ Slow braking
❏ Fuel economy

❏ **Quick acceleration**

When you press the accelerator sharply in an automatic, the gear box will 'kick-down' to a lower gear to give you greater acceleration.

5.86 — mark **two** answers

You are driving along this motorway. It is raining. When following this lorry you should

❏ allow at least a two-second gap
❏ move left and drive on the hard shoulder
❏ allow at least a four-second gap
❏ be aware of spray reducing your vision
❏ move right and stay in the right-hand lane

❏ **allow at least a four-second gap**

❏ **be aware of spray reducing your vision**

A four-second gap should (in wet conditions) give you the time and space to stop in an emergency. Remember large vehicles have bigger tyres which can throw up a large amount of spray

You are driving towards this left-hand bend. What dangers should you be aware of?

- ❏ A vehicle overtaking you
- ❏ No white lines in the centre of the road
- ❏ No sign to warn you of the bend
- ❏ Pedestrians walking towards you

❏ **Pedestrians walking towards you**

On a road with no pavement, pedestrians are advised to walk facing the oncoming traffic, i.e. on your side of the road.

The traffic ahead of you in the left-hand lane is slowing. You should

- ❏ be wary of cars on your right cutting in
- ❏ accelerate past the vehicles in the left-hand lane
- ❏ pull up on the left-hand verge
- ❏ move across and continue in the right-hand lane
- ❏ slow down, keeping a safe separation distance

❏ **be wary of cars on your right cutting in**

❏ **slow down, keeping a safe separation distance**

The road sign is giving you advanced warning of what is ahead – you should now assess what might happen and act accordingly.

5.89   mark **two** answers

As a provisional licence holder, you must not drive a motor car

- ❏ at more than 40 mph
- ❏ on your own
- ❏ on the motorway
- ❏ under the age of 18 years at night
- ❏ with passengers in the rear seats

❏ **on your own**

❏ **on the motorway**

This is the law.

5.90   mark **two** answers

You are not sure if your cough medicine will affect you. What TWO things should you do?

- ❏ Ask your doctor
- ❏ Check the medicine label
- ❏ Drive if you feel alright
- ❏ Ask a friend or relative for advice

❏ **Ask your doctor**

❏ **Check the medicine label**

It is easy to underestimate the effect of drugs on your system.

5.91   mark **one** answer

For which of these may you use hazard warning lights?

- ❏ When driving on a motorway to warn traffic behind of a hazard ahead
- ❏ When you are double-parked on a two-way road
- ❏ When your direction indicators are not working
- ❏ When warning oncoming traffic that you intend to stop

❏ **When driving on a motorway to warn traffic behind of a hazard ahead**

This is the only time you can use them when your car is moving. All the other options are either illegal or ambiguous.

mark **one** answer

You are waiting to emerge at a junction. Your view is restricted by parked vehicles. What can help you to see traffic on the road you are joining?

❑ Looking for traffic behind you
❑ Reflections of traffic in shop windows
❑ Making eye contact with other road users
❑ Checking for traffic in your interior mirror

❑ **Reflections of traffic in shop windows**

All the other options are irrelevant.

mark **one** answer

After passing your driving test, you suffer from ill health. This affects your driving. You MUST

❑ inform your local police station
❑ avoid using motorways
❑ always drive accompanied
❑ inform the licensing authority

❑ **inform the licensing authority**

In the event of a short-term illness, like flu, that affects your ability to drive, you would simply not drive until you are recovered.

mark **one** answer

Why should the junction on the left be kept clear?

❑ To allow vehicles to enter and emerge
❑ To allow the bus to reverse
❑ To allow vehicles to make a U-turn
❑ To allow vehicles to park

❑ **To allow vehicles to enter and emerge**

This is not only courteous but will help to speed up the general traffic flow and help avoid gridlock.

5.95   mark **one** answer

Your motorway journey seems boring and you feel drowsy. What should you do?

❏ Stop on the hard shoulder for a sleep
❏ Open a window and stop as soon as it's safe and legal
❏ Speed up to arrive at your destination sooner
❏ Slow down and let other drivers overtake

❏ **Open a window and stop as soon as it's safe and legal**

The best thing to do, should you feel this way, is to open a window and stop as soon as it's safe and legal to do so, for example, at the next service area. The other options increase the risks of danger.

5.96   mark **one** answer

You are driving on a motorway. The traffic ahead is braking sharply because of an incident. How could you warn traffic behind you?

❏ Briefly use the hazard warning lights
❏ Switch on the hazard warning lights continuously
❏ Briefly use the rear fog lights
❏ Switch on the headlights continuously

❏ **Briefly use the hazard warning lights**

This is the only occasion where you are legally allowed to use your hazard warning lights when your vehicle is moving. Be sure that you use them only for long enough to ensure that your warning has been observed.

Section 6
Vulnerable road users

There are 81 questions in this section covering the following subjects:

- ❏ Pedestrians
- ❏ Children
- ❏ Older drivers
- ❏ Disabled people
- ❏ Cyclists
- ❏ Motorcyclists
- ❏ Animals
- ❏ New drivers

You will need to think about:

- ❏ Safety – how you are going to deal with other people and objects that are at a much greater risk than you are in your car

- ❏ Dealing with large and/or slow vehicles and ones that are hard to pass.

Tips

Empathy – putting yourself in someone else's shoes – can be a key to parts of this section. For example, what would you want if you were the cyclist or pedestrian in the scenarios described in some of the questions? In fact if you look at the list above you may fit, or have fitted into, quite a few of the categories yourself, so you already have a head start.

Look for the safest option; this is always a good guide when dealing with vulnerable road users.

mark one answer

Which sign means that there may be people walking along the road?

Red triangles give warnings, in this case of people walking along the road. The lower left-hand sign is warning of a pedestrian crossing ahead.

mark one answer

You are turning left at a junction. Pedestrians have started to cross the road. You should

- ❑ go on, giving them plenty of room
- ❑ stop and wave at them to cross
- ❑ blow your horn and proceed
- ❑ give way to them

❑ **give way to them**

This is the safest option. Pedestrians have priority in this situation.

6.3   mark **one** answer

You are turning left from a main road into a side road. People are already crossing the road into which you are turning. You should

- ❏ continue, as it is your right of way
- ❏ signal to them to continue crossing
- ❏ wait and allow them to cross
- ❏ sound your horn to warn them of your presence

❏ **wait and allow them to cross**

Give way to pedestrians who are crossing the road.

6.4   mark **one** answer

You are at a road junction, turning into a minor road. There are pedestrians crossing the minor road. You should

- ❏ stop and wave the pedestrians across
- ❏ sound your horn to let the pedestrians know that you are there
- ❏ give way to the pedestrians who are already crossing
- ❏ carry on; the pedestrians should give way to you

❏ **give way to the pedestrians who are already crossing**

Look out for pedestrians. They have priority in this situation.

mark one answer

You are turning left into a side road. What hazards should you be especially aware of?

- ❏ One way street
- ❏ Pedestrians
- ❏ Traffic congestion
- ❏ Parked vehicles

❏ **Pedestrians**

Pedestrians may be waiting to, or have started to, cross the road. They have priority in this situation.

---

mark one answer

You intend to turn right into a side road. Just before turning you should check for motorcyclists who might be

- ❏ overtaking on your left
- ❏ following you closely
- ❏ emerging from the side road
- ❏ overtaking on your right

❏ **overtaking on your right**

Motorcyclists often overtake slower moving vehicles, sometimes quite quickly. Always check your mirrors before turning.

---

mark one answer

A toucan crossing is different from other crossings because

- ❏ moped riders can use it
- ❏ it is controlled by a traffic warden
- ❏ it is controlled by two flashing lights
- ❏ cyclists can use it

❏ **cyclists can use it**

This is the only type of crossing where cyclists are allowed to ride across. There will be a cycle lane as well as a pavement on either side of the road. On all other types of crossing cyclists are supposed to dismount before crossing.

---

mark one answer

How will a school crossing patrol signal you to stop?

- ❏ By pointing to children on the opposite pavement
- ❏ By displaying a red light
- ❏ By displaying a stop sign
- ❏ By giving you an arm signal

❏ **By displaying a stop sign**

The school crossing patrol person, commonly known as the 'lollipop man/lady', displays a circular sign and MUST be obeyed.

6.9   mark **one** answer

Where would you see this sign?

- ❑ In the window of a car taking children to school
- ❑ At the side of the road
- ❑ At playground areas
- ❑ On the rear of a school bus or coach

❑ **On the rear of a school bus or coach**

You will need to take care because children can be erratic pedestrians.

6.10   mark **one** answer

Which sign tells you that pedestrians may be walking in the road as there is no pavement?

❑   ❑

❑   ❑

❑

The other three refer to pedestrians crossing the road. They are side-on views on the sign.

What does this sign mean?

❏ No route for pedestrians and cyclists
❏ A route for pedestrians only
❏ A route for cyclists only
❏ A route for pedestrians and cyclists

❏ **A route for pedestrians and cyclists**

Because the sign is blue, it is a positive instruction.

You see a pedestrian with a white stick and red band. This means that the person is

❏ physically disabled
❏ deaf only
❏ blind only
❏ deaf and blind

❏ **deaf and blind**

A white stick for registered blind people. The red bands denote deafness.

What action would you take when elderly people are crossing the road?

❏ Wave them across so they know that you have seen them
❏ Be patient and allow them to cross in their own time
❏ Rev the engine to let them know that you are waiting
❏ Tap the horn in case they are hard of hearing

❏ **Be patient and allow them to cross in their own time**

The other three are either dangerous or inconsiderate.

6.14   mark **one** answer

You see two elderly pedestrians about to cross the road ahead. You should

❑ expect them to wait for you to pass
❑ speed up to get past them quickly
❑ stop and wave them across the road
❑ be careful, they may misjudge your speed

❑ **be careful, they may misjudge your speed**

The ability to judge speed tends to deteriorate as you get older.

6.15   mark **one** answer

You are coming up to a roundabout. A cyclist is signalling to turn right. What should you do?

❑ Overtake on the right
❑ Give a horn warning
❑ Signal the cyclist to move across
❑ Give the cyclist plenty of room

❑ **Give the cyclist plenty of room**

Cyclists are vulnerable and require time and space. They sometimes swerve unexpectedly.

6.16   mark **two** answers

Which TWO should you allow extra room when overtaking?

❑ Motorcycles
❑ Tractors
❑ Bicycles
❑ Road-sweeping vehicles

❑ **Motorcycles**

❑ **Bicycles**

Motorcyclists and bicyclists can easily swerve and you need to allow them extra room.

6.17   mark **one** answer

Why should you look particularly for motorcyclists and cyclists at junctions?

❑ They may want to turn into the side road
❑ They may slow down to let you turn
❑ They are harder to see
❑ They might not see you turn

❑ **They are harder to see**

Simply because of their size they can be easily hidden from view, by other vehicles or even your door pillars.

mark **one** answer

You are waiting to come out of a side road. Why should you watch carefully for motorcycles?

❏ Motorcycles are usually faster than cars
❏ Police patrols often use motorcycles
❏ Motorcycles are small and hard to see
❏ Motorcycles have right of way

❏ **Motorcycles are small and hard to see**

If you are waiting to emerge from a side road, look out particularly for motorcyclists. They are small and may be hiddem from view.

mark **one** answer

In daylight, an approaching motorcyclist is using a dipped headlight. Why?

❏ So that the rider can be seen more easily
❏ To stop the battery overcharging
❏ To improve the rider's vision
❏ The rider is inviting you to proceed

❏ **So that the rider can be seen more easily**

Because of their size they can be hard to see. Riders should also wear a reflective jacket or band.

mark **one** answer

Motorcyclists should wear bright clothing mainly because

❏ they must do so by law
❏ it helps keep them cool in summer
❏ the colours are popular
❏ drivers often do not see them

❏ **drivers often do not see them**

Motorcycles may be harder to see because of their size. Riders should wear bright clothing and also ride with dipped headlights at all times.

mark **one** answer

There is a slow-moving motorcyclist ahead of you. You are unsure what the rider is going to do. You should

❏ pass on the left
❏ pass on the right
❏ stay behind
❏ move closer

❏ **stay behind**

Never assume you know what someone else is going to do – stay back and give them space.

6.22   mark **one** answer

Motorcyclists will often look round over their right shoulder just before turning right. This is because

- ❑ they need to listen for following traffic
- ❑ motorcycles do not have mirrors
- ❑ looking around helps them balance as they turn
- ❑ they need to check for traffic in their blind area

❑ **they need to check for traffic in their blind area**

The blindspots on motorcycles are even greater than on cars. This check, sometimes known as the 'lifesaver', can give you a clue as to what the rider may do next.

6.23   mark **three** answers

At road junctions which of the following are most vulnerable?

- ❑ Cyclists
- ❑ Motorcyclists
- ❑ Pedestrians
- ❑ Car drivers
- ❑ Lorry drivers

❑ **Cyclists**

❑ **Motorcyclists**

❑ **Pedestrians**

Because they are unprotected in the event of an accident.

6.24   mark **one** answer

Motorcyclists are particularly vulnerable

- ❑ when moving off
- ❑ on dual carriageways
- ❑ when approaching junctions
- ❑ on motorways

❑ **when approaching junctions**

Junctions are where roads join and all kinds of traffic are crossing. Motorcyclists, because of their size they can be easily hidden from view, by other vehicles or even your door pillars.

6.25   mark **two** answers

You are approaching a roundabout. There are horses just ahead of you. You should

- ❑ be prepared to stop
- ❑ treat them like any other vehicle
- ❑ give them plenty of room
- ❑ accelerate past as quickly as possible
- ❑ sound your horn as a warning

❑ **be prepared to stop**

❑ **give them plenty of room**

Horses can be unpredictable; always approach them slowly and give them lots of space.

mark **one** answer

As you approach a pelican crossing the lights change to green. Elderly people are halfway across. You should

❑ wave them to cross as quickly as they can
❑ rev your engine to make them hurry
❑ flash your lights in case they have not heard you
❑ wait because they will take longer to cross

❑ **wait because they will take longer to cross**

This is the safest option and they have priority.

mark **one** answer

There are flashing amber lights under a school warning sign. What action should you take?

❑ Reduce speed until you are clear of the area
❑ Keep up your speed and sound the horn
❑ Increase your speed to clear the area quickly
❑ Wait at the lights until they change to green

❑ **Reduce speed until you are clear of the area**

The lights flash around the times when children will be going to or from school.

mark **one** answer

These road markings must be kept clear to allow

〰SCHOOL KEEP CLEAR〰

❑ school children to be dropped off
❑ for teachers to park
❑ school children to be picked up
❑ a clear view of the crossing area

❑ **a clear view of the crossing area**

You must not park on these yellow zig zag lines, not even to drop off or pick up children.

6.29   mark **one** answer

Where would you see this sign?

- Near a school crossing
- At a playground entrance
- On a school bus
- At a 'pedestrians only' area

❏ **On a school bus**

You will need to take care – children can be erratic pedestrians.

6.30   mark **one** answer

You are following two cyclists. They approach a roundabout in the left-hand lane. In which direction should you expect the cyclists to go?

- Left
- Right
- Any direction
- Straight ahead

❏ **Any direction**

Because of their size and speed it is often safer for cyclists to approach in the left-hand lane regardless of their final destination.

6.31   mark **one** answer

You are travelling behind a moped. You want to turn left just ahead. You should

- overtake the moped before the junction
- pull alongside the moped and stay level until just before the junction
- sound your horn as a warning and pull in front of the moped
- stay behind until the moped has passed the junction

❏ **stay behind until the moped has passed the junction**

This is the safest option. Overtaking will significantly increase the risk of a collision.

You see a horse rider as you approach a roundabout. They are signalling right but keeping well to the left. You should

- ❏ proceed as normal
- ❏ keep close to them
- ❏ cut in front of them
- ❏ stay well back

❏ **stay well back**

Because of their speed and unpredictable nature, it is usually safer for riders to approach in the left-hand lane regardless of their final destination.

How would you react to drivers who appear to be inexperienced?

- ❏ Sound your horn to warn them of your presence
- ❏ Be patient and prepare for them to react more slowly
- ❏ Flash your headlights to indicate that it is safe for them to proceed
- ❏ Overtake them as soon as possible

❏ **Be patient and prepare for them to react more slowly**

Novice drivers will have little experience and may respond to situations late. Be patient with them.

You are following a learner driver who stalls at a junction. You should

- ❏ be patient as you expect them to make mistakes
- ❏ stay very close behind and flash your headlights
- ❏ start to rev your engine if they take too long to restart
- ❏ immediately steer round them and drive on

❏ **be patient as you expect them to make mistakes**

Learning to drive is complex – all learners and inexperienced drivers need time and space to consolidate their skills.

6.35   mark **one** answer

You are on a country road. What should you expect to see coming towards you on YOUR side of the road?

❑ Motorcycles
❑ Bicycles
❑ Pedestrians
❑ Horse riders

❑ **Pedestrians**

Pedestrians are the most likely because country roads often have no pavements and pedestrians are advised to walk on the right. This is so that they can see oncoming traffic on their side of the road. However, you should always expect the unexpected when driving.

6.36   mark **one** answer

You are turning left into a side road. Pedestrians are crossing the road near the junction. You must

❑ wave them on
❑ sound your horn
❑ switch on your hazard lights
❑ wait for them to cross

❑ **wait for them to cross**

When you turn into a side road pedestrians who are already crossing have priority so you must give way.

6.37   mark **one** answer

You are following a car driven by an elderly driver. You should

❑ expect the driver to drive badly
❑ flash your lights and overtake
❑ be aware that the driver's reactions may not be as fast as yours
❑ stay very close behind but be careful

❑ **be aware that the driver's reactions may not be as fast as yours**

Everyone's reactions deteriorate as they get older.

     mark **one** answer

You are following a cyclist. You wish to turn left just ahead. You should

❏ overtake the cyclist before the junction
❏ pull alongside the cyclist and stay level until after the junction
❏ hold back until the cyclist has passed the junction
❏ go around the cyclist on the junction

❏ **hold back until the cyclist has passed the junction**

As the question states you are turning left JUST ahead, so you have no time to overtake the cyclist safely, which is why this is the correct answer.

     mark **one** answer

A horse rider is in the left-hand lane approaching a roundabout. You should expect the rider to

❏ go in any direction
❏ turn right
❏ turn left
❏ go ahead

❏ **go in any direction**

Because of their speed and unpredictable nature, it is usually safer for riders to approach in the left-hand lane regardless of their final destination.

     mark **one** answer

Powered vehicles used by disabled people are small and hard to see. How do they give early warning when on a dual carriageway?

❏ They will have a flashing red light
❏ They will have a flashing green light
❏ They will have a flashing blue light
❏ They will have a flashing amber light

❏ **They will have a flashing amber light**

Any potentially slow-moving vehicle will use a flashing orange light in this situation.

6.41 mark **one** answer

You should never attempt to overtake a cyclist

❏ just before you turn left
❏ on a left hand bend
❏ on a one-way street
❏ on a dual carriageway

❏ **just before you turn left**

This is the safest option. Overtaking will significantly increase the risk of a collision.

6.42 mark **one** answer

Ahead of you there is a moving vehicle with a flashing amber beacon. This means it is

❏ slow moving
❏ broken down
❏ a doctor's car
❏ a school crossing patrol

❏ **slow moving**

For example, a tractor or a breakdown recovery vehicle.

6.43 mark **one** answer

What does this sign mean?

❏ Contraflow pedal cycle lane
❏ With-flow pedal cycle lane
❏ Pedal cycles and buses only
❏ No pedal cycles or buses

❏ **With-flow pedal cycle lane**

Because the sign is blue, it is a positive instruction.

mark one answer

You notice horse riders in front. What should you do FIRST?

- ❏ Pull out to the middle of the road
- ❏ Slow down and be ready to stop
- ❏ Accelerate around them
- ❏ Signal right

❏ **Slow down and be ready to stop**

Horses and their riders can be unpredictable, so this is the safest first action.

mark one answer

You must not stop on these road markings because you may obstruct

- ❏ children's view of the crossing area
- ❏ teachers' access to the school
- ❏ delivery vehicles' access to the school
- ❏ emergency vehicles' access to the school

❏ **children's view of the crossing area**

Children can be erratic pedestrians; it is vital that the areas around school crossings are kept as safe as possible.

mark one answer

The left-hand pavement is closed due to street repairs. What should you do?

- ❏ Watch out for pedestrians walking in the road
- ❏ Use your right-hand mirror more often
- ❏ Speed up to get past the roadworks quicker
- ❏ Position close to the left-hand kerb

❏ **Watch out for pedestrians walking in the road**

Remember that pedestrians walking in the road may have their backs to you, so give them plenty of space.

6.47   mark **one** answer

You are following a motorcyclist on an uneven road. You should

- ❑ allow less room so you can be seen in their mirrors
- ❑ overtake immediately
- ❑ allow extra room in case they swerve to avoid potholes
- ❑ allow the same room as normal because road surfaces do not affect motorcyclists

❑ **allow extra room in case they swerve to avoid potholes**

Motorcyclists and cyclists have extra problems because of the nature of their vehicles. Always give them space.

6.48   mark **one** answer

What does this sign tell you?

- ❑ No cycling
- ❑ Cycle route ahead
- ❑ Cycle parking only
- ❑ End of cycle route

❑ **Cycle route ahead**

Triangles warn of a hazard ahead.

mark one answer

You are approaching this roundabout and see the cyclist signal right. Why is the cyclist keeping to the left?

- ❏ It is a quicker route for the cyclist
- ❏ The cyclist is going to turn left instead
- ❏ The cyclist thinks The Highway Code does not apply to bicycles
- ❏ The cyclist is slower and more vulnerable

❏ **The cyclist is slower and more vulnerable**

Because of their size and speed it is often safer for cyclists to approach in the left-hand lane regardless of their final destination.

mark one answer

You are approaching this crossing. You should

- ❏ prepare to slow down and stop
- ❏ stop and wave the pedestrians across
- ❏ speed up and pass by quickly
- ❏ continue unless the pedestrians step out

❏ **prepare to slow down and stop**

The pedestrian may want to cross; by slowing down and stopping you have selected the safest option.

6.51   mark **one** answer

You see a pedestrian with a dog. The dog has a yellow or burgundy coat. This especially warns you that the pedestrian is

❑ elderly
❑ dog training
❑ colour blind
❑ deaf

❑ **deaf**

This colour combination is designed to alert the driver's attention to a potential hazard.

6.52   mark **one** answer

At toucan crossings

❑ you only stop if someone is waiting to cross
❑ cyclists are not permitted
❑ there is a continuously flashing amber beacon
❑ pedestrians and cyclists may cross

❑ **pedestrians and cyclists may cross**

This is the only type of crossing where cyclists are allowed to ride across. There will be a cycle lane as well as a pavement on either side of the road. On all other types of crossing cyclists are supposed to dismount before crossing.

6.53   mark **one** answer

Some junctions controlled by traffic lights have a marked area between two stop lines. What is this for?

❑ To allow taxis to position in front of other traffic
❑ To allow people with disabilities to cross the road
❑ To allow cyclists and pedestrians to cross the road together
❑ To allow cyclists to position in front of other traffic

❑ **To allow cyclists to position in front of other traffic**

Expect cyclists to filter through stationary traffic and then wait in this position.

6.54   mark **one** answer

At some traffic lights there are advance stop lines and a marked area. What are these for?

☐ To allow cyclists to position in front of other traffic
☐ To let pedestrians cross when the lights change
☐ To prevent traffic from jumping the lights
☐ To let passengers get off a bus which is queuing

☐ **To allow cyclists to position in front of other traffic**

Cyclists will filter through stationary traffic; this gives them a safe area at the head of waiting traffic.

6.55   mark **one** answer

When you are overtaking a cyclist you should leave as much room as you would give to a car. What is the main reason for this?

☐ The cyclist might speed up
☐ The cyclist might get off the bike
☐ The cyclist might swerve
☐ The cyclist might have to make a left turn

☐ **The cyclist might swerve**

Cyclists will steer away from potholes and are affected by uneven road surfaces. Therefore, you need to give a cyclist plenty of room when overtaking.

6.56   mark **three** answers

Which THREE should you do when passing sheep on a road?

☐ Allow plenty of room
☐ Go very slowly
☐ Pass quickly but quietly
☐ Be ready to stop
☐ Briefly sound your horn

☐ **Allow plenty of room**

☐ **Go very slowly**

☐ **Be ready to stop**

Animals can be easily frightened by noise or vehicles passing to close to them, so slow down sufficiently and be prepared to stop.

6.57 mark **one** answer

At night you see a pedestrian wearing reflective clothing and carrying a bright red light. What does this mean?

❑ You are approaching roadworks
❑ You are approaching an organised walk
❑ You are approaching a slow-moving vehicle
❑ You are approaching a traffic danger spot

❑ **You are approaching an organised walk**

People on an organised walk will have their backs to you and may not know that you are there. You will need to pass slowly and carefully.

6.58 mark **one** answer

You have just passed your test. How can you reduce your risk of being involved in a collision?

❑ By always staying close to the vehicle in front
❑ By never going over 40 mph
❑ By staying only in the left-hand lane on all roads
❑ By taking further training

❑ **By taking further training**

The recommended further training consists of a six-module Pass-Plus Scheme. There is no exam, and successful completion can result in a reduced insurance premium.

6.59 mark **one** answer

You want to reverse into a side road. You are not sure that the area behind your car is clear. What should you do?

❑ Look through the rear window only
❑ Get out and check
❑ Check the mirrors only
❑ Carry on, assuming it is clear

❑ **Get out and check**

This is the only safe option available.

6.60   mark **one** answer

You are about to reverse into a side road.
A pedestrian wishes to cross behind you.
You should

- ❏ wave to the pedestrian to stop
- ❏ give way to the pedestrian
- ❏ wave to the pedestrian to cross
- ❏ reverse before the pedestrian starts to cross

❏ **give way to the pedestrian**

As well as being courteous, this will make your task easier by reducing your hazards.

6.61   mark **one** answer

Who is especially in danger of not being seen as you reverse your car?

- ❏ Motorcyclists
- ❏ Car drivers
- ❏ Cyclists
- ❏ Children

❏ **Children**

Children are small and you may not be able to see them through your rear windscreen.

6.62   mark **one** answer

You are reversing around a corner when you notice a pedestrian walking behind you. What should you do?

- ❏ Slow down and wave the pedestrian across
- ❏ Continue reversing and steer round the pedestrian
- ❏ Stop and give way
- ❏ Continue reversing and sound your horn

❏ **Stop and give way**

Give way to pedestrians crossing at junctions just as you would if you were driving forwards.

6.63   mark **one** answer

You want to turn right from a junction but your view is restricted by parked vehicles. What should you do?

❏ Move out quickly, but be prepared to stop
❏ Sound your horn and pull out if there is no reply
❏ Stop, then move slowly forward until you have a clear view
❏ Stop, get out and look along the main road to check

❏ **Stop, then move slowly forward until you have a clear view**

You should not turn right until you can see it is safe to do so. You should stop and then edge slowly forwards until you can see clearly to the left and right.

6.64   mark **one** answer

You are at the front of a queue of traffic waiting to turn right into a side road. Why is it important to check your right mirror just before turning?

❏ To look for pedestrians about to cross
❏ To check for overtaking vehicles
❏ To make sure the side road is clear
❏ To check for emerging traffic

❏ **To check for overtaking vehicles**

While you have been stationary other vehicles may be trying to overtake you (particularly motorcyclists).

6.65   mark **one** answer

What must a driver do at a pelican crossing when the amber light is flashing?

❏ Signal the pedestrian to cross
❏ Always wait for the green light before proceeding
❏ Give way to any pedestrians on the crossing
❏ Wait for the red-and-amber light before proceeding

❏ **Give way to any pedestrians on the crossing**

The amber flashing light only means 'go' if clear.

mark two answers

You have stopped at a pelican crossing.
A disabled person is crossing slowly in front of
you. The lights have now changed to green.
You should

- [ ] allow the person to cross
- [ ] drive in front of the person
- [ ] drive behind the person
- [ ] sound your horn
- [ ] be patient
- [ ] edge forward slowly

- [ ] **allow the person to cross**

- [ ] **be patient**

Treat the crossing as a zebra crossing at this
point, and wait until it is clear before
proceeding.

---

mark one answer

You are driving past a line of parked cars.
You notice a ball bouncing out into the road
ahead. What should you do?

- [ ] Continue driving at the same speed and
  sound your horn
- [ ] Continue driving at the same speed and
  flash your headlights
- [ ] Slow down and be prepared to stop for
  children
- [ ] Stop and wave the children across to fetch
  their ball

- [ ] **Slow down and be prepared to stop for
  children**

You have identified the hazard; now predict
what is likely to happen next, and act on it.

---

mark one answer

You want to turn right from a main road into a
side road. Just before turning you should

- [ ] cancel your right-turn signal
- [ ] select first gear
- [ ] check for traffic overtaking on your right
- [ ] stop and set the handbrake

- [ ] **check for traffic overtaking on your
  right**

Use your right-door mirror and look
particularly for motorcyclists.

6.69   mark **one** answer

You are driving in slow-moving queues of traffic. Just before changing lane you should

❏ sound the horn
❏ look for motorcyclists filtering through the traffic
❏ give a 'slowing down' arm signal
❏ change down to first gear

❏ **look for motorcyclists filtering through the traffic**

While you have been moving slowly other vehicles may have been filtering through the traffic.

6.70   mark **one** answer

You are driving in town. There is a bus at the bus stop on the other side of the road. Why should you be careful?

❏ The bus may have broken down
❏ Pedestrians may come from behind the bus
❏ The bus may move off suddenly
❏ The bus may remain stationary

❏ **Pedestrians may come from behind the bus**

You have identified the hazard; now predict what is likely to happen next and act on it.

6.71   mark **one** answer

How should you overtake horse riders?

❏ Drive up close and overtake as soon as possible
❏ Speed is not important but allow plenty of room
❏ Use your horn just once to warn them
❏ Drive slowly and leave plenty of room

❏ **Drive slowly and leave plenty of room**

Horses can be unpredictable and are easily frightened; always approach with caution.

6.72   mark **one** answer

You are driving on a main road. You intend to turn right into a side road. Just before turning you should

❏ adjust your interior mirror
❏ flash your headlamps
❏ steer over to the left
❏ check for traffic overtaking on your right

❏ **check for traffic overtaking on your right**

Always check your mirrors before turning especially for motorcycles.

mark **one** answer

Why should you allow extra room when overtaking a motorcyclist on a windy day?

❑ The rider may turn off suddenly to get out of the wind
❑ The rider may be blown across in front of you
❑ The rider may stop suddenly
❑ The rider may be travelling faster than normal

❑ **The rider may be blown across in front of you**

Motorcyclists are lighter and present a flat profile to the wind so they are easily blown off course.

mark **one** answer

Where in particular should you look out for motorcyclists?

❑ In a filling station
❑ At a road junction
❑ Near a service area
❑ When entering a car park

❑ **At a road junction**

At road junctions, think bike. Their smaller size might hide them from view.

mark **one** answer

Where should you take particular care to look out for motorcyclists and cyclists?

❑ On dual carriageways
❑ At junctions
❑ At zebra crossings
❑ On one-way streets

❑ **At junctions**

Simply because of their size they can be easily hidden from view by other vehicles or even your door pillars.

6.76   mark **one** answer

The road outside this school is marked with yellow zigzag lines. What do these lines mean?

❑ You may park on the lines when dropping off schoolchildren
❑ You may park on the lines when picking schoolchildren up
❑ You must not wait or park your vehicle here at all
❑ You must stay with your vehicle if you park here

❑ **You must not wait or park your vehicle here at all**

Children can be erratic pedestrians; it is vital that the areas around schools and school crossings are kept as safe as possible.

6.77   mark **one** answer

You are driving past parked cars. You notice a bicycle wheel sticking out between them. What should you do?

❑ Accelerate past quickly and sound your horn
❑ Slow down and wave the cyclist across
❑ Brake sharply and flash your headlights
❑ Slow down and be prepared to stop for a cyclist

❑ **Slow down and be prepared to stop for a cyclist**

You have identified the hazard, now predict what is likely to happen next, and act on it.

6.78   mark **one** answer

You are dazzled at night by a vehicle behind you. You should

❑ set your mirror to anti-dazzle
❑ set your mirror to dazzle the other driver
❑ brake sharply to a stop
❑ switch your rear lights on and off

❑ **set your mirror to anti-dazzle**

This is the only logical, safe option available.

You are driving towards a zebra crossing.
A person in a wheelchair is waiting to cross.
What should you do?

❏ Continue on your way
❏ Wave to the person to cross
❏ Wave to the person to wait
❏ Be prepared to stop

❏ **Be prepared to stop**

The person may want to cross, so by doing
this you have selected the safest option.

Yellow zigzag lines on the road outside
schools mean

⋏-SCHOOL KEEP CLEAR-⋏

❏ sound your horn to alert other road users
❏ stop to allow children to cross
❏ you should not park or stop on these lines
❏ you must not drive over these lines

❏ **you should not park or stop on these
lines**

Yellow zigzag lanes are intended to improve
road safety in the immediate outside the
school gates. Parking on these will restrict
the view of the schools entrance for drivers,
children and parents. Don't do it.

What do these road markings outside a school
mean?

⋏-SCHOOL KEEP CLEAR-⋏

❏ You may park here if you are a teacher
❏ Sound your horn before parking
❏ When parking, use your hazard warning
lights
❏ You should not wait or park your vehicle
here

❏ **You should not wait or park your
vehicle here**

Do not park on these as this will restrict the
view of the schools entrance for drivers,
children and parents. Show respect for the
yellow zigzag lanes as they are intended to
improve road safety in the immediate outside
the school gates.

Section 7
Other types of vehicle

There are 27 questions in this section covering the following subjects:

- ❑ Motorcycles
- ❑ Lorries
- ❑ Buses
- ❑ Trams

You will need to think about:

- ❑ The different problems that other road users may have when sharing the road with cars

- ❑ How these problems may affect you.

Tips

A lot of the problems motorcyclists have are the same as those that face cyclists, so if you have ridden a bicycle on the road, you have a good idea of what they might be. Of course you may already be a motorcyclist.

Quite a few of the lorry, bus and tram questions require sound judgement from you in recognising that they need to stop now and then, that they need more room to manoeuvre, or that they drive on rails. Some will need more study, like the maximum speed of a powered wheelchair (8 mph).

mark **one** answer

You are about to overtake a slow-moving motorcyclist. Which one of these signs would make you take special care?

❏   ❏

❏   ❏

❏

The motorcyclist may wobble as you pass by in a windy situation.

---

mark **one** answer

You are waiting to emerge left from a minor road. A large vehicle is approaching from the right. You have time to turn, but you should wait. Why?

❏ The large vehicle can easily hide an overtaking vehicle
❏ The large vehicle can turn suddenly
❏ The large vehicle is difficult to steer in a straight line
❏ The large vehicle can easily hide vehicles from the left

❏ **The large vehicle can easily hide an overtaking vehicle**

Large vehicles can hide other vehicles such as motorcyclists.

7.3   mark **one** answer

You are following a long vehicle. It approaches a crossroads and signals left, but moves out to the right. You should

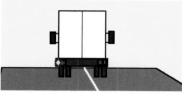

❑ get closer in order to pass it quickly
❑ stay well back and give it room
❑ assume the signal is wrong and it is really turning right
❑ overtake as it starts to slow down

❑ **stay well back and give it room**

Long vehicles require more space to turn and often need to position for this.

7.4   mark **one** answer

You are following a long vehicle approaching a crossroads. The driver signals right but moves close to the left-hand kerb. What should you do?

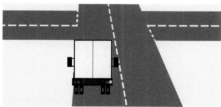

❑ Warn the driver of the wrong signal
❑ Wait behind the long vehicle
❑ Report the driver to the police
❑ Overtake on the right-hand side

❑ **Wait behind the long vehicle**

To prevent the rear end of the trailer cutting the corner, the driver needs to keep close to the left before turning right. Stay behind and wait for it to turn.

mark **one** answer

You are approaching a mini-roundabout. The long vehicle in front is signalling left but positioned over to the right. You should

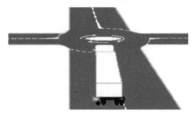

❑ sound your horn
❑ overtake on the left
❑ follow the same course as the lorry
❑ keep well back

❑ **keep well back**

Long vehicles require more space to turn and often need to reposition for this.

mark **one** answer

Before overtaking a large vehicle you should keep well back. Why is this?

❑ To give acceleration space to overtake quickly on blind bends
❑ To get the best view of the road ahead
❑ To leave a gap in case the vehicle stops and rolls back
❑ To offer other drivers a safe gap if they want to overtake you

❑ **To get the best view of the road ahead**

Staying well back opens your vision, giving you the chance to assess the danger properly.

mark **two** answers

You are travelling behind a bus that pulls up at a bus stop. What should you do?

❑ Accelerate past the bus sounding your horn
❑ Watch carefully for pedestrians
❑ Be ready to give way to the bus
❑ Pull in closely behind the bus

❑ **Watch carefully for pedestrians**

❑ **Be ready to give way to the bus**

Pedestrians may be hidden and try to cross from behind the bus. Giving way to the bus will speed up the general traffic flow.

7.8   mark **one** answer

You are following a large lorry on a wet road. Spray makes it difficult to see. You should

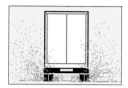

- ❑ drop back until you can see better
- ❑ put your headlights on full beam
- ❑ keep close to the lorry, away from the spray
- ❑ speed up and overtake quickly

❑ **drop back until you can see better**

Large vehicles have large tyres which create a large amount of spray; this will obscure your view.

7.9   mark **one** answer

You are following a large articulated vehicle. It is going to turn left into a narrow road. What action should you take?

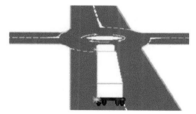

- ❑ Move out and overtake on the right
- ❑ Pass on the left as the vehicle moves out
- ❑ Be prepared to stop behind
- ❑ Overtake quickly before the lorry moves out

❑ **Be prepared to stop behind**

The large articulated vehicle may need to position to the right in order to turn left into the narrow road.

7.10   mark **one** answer

You keep well back while waiting to overtake a large vehicle. A car fills the gap. You should

- ❑ sound your horn
- ❑ drop back further
- ❑ flash your headlights
- ❑ start to overtake

❑ **drop back further**

Don't react to other drivers' errors or behaviour. Stay calm and regain your safety zone.

mark **one** answer

You are following a long lorry. The driver signals to turn left into a narrow road. What should you do?

❑ Overtake on the left before the lorry reaches the junction
❑ Overtake on the right as soon as the lorry slows down
❑ Do not overtake unless you can see there is no oncoming traffic
❑ Do not overtake, stay well back and be prepared to stop.

❑ **Do not overtake, stay well back and be prepared to stop.**

Drivers of unusual or large vehicles are professionals. Give them the time and space to do their job properly and they will be much quicker.

mark **one** answer

When you approach a bus signalling to move off from a bus stop you should

❑ get past before it moves
❑ allow it to pull away, if it is safe to do so
❑ flash your headlights as you approach
❑ signal left and wave the bus on

❑ **allow it to pull away, if it is safe to do so**

This helps traffic flow without giving confusing signals.

mark **one** answer

You wish to overtake a long, slow-moving vehicle on a busy road. You should

❑ follow it closely and keep moving out to see the road ahead
❑ flash your headlights for the oncoming traffic to give way
❑ stay behind until the driver waves you past
❑ keep well back until you can see that it is clear

❑ **keep well back until you can see that it is clear**

Staying well back opens your vision, giving you the chance to assess the danger properly.

7.14   mark **one** answer

Which of these is LEAST likely to be affected by crosswinds?

❏ Cyclists
❏ Motorcyclists
❏ High-sided vehicles
❏ Cars

❏ **Cars**

Of the four mentioned, cars are by far the most stable and least affected by crosswinds.

7.15   mark **one** answer

What should you do as you approach this lorry?

❏ Slow down and be prepared to wait
❏ Make the lorry wait for you
❏ Flash your lights at the lorry
❏ Move to the right-hand side of the road

❏ **Slow down and be prepared to wait**

Drivers of unusual or large vehicles are professionals; give them the time and space to do their job properly. They will be much quicker if you do.

7.16   mark **one** answer

You are following a large vehicle approaching crossroads. The driver signals to turn left. What should you do?

❏ Overtake if you can leave plenty of room
❏ Overtake only if there are no oncoming vehicles
❏ Do not overtake until the vehicle begins to turn
❏ Do not overtake when at or approaching a junction

❏ **Do not overtake when at or approaching a junction**

Overtaking at junctions is dangerous. You will be on the wrong side of the road, travelling quickly, hidden from the view of the vehicle you are overtaking, and hidden to other road users in an unexpected place.

mark one answer

Powered vehicles, such as wheelchairs or scooters, used by disabled people have a maximum speed of

❑ 8 mph
❑ 12 mph
❑ 16 mph
❑ 20 mph

❑ **8 mph**

These small vehicles can be used on the pavement as well as on the road. On dual carriageways they will have an amber flashing light but on other roads they can be difficult to see.

mark one answer

Why is it more difficult to overtake a large vehicle than a car?

❑ It takes longer to pass one
❑ They may suddenly pull up
❑ Their brakes are not as good
❑ They climb hills more slowly

❑ **It takes longer to pass one**

It will take longer to pass a large vehicle such as a lorry or a bus. You will need to be sure that it is going to be safe to complete the overtaking manoeuvre before you start it.

mark one answer

In front of you is a class-3 powered vehicle (powered wheelchair) driven by a disabled person. These vehicles have a maximum speed of

❑ 8 mph (12 km/h)
❑ 18 mph (29 km/h)
❑ 28 mph (45 km/h)
❑ 38 mph (61 km/h)

❑ **8 mph (12 km/h)**

These small mobility vehicles are powered by a battery. They are used by the elderly, disabled or infirm. Exercise particular care overtaking; these vehicles are extremely vulnerable because of their small size, low height and low speed.

mark one answer

It is very windy. You are behind a motorcyclist who is overtaking a high-sided vehicle. What should you do?

❑ Overtake the motorcyclist immediately
❑ Keep well back
❑ Stay level with the motorcyclist
❑ Keep close to the motorcyclist

❑ **Keep well back**

Let the motorcyclist complete the overtaking manoeuvre before even thinking about following.

7.21   mark **one** answer

It is very windy. You are about to overtake a motorcyclist. You should

- ❏ overtake slowly
- ❏ allow extra room
- ❏ sound your horn
- ❏ keep close as you pass

❏ **allow extra room**

Motorcycles may have problems with strong crosswinds.

7.22   mark **two** answers

You are driving in town. Ahead of you a bus is at a bus stop. Which TWO of the following should you do?

- ❏ Be prepared to give way if the bus suddenly moves off
- ❏ Continue at the same speed but sound your horn as a warning
- ❏ Watch carefully for the sudden appearance of pedestrians
- ❏ Pass the bus as quickly as you possibly can

❏ **Be prepared to give way if the bus suddenly moves off**

❏ **Watch carefully for the sudden appearance of pedestrians**

Giving way to the bus will speed up the general traffic flow. Pedestrians may be hidden and try to cross from behind the bus.

7.23   mark **one** answer

You are driving along this road. What should you be prepared to do?

- ❏ Sound your horn and continue
- ❏ Slow down and give way
- ❏ Report the driver to the police
- ❏ Squeeze through the gap

❏ **Slow down and give way**

Drivers of unusual or large vehicles are professionals. Give them the time and space to do their job and they will be much quicker.

7.24 — mark **one** answer

As a driver why should you be more careful where trams operate?

❏ Because they do not have a horn
❏ Because they do not stop for cars
❏ Because they do not have lights
❏ Because they cannot steer to avoid you

❏ **Because they cannot steer to avoid you**

Because they travel on rails they only have two options – slow down or speed up.

7.25 — mark **one** answer

You are towing a caravan. Which is the safest type of rear-view mirror to use?

❏ Interior wide-angle mirror
❏ Extended-arm side mirrors
❏ Ordinary door mirrors
❏ Ordinary interior mirror

❏ **Extended-arm side mirrors**

These will give you a view past the caravan which will most likely be wider than your vehicle.

7.26 — mark **two** answers

You are driving in heavy traffic on a wet road. Spray makes it difficult to be seen. You should use your

❏ full beam headlights
❏ rear fog lights if visibility is less than 100 metres (328 feet)
❏ rear fog lights if visibility is more than 100 metres (328 feet)
❏ dipped headlights
❏ sidelights only

❏ **rear fog lights if visibility is less than 100 metres (328 feet)**

❏ **dipped headlights**

Ensure that you can be seen by other road users. Use dipped headlights during the day and if it becomes very foggy use your rear fog lights. Remember to switch them off when the visibility improves.

7.27 — mark **one** answer

It is a very windy day and you are about to overtake a cyclist. What should you do?

❏ Overtake very closely
❏ Keep close as you pass
❏ Sound your horn repeatedly
❏ Allow extra room

❏ **Allow extra room**

Cyclists are vulnerable to the weather conditions. A strong gust of wind could blow a cyclist right off course, so it is important to allow extra room when overtaking.

Section 8
Vehicle handling

There are 62 questions in this section covering the following subjects:

- ❑ Weather conditions
- ❑ Road conditions
- ❑ Time of day
- ❑ Speed
- ❑ Traffic calming

You will need to think about:

- ❑ How your vehicle will react in a variety of situations and conditions

- ❑ How you will respond in the way you drive the vehicle.

Tips

Parts of this section require a degree of technical understanding – nothing too complicated, but things like the technique required for driving in snow, or what to do when you have driven through a ford. The explanations should help you with the reasons why, if you require them.

If that still isn't enough information, talk to your driving instructor or an experienced driver for more advice.

mark three answers

In which THREE of these situations may you overtake another vehicle on the left?

❑ When you are in a one-way street
❑ When approaching a motorway slip road where you will be turning off
❑ When the vehicle in front is signalling to turn right
❑ When a slower vehicle is travelling in the right-hand lane of a dual carriageway
❑ In slow-moving traffic queues when traffic in the right-hand lane is moving more slowly

❑ **When you are in a one-way street**

❑ **When the vehicle in front is signalling to turn right**

❑ **In slow-moving traffic queues when traffic in the right-hand lane is moving more slowly**

Generally overtaking on the left is dangerous because road users will not expect it. These are the exceptions.

mark one answer

You are travelling in very heavy rain. Your overall stopping distance is likely to be

❑ doubled
❑ halved
❑ up to ten times greater
❑ no different

❑ **doubled**

This is because your tyres have much less grip in the wet.

mark two answers

Which TWO of the following are correct? When overtaking at night you should

❑ wait until a bend so that you can see the oncoming headlights
❑ sound your horn twice before moving out
❑ be careful because you can see less
❑ beware of bends in the road ahead
❑ put headlights on full beam

❑ **be careful because you can see less**

❑ **beware of bends in the road ahead**

Even with good lights your vision is restricted, particularly as you approach a bend.

8.4   mark **one** answer

When may you wait in a box junction?

☐ When you are stationary in a queue of traffic
☐ When approaching a pelican crossing
☐ When approaching a zebra crossing
☐ When oncoming traffic prevents you turning right

☐ **When oncoming traffic prevents you turning right**

You may wait in a box junction if your exit is clear but oncoming traffic prevents you from turning right.

8.5   mark **one** answer

Which of these plates normally appear with this road sign?

☐ **Humps for ½ mile**

☐ **HumpBridge**

☐ **Low Bridge**

☐ **Soft Verge**

☐ **Humps for ½ mile**

The other plates require a different triangular sign.

8.6   mark **one** answer

Traffic calming measures are used to

☐ stop road rage
☐ help overtaking
☐ slow traffic down
☐ help parking

☐ **slow traffic down**

They are usually used in areas where pedestrians are at greatest risk.

mark one answer

You are on a motorway in fog. The left-hand edge of the motorway can be identified by reflective studs. What colour are they?

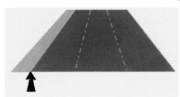

- ❏ Green
- ❏ Amber
- ❏ Red
- ❏ White

❏ **Red**

Red reflective studs separate the left-hand lane and the hard shoulder.

mark two answers

A rumble device is designed to

- ❏ give directions
- ❏ prevent cattle escaping
- ❏ alert you to low tyre pressure
- ❏ alert you to a hazard
- ❏ encourage you to reduce speed

❏ **alert you to a hazard**

❏ **encourage you to reduce speed**

A rumble device is usually a series of raised strips or markings on the surface of the road.

8.9   mark **one** answer

You have to make a journey in foggy conditions. You should

❑ follow other vehicles' tail lights closely
❑ avoid using dipped headlights
❑ leave plenty of time for your journey
❑ keep two seconds behind other vehicles

❑ **leave plenty of time for your journey**

The Highway Code advises you to allow more time for your journey in foggy conditions. However, always ask yourself if the journey really is necessary.

8.10   mark **one** answer

You are overtaking a car at night. You must be sure that

❑ you flash your headlights before overtaking
❑ you select a higher gear
❑ you have switched your lights to full beam before overtaking
❑ you do not dazzle other road users

❑ **you do not dazzle other road users**

You may need to switch to full-beam headlights as you overtake, but not before.

8.11   mark **one** answer

You are on a road which has speed humps. A driver in front is travelling slower than you. You should

❑ sound your horn
❑ overtake as soon as you can
❑ flash your headlights
❑ slow down and stay behind

❑ **slow down and stay behind**

Speed humps are traffic-calming measures. They are found in areas where pedestrians are at greatest risk.

You see these markings on the road. Why are they there?

❑ To show a safe distance between vehicles
❑ To keep the area clear of traffic
❑ To make you aware of your speed
❑ To warn you to change direction

❑ **To make you aware of your speed**

The spacing of these lines affects perception, drawing your attention to your speed.

Areas reserved for trams may have

❑ metal studs around them
❑ white line markings
❑ zigzag markings
❑ a different coloured surface
❑ yellow hatch markings
❑ a different surface texture

❑ **white line markings**

❑ **a different coloured surface**

❑ **a different surface texture**

They are all there to draw your attention to the tram and its special requirements.

You see a vehicle coming towards you on a single-track road. You should

❑ go back to the main road
❑ do an emergency stop
❑ stop at a passing place
❑ put on your hazard warning lights

❑ **stop at a passing place**

Bear in mind that single-track roads may have passing places at long intervals. You may meet an oncoming vehicle at a point where one of you will need to reverse to the previous nearest passing point.

8.15
mark **one** answer

The road is wet. Why might a motorcyclist steer round drain covers on a bend?

❏ To avoid puncturing the tyres on the edge of the drain covers
❏ To prevent the motorcycle sliding on the metal drain covers
❏ To help judge the bend using the drain covers as marker points
❏ To avoid splashing pedestrians on the pavement

❏ **To prevent the motorcycle sliding on the metal drain covers**

Because of their weight and the fact that they only have two wheels, motorcycles and cycles are much more susceptible to this type of problem.

8.16
mark **one** answer

After this hazard you should test your brakes. Why is this?

❏ You will be on a slippery road
❏ Your brakes will be soaking wet
❏ You will be going down a long hill
❏ You will have just crossed a long bridge

❏ **Your brakes will be soaking wet**

As you have just driven through fairly deep water, you must test your brakes.

8.17
mark **one** answer

Why should you always reduce your speed when travelling in fog?

❏ The brakes do not work as well
❏ You will be dazzled by other headlights
❏ The engine will take longer to warm up
❏ It is more difficult to see events ahead

❏ **It is more difficult to see events ahead**

Everybody knows this but an alarming number of people don't put the knowledge into practice. Collisions happen as a result.

mark **two** answers

Hills can affect the performance of your vehicle. Which TWO apply when driving up steep hills?

❑ Higher gears will pull better
❑ You will slow down sooner
❑ Overtaking will be easier
❑ The engine will work harder
❑ The steering will feel heavier

❑ **You will slow down sooner**

❑ **The engine will work harder**

Think about riding a bike – it is much harder work up a hill!

mark **one** answer

You are driving on the motorway in windy conditions. When passing high-sided vehicles you should

❑ increase your speed
❑ be wary of a sudden gust
❑ drive alongside very closely
❑ expect normal conditions

❑ **be wary of a sudden gust**

The flat slab sides of these vehicles will make them more susceptible to windy conditions.

mark **one** answer

To correct a rear-wheel skid you should

❑ not steer at all
❑ steer away from it
❑ steer into it
❑ apply your handbrake

❑ **steer into it**

If the back of your car has moved to the right you will need to steer right to correct it, and vice-versa on the left.

mark **one** answer

You are driving in fog. Why should you keep well back from the vehicle in front?

❑ In case it changes direction suddenly
❑ In case its fog lights dazzle you
❑ In case it stops suddenly
❑ In case its brake lights dazzle you

❑ **In case it stops suddenly**

If the car in front stops suddenly, you may run into it if you have been driving too close.

8.22   mark **one** answer

You should switch your rear fog lights on when visibility drops below

❑ your overall stopping distance
❑ ten car lengths
❑ 200 metres (656 feet)
❑ 100 metres (328 feet)

❑ **100 metres (328 feet)**

Remember to switch them off when visibility improves.

8.23   mark **one** answer

While driving, the fog clears and you can see more clearly. You must remember to

❑ switch off the fog lights
❑ reduce your speed
❑ switch off the demister
❑ close any open windows

❑ **switch off the fog lights**

Fog lights should only be used where visibility is down to about 100 metres, otherwise you risk dazzling other drivers.

8.24   mark **one** answer

You have to park on the road in fog. You should

❑ leave sidelights on
❑ leave dipped headlights and fog lights on
❑ leave dipped headlights on
❑ leave main beam headlights on

❑ **leave sidelights on**

This is important so that you can be seen by other road users.

8.25   mark **one** answer

On a foggy day you unavoidably have to park your car on the road. You should

❑ leave your headlights on
❑ leave your fog lights on
❑ leave your sidelights on
❑ leave your hazard lights on

❑ **leave your sidelights on**

This will reduce the risk of someone colliding with your vehicle.

You are travelling at night. You are dazzled by headlights coming towards you. You should

- ❏ pull down your sun visor
- ❏ slow down or stop
- ❏ switch on your main beam headlights
- ❏ put your hand over your eyes

❏ **slow down or stop**

You are unable to see clearly, so this is the only safe option.

Front fog lights may be used ONLY if

- ❏ visibility is seriously reduced
- ❏ they are fitted above the bumper
- ❏ they are not as bright as the headlights
- ❏ an audible warning device is used

❏ **visibility is seriously reduced**

Do check that the fog lights have been switched off once conditions improve.

Front fog lights may be used ONLY if
- ❏ your headlights are not working
- ❏ they are operated with rear fog lights
- ❏ they were fitted by the vehicle manufacturer
- ❏ visibility is seriously reduced

❏ **visibility is seriously reduced**

Fog lights will help others to see you, but they must only be used if visibility is seriously reduced, that is, to less than 100 meters.

8.29   mark **one** answer

You are driving with your front fog lights switched on. Earlier fog has now cleared. What should you do?

❏ Leave them on if other drivers have their lights on
❏ Switch them off as long as visibility remains good
❏ Flash them to warn oncoming traffic that it is foggy
❏ Drive with them on instead of your headlights

❏ **Switch them off as long as visibility remains good**

They may dazzle other road users.

8.30   mark **one** answer

Front fog lights should be used ONLY when

❏ travelling in very light rain
❏ visibility is seriously reduced
❏ daylight is fading
❏ driving after midnight

❏ **visibility is seriously reduced**

Use them where visibility is down to 100 metres or less. They are unnecessary at other times.

8.31   mark **three** answers

You forget to switch off your rear fog lights when the fog has cleared. This may

❏ dazzle other road users
❏ reduce battery life
❏ cause brake lights to be less clear
❏ be breaking the law
❏ seriously affect engine power

❏ **dazzle other road users**

❏ **cause brake lights to be less clear**

❏ **be breaking the law**

Rear fog lights should only be used when visibility is seriously reduced, down to 100 metres or less.

mark **one** answer

You have been driving in thick fog which has now cleared. You must switch OFF your rear fog lights because

❏ they use a lot of power from the battery
❏ they make your brake lights less clear
❏ they will cause dazzle in your rear view mirrors
❏ they may not be properly adjusted

❏ **they make your brake lights less clear**

Following traffic needs to be warned when you brake. Leaving the rear fog lights on makes it hard for others to see your brake lights.

mark **one** answer

Front fog lights should be used

❏ when visibility is reduced to 100 metres (328 feet)
❏ as a warning to oncoming traffic
❏ when driving during the hours of darkness
❏ in any conditions and at any time

❏ **when visibility is reduced to 100 metres (328 feet)**

They are unnecessary at other times, and may dazzle other road users.

mark **one** answer

Using rear fog lights in clear daylight will

❏ be useful when towing a trailer
❏ give extra protection
❏ dazzle other drivers
❏ make following drivers keep back

❏ **dazzle other drivers**

Rear fog lights should only be used when visibility is seriously reduced, down to 100 metres or less.

mark **one** answer

Using front fog lights in clear daylight will

❏ flatten the battery
❏ dazzle other drivers
❏ improve your visibility
❏ increase your awareness

❏ **dazzle other drivers**

Fog lights should only be used when visibility is seriously reduced, down to 100 metres or less. They are unnecessary at other times.

8.36   mark **one** answer

You may use front fog lights with headlights ONLY when visibility is reduced to less than

❑ 100 metres (328 feet)
❑ 200 metres (656 feet)
❑ 300 metres (984 feet)
❑ 400 metres (1312 feet)

❑ **100 metres (328 feet)**

Fog lights should only be used when visibility is seriously reduced.

8.37   mark **one** answer

Chains can be fitted to your wheels to help prevent

❑ damage to the road surface
❑ wear to the tyres
❑ skidding in deep snow
❑ the brakes locking

❑ **skidding in deep snow**

The chain fits across the tyre surface and effectively bites into the snow surface as the wheel turns.

8.38   mark **one** answer

How can you use the engine of your vehicle to control your speed?

❑ By changing to a lower gear
❑ By selecting reverse gear
❑ By changing to a higher gear
❑ By selecting neutral

❑ **By changing to a lower gear**

On a long, downhill slope, changing to a lower gear before the descent means that you may not need to use the footbrake the whole time, thereby lowering the risk of the brakes overheating.

8.39   mark **one** answer

Why could keeping the clutch down or selecting neutral for long periods of time be dangerous?

❑ Fuel spillage will occur
❑ Engine damage may be caused
❑ You will have less steering and braking control
❑ It will wear tyres out more quickly

❑ **You will have less steering and braking control**

This is called 'coasting', and it increases the risk of an accident because it reduces your control options.

mark **one** answer

You are driving on an icy road. What distance should you drive from the car in front?

❏ four times the normal distance
❏ six times the normal distance
❏ eight times the normal distance
❏ ten times the normal distance

❏ **ten times the normal distance**

Stopping distances can be up to ten times longer in snow and ice. Give yourself plenty of time to stop.

mark **one** answer

You are on a well-lit motorway at night. You must

❏ use only your sidelights
❏ always use your headlights
❏ always use rear fog lights
❏ use headlights only in bad weather

❏ **always use your headlights**

Remember, see and be seen.

mark **one** answer

You are on a motorway at night with other vehicles just ahead of you. Which lights should you have on?

❏ Front fog lights
❏ Main beam headlights
❏ Sidelights only
❏ Dipped headlights

❏ **Dipped headlights**

Full-beam headlights would dazzle the drivers in front by reflecting in their mirrors.

mark **three** answers

Which THREE of the following will affect your stopping distance?

❏ How fast you are going
❏ The tyres on your vehicle
❏ The time of day
❏ The weather
❏ The street lighting

❏ **How fast you are going**

❏ **The tyres on your vehicle**

❏ **The weather**

The higher the speed, the longer the stopping distance. The better the tyres grip on the road, the less chance there is of skidding.

8.44   mark **one** answer

You are on a motorway at night. You MUST have your headlights switched on unless

❏ there are vehicles close in front of you
❏ you are travelling below 50 mph
❏ the motorway is lit
❏ your vehicle is broken down on the hard shoulder

❏ **your vehicle is broken down on the hard shoulder**

You must use your headlights when driving on a motorway at night, even if the motorway is lit.

8.45   mark **one** answer

You will feel the effects of engine braking when you

❏ only use the handbrake
❏ only use neutral
❏ change to a lower gear
❏ change to a higher gear

❏ **change to a lower gear**

As you re-engage the engine with the clutch, the engine is forced to turn over (rev) higher, and if you don't touch the accelerator this will make the engine slow the car quicker.

8.46   mark **one** answer

Daytime visibility is poor but not seriously reduced. You should switch on

❏ headlights and fog lights
❏ front fog lights
❏ dipped headlights
❏ rear fog lights

❏ **dipped headlights**

You need to see and be seen. Fog lights should only be used when visibility is seriously reduced.

8.47   mark **one** answer

Why are vehicles fitted with rear fog lights?

❏ To be seen when driving at high speed
❏ To use if broken down in a dangerous position
❏ To make them more visible in thick fog
❏ To warn drivers following closely to drop back

❏ **To make them more visible in thick fog**

The fog light is of a higher intensity – therefore it is easier to see.

mark one answer

While you are driving in fog, it becomes necessary to use front fog lights. You should

❏ only turn them on in heavy traffic conditions
❏ remember not to use them on motorways
❏ only use them on dual carriageways
❏ remember to switch them off as visibility improves

❏ **remember to switch them off as visibility improves**

Fog lights should only be used when visibility is seriously reduced, down to 100 metres or less. They are unnecessary at other times.

mark one answer

When snow is falling heavily you should

❏ only drive with your hazard lights on
❏ not drive unless you have a mobile phone
❏ only drive when your journey is short
❏ not drive unless it is essential

❏ **not drive unless it is essential**

Driving in snow is clearly more dangerous than driving in normal conditions.

mark one answer

You are driving down a long steep hill. You suddenly notice your brakes are not working as well as normal. What is the usual cause of this?

❏ The brakes overheating
❏ Air in the brake fluid
❏ Oil on the brakes
❏ Badly adjusted brakes

❏ **The brakes overheating**

Selecting a lower gear before descending a long, steep hill allows the engine to control the speed of the car and helps prevent the brakes overheating. With a lower gear selected, the footbrake can be used when necessary rather than the whole time.

mark two answers

You have to make a journey in fog. What are the TWO most important things you should do before you set out?

❏ Top up the radiator with anti-freeze
❏ Make sure that you have a warning triangle in the vehicle
❏ Check that your lights are working
❏ Check the battery
❏ Make sure that the windows are clean

❏ **Check that your lights are working**

❏ **Make sure that the windows are clean**

See and be seen are the two most crucial safety aspects of driving in fog.

8.52   mark **one** answer

You have just driven out of fog. Visibility is now good. You MUST

- ❏ switch off all your fog lights
- ❏ keep your rear fog lights on
- ❏ keep your front fog lights on
- ❏ leave fog lights on in case fog returns

❏ **switch off all your fog lights**

They are unnecessary now and may dazzle other road users.

8.53   mark **one** answer

You may drive with front fog lights switched on

N 512 CTW

- ❏ when visibility is less than 100 metres (328 feet)
- ❏ at any time to be noticed
- ❏ instead of headlights on high speed roads
- ❏ when dazzled by the lights of oncoming vehicles

❏ **when visibility is less than 100 metres (328 feet)**

Fog lights should only be used when visibility is seriously reduced. They are unnecessary at other times and may dazzle other road users.

8.54   mark **two** answers

Why is it dangerous to leave rear fog lights on when they are not needed?

- ❏ Brake lights are less clear
- ❏ Following drivers can be dazzled
- ❏ Electrical systems could be overloaded
- ❏ Direction indicators may not work properly
- ❏ The battery could fail

❏ **Brake lights are less clear**

❏ **Following drivers can be dazzled**

Because they are of a higher intensity, they cause problems when used in good conditions.

Holding the clutch pedal down or rolling in neutral for too long while driving will

❏ use more fuel
❏ cause the engine to overheat
❏ reduce your control
❏ improve tyre wear

❏ **reduce your control**

This is called 'coasting', and it increases the risk of an accident, because you will have less steering and braking control.

You are driving down a steep hill. Why could keeping the clutch down or rolling in neutral for too long be dangerous?

❏ Fuel consumption will be higher
❏ Your vehicle will pick up speed
❏ It will damage the engine
❏ It will wear tyres out more quickly

❏ **Your vehicle will pick up speed**

This is called 'coasting' – it increases the risk of an accident because you will have less control over steering and braking.

What are TWO main reasons why coasting downhill is wrong?

❏ Fuel consumption will be higher
❏ The vehicle will get faster
❏ It puts more wear and tear on the tyres
❏ You have less braking and steering control
❏ It damages the engine

❏ **The vehicle will get faster**

❏ **You have less braking and steering control**

You cannot utilise engine braking, and you have increased the chances of skidding.

8.58   mark **four** answers

Which FOUR of the following may apply when dealing with this hazard?

❏ It could be more difficult in winter
❏ Use a low gear and drive slowly
❏ Use a high gear to prevent wheelspin
❏ Test your brakes afterwards
❏ Always switch on fog lamps
❏ There may be a depth gauge

❏ **It could be more difficult in winter**

❏ **Use a low gear and drive slowly**

❏ **Test your brakes afterwards**

❏ **There may be a depth gauge**

You could be driving through fairly deep water. You will need to maintain full control, and may need to dry your brakes afterwards.

8.59   mark **one** answer

Why is travelling in neutral for long distances (known as coasting) wrong?

❏ It will cause the car to skid
❏ It will make the engine stall
❏ The engine will run faster
❏ There is no engine braking

❏ **There is no engine braking**

You cannot utilise engine braking, or accelerate quickly, and you have increased the chances of skidding.

8.60   mark **one** answer

When MUST you use dipped headlights during the day?

❏ All the time
❏ Along narrow streets
❏ In poor visibility
❏ When parking

❏ **In poor visibility**

Don't forget – see and be seen. Fog lights should only be used when visibility is seriously reduced, down to 100 metres or less.

8.61   mark **one** answer

You are braking on a wet road. Your vehicle begins to skid. It does not have anti-lock brakes. What is the FIRST thing you should do?

❏ Quickly pull up the handbrake
❏ Release the footbrake
❏ Push harder on the brake pedal
❏ Gently use the accelerator

❏ **Release the footbrake**

It is important to remove the cause of the skid. In this case it is the braking, therefore you will need to release the footbrake. What you do next will depend on the circumstances.

8.62   mark **two** answers

Using rear fog lights on a clear dry night will

❏ reduce glare from the road surface
❏ make your brake lights less visible
❏ give a better view of the road ahead
❏ dazzle following drivers
❏ help your indicators to be seen more clearly

❏ **make your brake lights less visible**

❏ **dazzle following drivers**

Rear fog lights have a high intensity, therefore, if you are using them when they're not needed, following drivers will be dazzled and will be less likely to see when you are braking.

Section 9
Motorway rules

There are 67 questions in this section covering the following subjects:

- ❏ Speed limits
- ❏ Lane discipline
- ❏ Stopping
- ❏ Lighting
- ❏ Parking

You will need to think about:

- ❏ The rules of motorway driving

- ❏ How these rules differ from other road regulations

- ❏ Why these rules differ from other regulations.

Tips

Most people have been a car passenger on a motorway, so even though – as a learner – you will not yet have driven on a motorway, the subject is not as unfamiliar as you might think. Next time you are in a car on a motorway, take the time to read the displayed signs and signals and check your knowledge with the driver. You should ask first if this is OK with the driver, but most will be glad of the distraction to alleviate the boredom, while still concentrating on driving!

Motorways are evolving, and there are some new rules emerging as a consequence. As an example, look out for questions on Active Traffic Management or ATM and variable speed limits in this section. These rules will be new to experienced drivers as well.

mark **one** answer

When joining a motorway you must always

❑ use the hard shoulder
❑ stop at the end of the acceleration lane
❑ come to a stop before joining the motorway
❑ give way to traffic already on the motorway

❑ **give way to traffic already on the motorway**

They have priority. Match your speed to the traffic in the left-hand lane, and slot into a suitable gap. Don't force your way in.

mark **one** answer

What is the national speed limit for cars and motorcycles in the centre lane of a three-lane motorway?

❑ 40 mph
❑ 50 mph
❑ 60 mph
❑ 70 mph

❑ **70 mph**

The speed limit for motorways is 70 mph. This applies in all lanes unless otherwise indicated.

mark **one** answer

What is the national speed limit on motorways for cars and motorcycles?

❑ 30 mph
❑ 50 mph
❑ 60 mph
❑ 70 mph

❑ **70 mph**

Speed limits may be altered due to weather conditions. Look out for signs on the central reservation or above your lane.

mark **one** answer

The left-hand lane on a three-lane motorway is for use by

❑ any vehicle
❑ large vehicles only
❑ emergency vehicles only
❑ slow vehicles only

❑ **any vehicle**

Strictly speaking, any vehicle which is allowed on a motorway.

9.5   mark **one** answer

Which of these IS NOT allowed to travel in the right-hand lane of a three-lane motorway?

❑ A small delivery van
❑ A motorcycle
❑ A vehicle towing a trailer
❑ A motorcycle and side-car

❑ **A vehicle towing a trailer**

Because a vehicle towing a trailer is restricted to 60 mph, it is prohibited from the outside lane where the speed limit is likely to be 70 mph as it would become an obstruction.

9.6   mark **one** answer

You break down on a motorway. You need to call for help. Why may it be better to use an emergency roadside telephone rather than a mobile phone?

❑ It connects you to a local garage
❑ Using a mobile phone will distract other drivers
❑ It allows easy location by the emergency services
❑ Mobile phones do not work on motorways

❑ **It allows easy location by the emergency services**

The telephone operator will instantly know where you are, from the emergency phone you are using.

9.7   mark **one** answer

After a breakdown you need to rejoin the main carriageway of a motorway from the hard shoulder. You should

❑ move out onto the carriageway then build up your speed
❑ move out onto the carriageway using your hazard lights
❑ gain speed on the hard shoulder before moving out onto the carriageway
❑ wait on the hard shoulder until someone flashes their headlights at you

❑ **gain speed on the hard shoulder before moving out onto the carriageway**

You should treat it in a similar way to joining from a slip road. Match your speed to the traffic in the left-hand lane, signal early, and slot into a suitable gap. Don't force your way in.

A crawler lane on a motorway is found

- ❑ on a steep gradient
- ❑ before a service area
- ❑ before a junction
- ❑ along the hard shoulder

❑ **on a steep gradient**

This allows slow-moving vehicles to move to a designated lane, which aids traffic flow and reduces congestion.

What do these motorway signs show?

- ❑ They are countdown markers to a bridge
- ❑ They are distance markers to the next telephone
- ❑ They are countdown markers to the next exit
- ❑ They warn of a police control ahead

❑ **They are countdown markers to the next exit**

They are displayed approximately 300, 200 and 100 metres from the start of the exit lane.

On a motorway the amber reflective studs can be found between

- ❑ the hard shoulder and the carriageway
- ❑ the acceleration lane and the carriageway
- ❑ the central reservation and the carriageway
- ❑ each pair of the lanes

❑ **the central reservation and the carriageway**

Amber studs mark the right-hand edge of the carriageway.

9.11   mark **one** answer

What colour are the reflective studs between the lanes on a motorway?

❑ **White**

White studs separate lanes on the carriageway. Your headlights will reflect back on these.

❑ Green
❑ Amber
❑ White
❑ Red

9.12   mark **one** answer

What colour are the reflective studs between a motorway and its slip road?

❑ Amber
❑ White
❑ Green
❑ Red

❑ **Green**

Green studs mark the entrance and exit to slip roads (acceleration/deceleration lanes).

9.13   mark **one** answer

You have broken down on a motorway. To find the nearest emergency telephone you should always walk

❑ with the traffic flow
❑ facing oncoming traffic
❑ in the direction shown on the marker posts
❑ in the direction of the nearest exit

❑ **in the direction shown on the marker posts**

They will be placed every 100 metres and will direct you to the closest phone. The operator will then instantly know where you are by the phone you are using.

mark **one** answer

You are joining a motorway. Why is it important to make full use of the slip road?

❑ Because there is space available to turn round if you need to
❑ To allow you direct access to the overtaking lanes
❑ To build up a speed similar to traffic on the motorway
❑ Because you can continue on the hard shoulder

❑ **To build up a speed similar to traffic on the motorway**

You need to build up your speed to that of the traffic already on the motorway so you can ease into a gap in the flow of traffic.

mark **one** answer

How should you use the emergency telephone on a motorway?

❑ Stay close to the carriageway
❑ Face the oncoming traffic
❑ Keep your back to the traffic
❑ Stand on the hard shoulder

❑ **Face the oncoming traffic**

You will be able to see approching cars and take the appropriate action; this is to avoid an accident.

mark **one** answer

You are on a motorway. What colour are the reflective studs on the left of the carriageway?

❑ Green
❑ Red
❑ White
❑ Amber

❑ **Red**

Red studs mark the left edge of the carriageway. Green mark the entrance and exit to slip roads (acceleration/deceleration lanes).

mark **one** answer

On a three-lane motorway which lane should you normally use?

❑ Left
❑ Right
❑ Centre
❑ Either the right or centre

❑ **Left**

The other lanes should be used for overtaking.

9.18   mark **one** answer

When going through a contraflow system on a motorway you should

❑ ensure that you do not exceed 30 mph
❑ keep a good distance from the vehicle ahead
❑ switch lanes to keep the traffic flowing
❑ stay close to the vehicle ahead to reduce queues

❑ **keep a good distance from the vehicle ahead**

In these circumstances there may also be a speed limit – keep to it.

9.19   mark **one** answer

You are on a three-lane motorway. There are red reflective studs on your left and white ones to your right. Where are you?

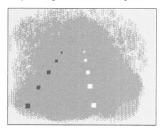

❑ In the right-hand lane
❑ In the middle lane
❑ On the hard shoulder
❑ In the left-hand lane

❑ **In the left-hand lane**

Red studs mark the left edge of the carriageway. Green mark the entrance and exit to slip roads (acceleration/deceleration lanes). White studs separate lanes on the carriageway. Amber studs mark the right-hand edge of the carriageway. This is so that in poor visibility you can tell your position on the motorway by the colour of the studs around your vehicle.

mark one answer

You are approaching roadworks on a motorway. What should you do?

❏ Speed up to clear the area quickly
❏ Always use the hard shoulder
❏ Obey all speed limits
❏ Stay very close to the vehicle in front

❏ **Obey all speed limits**

In motorway roadworks you are sometimes, but not always, directed to use the hard shoulder, especially where the right-hand lane is closed. Therefore, the second answer is not correct. There often are lower speed limits to protect the traffic in contraflows or narrow lanes and you must obey these.

mark four answers

Which FOUR of these must NOT use motorways?

❏ Learner car drivers
❏ Motorcycles over 50cc
❏ Double-deck buses
❏ Farm tractors
❏ Horse riders
❏ Cyclists

❏ **Learner car drivers**

❏ **Farm tractors**

❏ **Horse riders**

❏ **Cyclists**

Slow vehicles and horse riders are prevented by law from using motorways.

mark four answers

Which FOUR of these must NOT use motorways?

❏ Learner car drivers
❏ Motorcycles over 50cc
❏ Double-deck buses
❏ Farm tractors
❏ Learner motorcyclists
❏ Cyclists

❏ **Learner car drivers**

❏ **Farm tractors**

❏ **Learner motorcyclists**

❏ **Cyclists**

For safety reasons, the law prevents these road users from using the motorway.

9.23   mark **one** answer

Immediately after joining a motorway you should normally

❏ try to overtake
❏ re-adjust your mirrors
❏ position your vehicle in the centre lane
❏ keep in the left-hand lane

❏ **keep in the left-hand lane**

Wait until you are accustomed to the higher speed before overtaking.

9.24   mark **one** answer

What is the right-hand lane used for on a three-lane motorway?

❏ Emergency vehicles only
❏ Overtaking
❏ Vehicles towing trailers
❏ Coaches only

❏ **Overtaking**

You should use the left-hand lane for driving, and the centre or right-hand lanes for overtaking. Once an overtaking manoeuvre is completed you should move back to the left.

9.25   mark **one** answer

What should you use the hard shoulder of a motorway for?

❏ Stopping in an emergency
❏ Leaving the motorway
❏ Stopping when you are tired
❏ Joining the motorway

❏ **Stopping in an emergency**

You may only stop on the hard shoulder in an emergency.

mark **one** answer

You are in the right-hand lane on a motorway. You see these overhead signs. This means

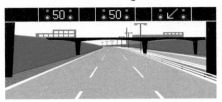

- move to the left and reduce your speed to 50 mph
- there are roadworks 50 metres (55 yards) ahead
- use the hard shoulder until you have passed the hazard
- leave the motorway at the next exit

- **move to the left and reduce your speed to 50 mph**

These signs are mandatory – follow them. It is not always possible to see or understand the nature of the hazard ahead.

mark **one** answer

You are allowed to stop on a motorway when you

- need to walk and get fresh air
- wish to pick up hitchhikers
- are told to do so by flashing red lights
- need to use a mobile telephone

- **are told to do so by flashing red lights**

The other options are dangerous. Remember these lights are mandatory – obey them. It is not always possible to see or understand the nature of the hazard ahead.

mark **one** answer

You are travelling along the left-hand lane of a three-lane motorway. Traffic is joining from a slip road. You should

- race the other vehicles
- move to another lane
- maintain a steady speed
- switch on your hazard flashers

- **move to another lane**

This will reduce the risk of an incident and will help to keep the traffic flowing.

9.29   mark **one** answer

A basic rule when on motorways is

❏ use the lane that has least traffic
❏ keep to the left-hand lane unless overtaking
❏ overtake on the side that is clearest
❏ try to keep above 50 mph to prevent congestion

❏ **keep to the left-hand lane unless overtaking**

You should use the left-hand lane for driving, and the centre or right-hand lanes for overtaking. Once an overtaking manoeuvre is completed you should move back to the left.

9.30   mark **one** answer

On motorways you should never overtake on the left unless

❏ you can see well ahead that the hard shoulder is clear
❏ the traffic in the right-hand lane is signalling right
❏ you warn drivers behind by signalling left
❏ there is a queue of slow-moving traffic to your right that is moving more slowly than you are

❏ **there is a queue of slow-moving traffic to your right that is moving more slowly than you are**

Other road users would not expect it, might not look for it, and it would therefore be a very risky manoeuvre.

9.31   mark **one** answer

Motorway emergency telephones are usually linked to the police. In some areas they are now linked to

❏ the Highways Agency Control Centre
❏ the Driver Vehicle Licensing Agency
❏ the Driving Standards Agency
❏ the local Vehicle Registration Office

❏ **the Highways Agency Control Centre**

In some areas the Highways Agency Control Centre operates the phone network, taking the calls and passing the information on where appropriate to the relevant emergency service.

9.32   mark **one** answer

An Emergency Refuge Area is an area

❑ on a motorway for use in cases of
emergency or breakdown
❑ for use if you think you will be involved in a
road rage incident
❑ on a motorway for a police patrol to park
and watch traffic
❑ for construction and road workers to store
emergency equipment

❑ **on a motorway for use in cases of
emergency or breakdown**

Emergency refuge areas will be available in
areas where the hard shoulder is being used
as a running lane. They are 100 metres long,
wider than the hard shoulder and are located
every 500 metres. They are designed to be
used in cases of emergency or breakdown.

9.33   mark **one** answer

What is an Emergency Refuge Area on a
motorway for?

❑ An area to park in when you want to use a
mobile phone
❑ To use in cases of emergency or
breakdown
❑ For an emergency recovery vehicle to park
in a contra-flow system
❑ To drive in when there is queuing traffic
ahead

❑ **To use in cases of emergency or
breakdown**

These are often provided in areas where
there is no hard shoulder, or in an Active
Traffic Management (ATM) area where the
hard shoulder is sometimes used as a
normal part of the carriageway. Use
emergency refuge areas if they are available,
it will be much safer.

9.34   mark **one** answer

Highways Agency Traffic Officers

❑ will not be able to assist at a breakdown or
emergency
❑ are not able to stop and direct anyone on a
motorway
❑ will tow a broken down vehicle and its
passengers home
❑ are able to stop and direct anyone on a
motorway

❑ **are able to stop and direct anyone on
a motorway**

Highways Agency Traffic Officers are there to
help and guide you, usually at the scene of
an accident or at road works. Follow their
directions.

9.35   mark **one** answer

You are on a motorway. A red cross is displayed above the hard shoulder. What does this mean?

- ❏ Pull up in this lane to answer your mobile phone
- ❏ Use this lane as a running lane
- ❏ This lane can be used if you need a rest
- ❏ You should not travel in this lane

❏ **You should not travel in this lane**

The red cross means the same displayed above any lane – do not travel any further in this lane. When it is displayed above the hard shoulder it indicates you are travelling in an Active Traffic Management (ATM) area.

9.36   mark **one** answer

You are on a motorway in an Active Traffic Management (ATM) area. A mandatory speed limit is displayed above the hard shoulder. What does this mean?

- ❏ You should not travel in this lane
- ❏ The hard shoulder can be used as a running lane
- ❏ You can park on the hard shoulder if you feel tired
- ❏ You can pull up in this lane to answer a mobile phone

❏ **The hard shoulder can be used as a running lane**

Active Traffic Management (ATM) aims to reduce congestion and make journey times more reliable.

mark **one** answer

The aim of an Active Traffic Management scheme on a motorway is to

❏ prevent overtaking
❏ reduce rest stops
❏ prevent tailgating
❏ reduce congestion

❏ **reduce congestion**

Active Traffic Management aims to reduce congestion and make journey times more reliable.

mark **one** answer

You are in an Active Traffic Management area on a motorway. When the actively managed mode is operating

❏ speed limits are only advisory
❏ the national speed limit will apply
❏ the speed limit is always 30 mph
❏ all speed limit signals are set

❏ **all speed limit signals are set**

This allows the managed area to be controlled so that congestion is reduced.

mark **one** answer

You are travelling on a motorway. A red cross is shown above the hard shoulder. What does this mean?

❏ Use this lane as a rest area
❏ Use this as a normal running lane
❏ Do not use this lane to travel in
❏ National speed limit applies in this lane

❏ **Do not use this lane to travel in**

The red cross means the same when displayed above any lane – do not travel any further in this lane. When it is displayed above the hard shoulder it means you are in an Active Traffic Management area.

9.40   mark **one** answer

Why can it be an advantage for traffic speed to stay constant over a longer distance?

❏ You will do more stop-start driving
❏ You will use far more fuel
❏ You will be able to use more direct routes
❏ Your overall journey time will normally improve

❏ **Your overall journey time will normally improve**

It has been proven on roads such as the M25 that managing traffic speed to be more constant reduces journey time, pollution and the risk of accidents.

9.41   mark **one** answer

You should not normally travel on the hard shoulder of a motorway. When can you use it?

❏ When taking the next exit
❏ When traffic is stopped
❏ When signs direct you to
❏ When traffic is slow moving

❏ **When signs direct you to**

You could be travelling through roadworks, in a contraflow system, or in an area with Active Traffic Management.

9.42   mark **one** answer

For what reason may you use the right-hand lane of a motorway?

❏ For keeping out of the way of lorries
❏ For travelling at more than 70 mph
❏ For turning right
❏ For overtaking other vehicles

❏ **For overtaking other vehicles**

You should use the left-hand lane for driving, and the centre or right-hand lanes for overtaking. Once an overtaking manoeuvre is completed you should move back to the left.

9.43 — mark **one** answer

On a motorway what is used to reduce traffic bunching?

- Variable speed limits
- Contraflow systems
- National speed limits
- Lane closures

Variable speed limits

When traffic is heavy on certain stretches of motorway, variable speed limits are used. The traffic might be limited to a maximum of 50 mph over a certain distance which helps spread the traffic out and avoid congestion.

9.44 — mark **three** answers

When should you stop on a motorway?

- If you have to read a map
- When you are tired and need a rest
- If red lights show above every lane
- When told to by the police
- If your mobile phone rings
- When signalled by a Highways Agency Traffic Officer

If red lights show above every lane

When told to by the police

When signalled by a Highways Agency Traffic Officer

Motorways are statistically the safest roads to drive on because the traffic travels at a constant speed and there are few distractions, such as stationary vehicles. You may only stop on a motorway in an emergency.

9.45 — mark **one** answer

When may you stop on a motorway?

- If you have to read a map
- When you are tired and need a rest
- If your mobile phone rings
- In an emergency or breakdown

In an emergency or breakdown

You may not generally stop on a motorway. Make use of the motorway services or leave at the next exit for the other options.

9.46 — mark **one** answer

You are travelling on a motorway. Unless signs show a lower speed limit you must NOT exceed

- 50 mph
- 60 mph
- 70 mph
- 80 mph

70 mph

This is the national speed limit for cars on a motorway. Signs overhead or to the side of the carriageway will alert you to any changes, for example at roadworks.

9.47   mark **one** answer

Motorway emergency telephones are usually linked to the police. In some areas they are now linked to

❑ the local ambulance service
❑ a Highways Agency control centre
❑ the local fire brigade
❑ a breakdown service control centre

❑ **a Highways Agency control centre**

They will be placed every 100 metres and will direct you to the closest phone. The operator will then instantly know where you are by the phone you are using.

9.48   mark **one** answer

You are on a motorway. There are red flashing lights above every lane. You must

❑ pull onto the hard shoulder
❑ slow down and watch for further signals
❑ leave at the next exit
❑ stop and wait

❑ **stop and wait**

These lights are mandatory, so obey them. It is not always possible to see or understand the nature of the hazard ahead.

9.49   mark **one** answer

You are on a three-lane motorway. A red cross is shown above the hard shoulder and mandatory speed limits above all other lanes. This means

❑ the hard shoulder can be used as a rest area if you feel tired
❑ the hard shoulder is for emergency or breakdown use only
❑ the hard shoulder can be used as a normal running lane
❑ the hard shoulder has a speed limit of 50 mph

❑ **the hard shoulder is for emergency or breakdown use only**

The red cross indicates you are driving in an Active Traffic Management area under normal motorway conditions, so the hard shoulder may only be used for emergency or breakdown.

You are on a three-lane motorway and see this sign. It means you can use

❑ any lane except the hard shoulder
❑ the hard shoulder only
❑ the three right hand lanes only
❑ all the lanes including the hard shoulder

❑ **all the lanes including the hard shoulder**

You are in an Active Traffic Management area which is in operation. Treat the hard shoulder as a normal traffic lane. In an emergency use the emergency refuge areas.

You are travelling on a motorway. You decide you need a rest. You should

❑ stop on the hard shoulder
❑ pull in at the nearest service area
❑ pull up on a slip road
❑ park on the central reservation

❑ **pull in at the nearest service area**

Plan your rest stops before you start a motorway journey. You are not permitted to stop on the motorway or hard shoulder, unless there is an emergency or when directed by the police or traffic signals.

You are on a motorway. You become tired and decide you need to rest. What should you do?

❑ Stop on the hard shoulder
❑ Pull up on a slip road
❑ Park on the central reservation
❑ Leave at the next exit

❑ **Leave at the next exit**

You are not permitted to stop on the motorway or hard shoulder, unless there is an emergency or when directed by the police or traffic signals. If you become tired and decide that you need to rest, the best option might well be to leave at the next exit and find somewhere that is both safe and convenient to pull over.

9.53   mark **one** answer

You are towing a trailer on a motorway. What is your maximum speed limit?

❏ 40 mph
❏ 50 mph
❏ 60 mph
❏ 70 mph

❏ **60 mph**

The speed limit for motorways is 70 mph unless signs or signals dictate otherwise. The limit for a vehicle towing a trailer is 60 mph; it is also prohibited from the outside lane where it would become an obstruction because of the lower speed travelled.

9.54   mark **one** answer

The left-hand lane of a motorway should be used for

❏ breakdowns and emergencies only
❏ overtaking slower traffic in the other lanes
❏ slow vehicles only
❏ normal driving

❏ **normal driving**

You should use the left-hand lane for driving, and the centre or right-hand lanes for overtaking. Once an overtaking manoeuvre is completed you should move back to the left.

9.55   mark **one** answer

You are driving on a motorway. You have to slow down quickly due to a hazard. You should

❏ switch on your hazard lights
❏ switch on your headlights
❏ sound your horn
❏ flash your headlights

❏ **switch on your hazard lights**

This will warn the drivers behind you of a hazard ahead. It is the only time you are allowed to use the hazard lights while on the move.

mark **one** answer

You get a puncture on the motorway. You manage to get your vehicle onto the hard shoulder. You should

❑ change the wheel yourself immediately
❑ use the emergency telephone and call for assistance
❑ try to wave down another vehicle for help
❑ only change the wheel if you have a passenger to help you

❑ **use the emergency telephone and call for assistance**

It is dangerous to attempt to change the wheel yourself. Try to keep as far from the carriageway as possible while waiting for assistance.

mark **one** answer

You are driving on a motorway. By mistake, you go past the exit that you wanted to take. You should

❑ carefully reverse on the hard shoulder
❑ carry on to the next exit
❑ carefully reverse in the left-hand lane
❑ make a U-turn at the next gap in the central reservation

❑ **carry on to the next exit**

As well as the dangers of the alternatives, these options are illegal.

mark **one** answer

You are driving at 70 mph on a three-lane motorway. There is no traffic ahead. Which lane should you use?

❑ Any lane
❑ Middle lane
❑ Right lane
❑ Left lane

❑ **Left lane**

You should always use the left-hand lane for normal driving.

9.59 mark **one** answer

Your vehicle has broken down on a motorway. You are not able to stop on the hard shoulder. What should you do?

❑ Switch on your hazard warning lights
❑ Stop following traffic and ask for help
❑ Attempt to repair your vehicle quickly
❑ Stand behind your vehicle to warn others

❑ **Switch on your hazard warning lights**

All the other options are extremely dangerous.

9.60 mark **one** answer

Why is it particularly important to carry out a check on your vehicle before making a long motorway journey?

❑ You will have to do more harsh braking on motorways
❑ Motorway service stations do not deal with breakdowns
❑ The road surface will wear down the tyres faster
❑ Continuous high speeds may increase the risk of your vehicle breaking down

❑ **Continuous high speeds may increase the risk of your vehicle breaking down**

Check oil and windscreen washer levels and also check the tyres. Plan your rest stops.

9.61 mark **one** answer

You are driving on a motorway. The car ahead shows its hazard lights for a short time. This tells you that

❑ the driver wants you to overtake
❑ the other car is going to change lanes
❑ traffic ahead is slowing or stopping suddenly
❑ there is a police speed check ahead

❑ **traffic ahead is slowing or stopping suddenly**

This should warn you of a hazard ahead. It is the only time drivers are allowed to use the hazard lights while on the move.

mark **one** answer

You are intending to leave the motorway at the next exit. Before you reach the exit you should normally position your vehicle

❏ in the middle lane
❏ in the left-hand lane
❏ on the hard shoulder
❏ in any lane

❏ **in the left-hand lane**

Do so well before you reach the exit. Adjust your speed to the speed of the traffic in the lane, if needed, and gently ease off at the exit. Motorway driving must be smooth, consistent, and controlled at all times.

mark **one** answer

As a provisional licence holder you should not drive a car

❏ over 30 mph
❏ at night
❏ on the motorway
❏ with passengers in rear seats

❏ **on the motorway**

It is against the law for learner drivers to use the motorway. However, it is strongly recommended that once a driver passes their test they take a course of motorway tuition before embarking on their first unaccompanied motorway journey.

mark **one** answer

Your vehicle breaks down on the hard shoulder of a motorway. You decide to use your mobile phone to call for help. You should

❏ stand at the rear of the vehicle while making the call
❏ try to repair the vehicle yourself
❏ get out of the vehicle by the right-hand door
❏ check your location from the marker posts on the left

❏ **check your location from the marker posts on the left**

They will be placed every 100 metres. Each post has a unique number which helps the operator to guide the emergency services to your location.

9.65
mark **one** answer

You are on a three-lane motorway towing a trailer. You may use the right-hand lane when

❏ there are lane closures
❏ there is slow moving traffic
❏ you can maintain a high speed
❏ large vehicles are in the left and centre lanes

❏ **there are lane closures**

Because a vehicle towing a trailer is restricted to 60 mph, it is normally prohibited from using the outside lane where the speed limit is likely to be 70 mph, because it would become an obstruction. This is the exception.

9.66
mark **one** answer

You are on a motorway. There is a contraflow system ahead. What would you expect to find?

❏ Temporary traffic lights
❏ Lower speed limits
❏ Wider lanes than normal
❏ Speed humps

❏ **Lower speed limits**

Contraflow systems are by their nature more dangerous than the normal road layout and consequently normally have lower speed limits.

9.67
mark **one** answer

On a motorway you may only stop on the hard shoulder

❏ in an emergency
❏ if you feel tired and need to rest
❏ if you miss the exit that you wanted
❏ to pick up a hitchhiker

❏ **in an emergency**

You should not normally stop on a motorway. If however, you experience an emergency, such as your vehicle breaking down, you will have little choice than to pull onto the hard shoulder. Try to position your vehicle as far to the left as you can.

Section 10
Rules of the road

There are 75 questions in this section covering the following subjects:

❑ Speed limits
❑ Lane discipline
❑ Parking
❑ Lighting

You will need to think about:

❑ Rules and regulations covering most aspects of road procedure

❑ how fast can you go

❑ where can you park

❑ can you turn round, turn right, or turn your lights off, etc.

Tips

There's a lot to cover in this section and some of it will need to be memorised – 'how far may you park from a junction' for example (10 metres). However, some information has already been covered in other sections, such as dealing with long vehicles, and some is straightforward – 'You meet an obstruction on your side of the road you should… give way to oncoming traffic'.

If you are having difficulty remembering facts, and coping with the diversity of this section, you could group the questions into sub-sections, putting together questions on speed limits, or questions on schools, etc, as this may help you to learn a large and varied section more easily, by making it more manageable.

10.1 **mark one answer**

What is the meaning of this sign?

❑ Local speed limit applies
❑ No waiting on the carriageway
❑ National speed limit applies
❑ No entry to vehicular traffic

❑ **National speed limit applies**

The actual speed limit will depend on the vehicle you are driving, and the type of road you are driving on.

10.2 **mark one answer**

What is the national speed limit for cars and motorcycles on a dual carriageway?

❑ 30 mph
❑ 50 mph
❑ 60 mph
❑ 70 mph

❑ **70 mph**

The national speed limit is 70 mph on a motorway or dual carriageway and 60 mph on two-way roads unless traffic signs denote anything different.

10.3 **mark one answer**

There are no speed limit signs on the road. How is a 30 mph limit indicated?

❑ By hazard warning lines
❑ By street lighting
❑ By pedestrian islands
❑ By double or single yellow lines

❑ **By street lighting**

In a 'built up area' a 30 mph speed limit applies – this area is defined by street lights. If a higher or lower limit applies there will be signs to advise you of this.

10.4 **mark one answer**

Where you see street lights but no speed limit signs the limit is usually

❑ 30 mph
❑ 40 mph
❑ 50 mph
❑ 60 mph

❑ **30 mph**

A 30 mph speed limit applies where there are street lights and no other speed limit signs.

10.5   mark **one** answer

What does this sign mean?

❏ **End of minimum speed**

A blue sign gives a positive instruction (something you must do). The red line through it denotes the end of this instruction.

❏ Minimum speed 30 mph
❏ End of maximum speed
❏ End of minimum speed
❏ Maximum speed 30 mph

10.6   mark **one** answer

There is a tractor ahead of you. You wish to overtake but you are NOT sure if it is safe to do so. You should

❏ **not overtake if you are in doubt**

Use discretion – only overtake if it is necessary, safe and permissible.

❏ follow another overtaking vehicle through
❏ sound your horn to the slow vehicle to pull over
❏ speed through but flash your lights to oncoming traffic
❏ not overtake if you are in doubt

10.7   mark **three** answers

Which three of the following are most likely to take an unusual course at roundabouts?

❏ **Horse riders**

❏ **Long vehicles**

❏ **Cyclists**

❏ Horse riders
❏ Milk floats
❏ Delivery vans
❏ Long vehicles
❏ Estate cars
❏ Cyclists

Because of their size and speed it is often safer for cyclists and horse riders to approach in the left-hand lane regardless of their final destination. Long vehicles require more space to turn and often need to reposition for this.

mark **one** answer

On a clearway you must not stop

❏ at any time
❏ when it is busy
❏ in the rush hour
❏ during daylight hours

❏ **at any time**

The whole purpose of a clearway is to keep the traffic flowing. Don't stop or park on one.

mark **one** answer

What is the meaning of this sign?

❏ No entry
❏ Waiting restrictions
❏ National speed limit
❏ School crossing patrol

❏ **Waiting restrictions**

You will normally find a plate below this telling you when the restrictions apply.

mark **one** answer

You can park on the right-hand side of a road at night

❏ in a one-way street
❏ with your sidelights on
❏ more than 10 metres (32 feet) from a junction
❏ under a lamp-post

❏ **in a one-way street**

It is normally safer to park on the left, because the red reflectors fitted to the back of your vehicle (in the light cluster) will be easily picked up by the headlights of traffic using the road.

10.11 mark **one** answer

On a three-lane dual carriageway the right-hand lane can be used for

❏ overtaking only, never turning right
❏ overtaking or turning right
❏ fast-moving traffic only
❏ turning right only, never overtaking

❏ **overtaking or turning right**

You should use the left-hand lane for driving, and the centre lane for overtaking and the right-hand lane for overtaking or turning right. Once an overtaking manoeuvre is completed you should move back to the left.

10.12 mark **one** answer

You are approaching a busy junction. There are several lanes with road markings. At the last moment you realise that you are in the wrong lane. You should

❏ continue in that lane
❏ force your way across
❏ stop until the area has cleared
❏ use clear arm signals to cut across

❏ **continue in that lane**

All the other actions suggested could be dangerous.

10.13 mark **one** answer

Where may you overtake on a one-way street?

❏ Only on the left-hand side
❏ Overtaking is not allowed
❏ Only on the right-hand side
❏ Either on the right or the left

❏ **Either on the right or the left**

Normally you should overtake only on the right. This is the exception.

mark **one** answer

When going straight ahead at a roundabout you should

❑ indicate left before leaving the roundabout
❑ not indicate at any time
❑ indicate right when approaching the roundabout
❑ indicate left when approaching the roundabout

❑ **indicate left before leaving the roundabout**

You should signal left just as you pass the exit before the one you want to take.

mark **one** answer

Which vehicle might have to use a different course to normal at roundabouts?

❑ Sports car
❑ Van
❑ Estate car
❑ Long vehicle

❑ **Long vehicle**

Long vehicles require more space to turn and often need to reposition for this.

mark **one** answer

You may only enter a box junction when

❑ there are less than two vehicles in front of you
❑ the traffic lights show green
❑ your exit road is clear
❑ you need to turn left

❑ **your exit road is clear**

These markings are designed to keep busy junctions clear and free flowing. Stopping on them will hinder traffic flow and can lead to gridlock (where no one can move). However when you are turning right you're allowed to wait on them, providing you are only prevented from turning right by oncoming traffic.

10.17 — mark **one** answer

You may wait in a yellow box junction when

❑ oncoming traffic is preventing you from turning right
❑ you are in a queue of traffic turning left
❑ you are in a queue of traffic to go ahead
❑ you are on a roundabout

❑ **oncoming traffic is preventing you from turning right**

The purpose of the yellow box is to keep the junction clear of queing traffic. If you are turning right and need to wait for approaching traffic, you can drive into and wait in this box, provided that that your exit is clear.

10.18 — mark **three** answers

You MUST stop when signalled to do so by which THREE of these?

❑ A police officer
❑ A pedestrian
❑ A school crossing patrol
❑ A bus driver
❑ A red traffic light

❑ **A police officer**

❑ **A school crossing patrol**

❑ **A red traffic light**

Note the word 'MUST' in the question, which is asking what the law says.

10.19 — mark **one** answer

Someone is waiting to cross at a zebra crossing. They are standing on the pavement. You should normally

❑ go on quickly before they step onto the crossing
❑ stop before you reach the zigzag lines and let them cross
❑ stop, let them cross, wait patiently
❑ ignore them as they are still on the pavement

❑ **stop, let them cross, wait patiently**

This is the safest option. You are controlling the situation.

At toucan crossings, apart from pedestrians you should be aware of

❏ emergency vehicles emerging
❏ buses pulling out
❏ trams crossing in front
❏ cyclists riding across

❏ **cyclists riding across**

Cyclists are allowed to ride across toucan crossings, unlike other crossings where they must dismount.

Who can use a toucan crossing?

❏ Trains
❏ Cyclists
❏ Buses
❏ Pedestrians
❏ Trams

❏ **Cyclists**

❏ **Pedestrians**

Toucan crossings are shared by pedestrians and cyclists together.

At a pelican crossing, what does a flashing amber light mean?

❏ You must not move off until the lights stop flashing
❏ You must give way to pedestrians still on the crossing
❏ You can move off, even if pedestrians are still on the crossing
❏ You must stop because the lights are about to change to red

❏ **You must give way to pedestrians still on the crossing**

You may drive on as soon as the crossing is clear and before the flashing amber light changes to green.

10.23   mark **one** answer

You are waiting at a pelican crossing. The red light changes to flashing amber. This means you must

❏ wait for pedestrians on the crossing to clear
❏ move off immediately without any hesitation
❏ wait for the green light before moving off
❏ get ready and go when the continuous amber light shows

❏ **wait for pedestrians on the crossing to clear**

Treat the crossing as a zebra crossing at this point, and wait until it is clear before proceeding.

10.24   mark **one** answer

When can you park on the left opposite these road markings?

❏ If the line nearest to you is broken
❏ When there are no yellow lines
❏ To pick up or set down passengers
❏ During daylight hours only

❏ **To pick up or set down passengers**

Stopping or parking is prohibited on any road with double white lines down the centre (regardless of whether they are solid or broken), unless it is to pick up or set down passengers.

10.25   mark **one** answer

You are intending to turn right at a crossroads. An oncoming driver is also turning right. It will normally be safer to

❏ keep the other vehicle to your RIGHT and turn behind it (offside to offside)
❏ keep the other vehicle to your LEFT and turn in front of it (nearside to nearside)
❏ carry on and turn at the next junction instead
❏ hold back and wait for the other driver to turn first

❏ **keep the other vehicle to your RIGHT and turn behind it (offside to offside)**

This is because when passing offside-to-offside your view will not be blocked by the oncoming car whose driver also wishes to turn right.

mark **one** answer

You are on a road that has no traffic signs. There are street lights. What is the speed limit?

❏ 20 mph
❏ 30 mph
❏ 40 mph
❏ 60 mph

❏ **30 mph**

If there are street lights, the speed limit is 30 mph, unless a road sign states otherwise.

mark **three** answers

You are going along a street with parked vehicles on the left-hand side. For which THREE reasons should you keep your speed down?

❏ So that oncoming traffic can see you more clearly
❏ You may set off car alarms
❏ Vehicles may be pulling out
❏ Drivers' doors may open
❏ Children may run out from between the vehicles

❏ **Vehicles may be pulling out**

❏ **Drivers' doors may open**

❏ **Children may run out from between the vehicles**

Because of the parked cars the road is much more hazardous; things will happen quickly, even at a slow speed. These are common hazards.

mark **one** answer

You meet an obstruction on your side of the road. You should

❏ carry on, you have priority
❏ give way to oncoming traffic
❏ wave oncoming vehicles through
❏ accelerate to get past first

❏ **give way to oncoming traffic**

It is your responsibility to allow oncoming vehicles through a gap narrowed by a vehicle parked on your side of the road if there isn't enough room for you both to continue safely.

10.29   mark **two** answers

You are on a two-lane dual carriageway. For which TWO of the following would you use the right-hand lane?

- ❏ Turning right
- ❏ Normal progress
- ❏ Staying at the minimum allowed speed
- ❏ Constant high speed
- ❏ Overtaking slower traffic
- ❏ Mending punctures

❏ **Turning right**

❏ **Overtaking slower traffic**

You should use the left-hand lane for driving, and the right-hand lane for overtaking or turning right. Once an overtaking manoeuvre is completed you should move back to the left.

10.30   mark **one** answer

Who has priority at an unmarked crossroads?

- ❏ The larger vehicle
- ❏ No one has priority
- ❏ The faster vehicle
- ❏ The smaller vehicle

❏ **No one has priority**

An unmarked crossroads has no road signs or road markings and no vehicle has priority even if one road is wider or busier than the other.

10.31   mark **one** answer

What is the nearest you may park to a junction?

- ❏ 10 metres (32 feet)
- ❏ 12 metres (39 feet)
- ❏ 15 metres (49 feet)
- ❏ 20 metres (66 feet)

❏ **10 metres (32 feet)**

This is the case unless there is a marked parking place. These restrictions are in place to keep junctions safe, by ensuring good visibility for all road users.

10.32   mark **three** answers

In which THREE places must you NOT park?

- ❏ Near the brow of a hill
- ❏ At or near a bus stop
- ❏ Where there is no pavement
- ❏ Within 10 metres (32 feet) of a junction
- ❏ On a 40 mph road

❏ **Near the brow of a hill**

❏ **At or near a bus stop**

❏ **Within 10 metres (32 feet) of a junction**

These options would be inconvenient at best but could cause danger.

mark one answer

You are waiting at a level crossing. A train has passed but the lights keep flashing. You must

❏ carry on waiting
❏ phone the signal operator
❏ edge over the stop line and look for trains
❏ park and investigate

❏ **carry on waiting**

Most likely there is another train coming.

---

mark one answer

At a crossroads there are no signs or road markings. Two vehicles approach. Which has priority?

❏ Neither of the vehicles
❏ The vehicle travelling the fastest
❏ Oncoming vehicles turning right
❏ Vehicles approaching from the right

❏ **Neither of the vehicles**

You often find these on housing estates. Approach with caution and be prepared to give way.

---

mark one answer

What does this sign tell you?

❏ That it is a no-through road
❏ End of traffic calming zone
❏ Free parking zone ends
❏ No waiting zone ends

❏ **No waiting zone ends**

The circular sign on its own would mean parking restrictions; this sign means what it says: 'zone ends'.

10.36   mark **one** answer

You are entering an area of roadworks. There is a temporary speed limit displayed. You should

- ❏ not exceed the speed limit
- ❏ obey the limit only during rush hour
- ❏ ignore the displayed limit
- ❏ obey the limit except at night

❏ **not exceed the speed limit**

Even though the signs are temporary, they are still compulsory. They are there to protect the people working on the road.

10.37   mark **two** answers

In which TWO places should you NOT park?

- ❏ Near a school entrance
- ❏ Near a police station
- ❏ In a side road
- ❏ At a bus stop
- ❏ In a one-way street

❏ **Near a school entrance**

❏ **At a bus stop**

Parking here would be inconvenient at best, but could cause danger.

10.38   mark **one** answer

You are travelling on a well-lit road at night in a built-up area. By using dipped headlights you will be able to

- ❏ see further along the road
- ❏ go at a much faster speed
- ❏ switch to main beam quickly
- ❏ be easily seen by others

❏ **be easily seen by others**

Remember – you need to see and be seen.

10.39   mark **one** answer

The dual carriageway you are turning right onto has a very narrow central reservation. What should you do?

- ❏ Proceed to the central reservation and wait
- ❏ Wait until the road is clear in both directions
- ❏ Stop in the first lane so that other vehicles give way
- ❏ Emerge slightly to show your intentions

❏ **Wait until the road is clear in both directions**

Because the central reservation is narrow, you would partly block the road if you drove to the middle and had to wait.

mark **one** answer

What is the national speed limit on a single carriageway road for cars and motorcycles?

❏ 30 mph
❏ 50 mph
❏ 60 mph
❏ 70 mph

❏ **60 mph**

The national speed limit varies, depending on the vehicle you are driving and the type of road you are driving on. In this case it is 60 mph.

mark **one** answer

You park at night on a road with a 40 mph speed limit. You should park

❏ facing the traffic
❏ with parking lights on
❏ with dipped headlights on
❏ near a street light

❏ **with parking lights on**

This is true on any road at night, where the speed limit is greater than 30 mph. You should also park on the left, because the red reflectors fitted to the back of your vehicle (in the light cluster) will be easily picked up by the headlights of traffic using the road.

mark **one** answer

You will see these red and white markers when approaching

❏ the end of a motorway
❏ a concealed level crossing
❏ a concealed speed limit sign
❏ the end of a dual carriageway

❏ **a concealed level crossing**

These countdown markers indicate the distance to the stop line at the concealed level crossing.

10.43   mark **one** answer

You are travelling on a motorway. You MUST stop when signalled to do so by which of these?

❏ Flashing amber lights above your lane
❏ A Highways Agency Traffic Officer
❏ Pedestrians on the hard shoulder
❏ A driver who has broken down

❏ **A Highways Agency Traffic Officer**

Amber lights mean caution, red lights mean stop. The Highway Agency Traffic Officer is the only option available that has authority to give directions.

10.44   mark **one** answer

At a busy unmarked crossroads, which of the following has priority?

❏ Vehicles going straight ahead
❏ Vehicles turning right
❏ None of the vehicles
❏ The vehicles that arrived first

❏ **None of the vehicles**

There are no road markings and therefore no one has priority. You should approach with caution, ready to stop and give way.

10.45   mark **one** answer

You are going straight ahead at a roundabout. How should you signal?

❏ Signal right on the approach and then left to leave the roundabout
❏ Signal left after you leave the roundabout and enter the new road
❏ Signal right on the approach to the roundabout and keep the signal on
❏ Signal left just after you pass the exit before the one you will take.

❏ **Signal left just after you pass the exit before the one you will take**

Your signals must be both clear and unmistakable. There will be no need to signal on the approach to a roundabout if you are going straight ahead. You will only need to signal left just after you pass the exit before the one you wish to take.

10.46   mark **one** answer

You may drive over a footpath

❏ to overtake slow-moving traffic
❏ when the pavement is very wide
❏ if no pedestrians are near
❏ to get into a property

❏ **to get into a property**

This is the only safe option offered.

mark **one** answer

A single carriageway road has this sign. What is the maximum permitted speed for a car towing a trailer?

❑ 30 mph
❑ 40 mph
❑ 50 mph
❑ 60 mph

❑ **50 mph**

The national speed limit varies, depending on the vehicle you are driving and the type of road you are driving on. In this case it is 50 mph.

mark **one** answer

You are towing a small caravan on a dual carriageway. You must not exceed

❑ 50 mph
❑ 40 mph
❑ 70 mph
❑ 60 mph

❑ **60 mph**

Speed limits vary, depending on the vehicle you are driving, and the type of road you are driving on. In this case the limit is 60 mph.

10.49   mark **one** answer

You want to park and you see this sign.
On the days and times shown you should

Meter
ZONE

Mon - Fri
8.30 am - 6.30 pm
Saturday
8.30 am - 1.30 pm

- ❏ park in a bay and not pay
- ❏ park on yellow lines and pay
- ❏ park on yellow lines and not pay
- ❏ park in a bay and pay

❏ **park in a bay and pay**

Time plates like this give information on when the restrictions are in place.

10.50   mark **one** answer

You are driving along a road that has a cycle lane. The lane is marked by a solid white line. This means that during its period of operation

- ❏ the lane may be used for parking your car
- ❏ you may drive in that lane at any time
- ❏ the lane may be used when necessary
- ❏ you must not drive in that lane

❏ **you must not drive in that lane**

Like bus lanes, the times shown on the accompanying time plates tell you when the cycle lane is in operation.

10.51   mark **one** answer

A cycle lane is marked by a solid white line. You must not drive or park in it

- ❏ at any time
- ❏ during the rush hour
- ❏ if a cyclist is using it
- ❏ during its period of operation

❏ **during its period of operation**

Like bus lanes, the times shown on the accompanying time plates tell you when the cycle lane is in operation.

mark **one** answer

While driving, you intend to turn left into a minor road. On the approach you should

❏ keep just left of the middle of the road
❏ keep in the middle of the road
❏ swing out wide just before turning
❏ keep well to the left of the road

❏ **keep well to the left of the road**

Your road position will reinforce your signal telling people of your intention.

mark **one** answer

You are waiting at a level crossing. The red warning lights continue to flash after a train has passed by. What should you do?

❏ Get out and investigate
❏ Telephone the signal operator
❏ Continue to wait
❏ Drive across carefully

❏ **Continue to wait**

You should wait for three minutes. If no further train passes you should telephone the signal operator.

mark **one** answer

You are driving over a level crossing.
The warning lights come on and a bell rings.
What should you do?

❏ Get everyone out of the vehicle immediately
❏ Stop and reverse back to clear the crossing
❏ Keep going and clear the crossing
❏ Stop immediately and use your hazard warning lights

❏ **Keep going and clear the crossing**

You are already on the crossing when the warning lights come on, so 'keep going and clear the crossing'.

10.55   mark **one** answer

You are on a busy main road and find that you are travelling in the wrong direction. What should you do?

❑ Turn into a side road on the right and reverse into the main road
❑ Make a U-turn in the main road
❑ Make a 'three-point' turn in the main road
❑ Turn round in a side road

❑ **Turn round in a side road**

It is illegal to reverse from a minor to a major road, so the first option is wrong. The second and third answers would be dangerous because the road is busy.

10.56   mark **one** answer

You may remove your seat belt when carrying out a manoeuvre that involves

❑ reversing
❑ a hill start
❑ an emergency stop
❑ driving slowly

❑ **reversing**

Do this if necessary to get a better view. Put the seat belt back on as soon as the manoeuvre is finished.

10.57   mark **one** answer

You must not reverse

❑ for longer than necessary
❑ for more than a car's length
❑ into a side road
❑ in a built-up area

❑ **for longer than necessary**

To do so would only increase the risk of an accident.

10.58   mark **one** answer

When you are NOT sure that it is safe to reverse your vehicle you should

❑ use your horn
❑ rev your engine
❑ get out and check
❑ reverse slowly

❑ **get out and check**

Do not carry out any manoeuvre unless you are sure it is safe to do so.

mark **one** answer

When may you reverse from a side road into a main road?

❏ Only if both roads are clear of traffic
❏ Not at any time
❏ At any time
❏ Only if the main road is clear of traffic

❏ **Not at any time**

This would be dangerous. Drivers may reverse from a main road into a side road.

mark **one** answer

You want to turn right at a box junction. There is oncoming traffic. You should

❏ wait in the box junction if your exit is clear
❏ wait before the junction until it is clear of all traffic
❏ drive on, you cannot turn right at a box junction
❏ drive slowly into the box junction when signalled by oncoming traffic

❏ **wait in the box junction if your exit is clear**

Box junctions are designed to keep busy intersections clear and free flowing. Stopping on them will hinder traffic flow and can lead to gridlock. However, when you are turning right you're allowed to wait on them, provided you are only prevented from turning right by oncoming traffic.

mark **one** answer

You are reversing your vehicle into a side road. When would the greatest hazard to passing traffic occur?

❏ After you've completed the manoeuvre
❏ Just before you actually begin to manoeuvre
❏ After you've entered the side road
❏ When the front of your vehicle swings out

❏ **When the front of your vehicle swings out**

Always remember to check all round just before steering and give way to any road users.

mark **one** answer

Where is the safest place to park your vehicle at night?

❏ In a garage
❏ On a busy road
❏ In a quiet car park
❏ Near a red route

❏ **In a garage**

Where the car will be out of sight and under an additional lock and key.

10.63 · mark **one** answer

You are driving on an urban clearway. You may stop only to

❑ set down and pick up passengers
❑ use a mobile telephone
❑ ask for directions
❑ load or unload goods

❑ **set down and pick up passengers**

The whole purpose of an urban clearway is to keep the traffic flowing; don't stop or park on one, unless it is to pick up or set down passengers.

10.64 · mark **one** answer

You are looking for somewhere to park your vehicle. The area is full EXCEPT for spaces marked 'disabled use'. You can

❑ use these spaces when elsewhere is full
❑ park if you stay with your vehicle
❑ use these spaces, disabled or not
❑ not park there unless permitted

❑ **not park there unless permitted**

They are there to allow disabled people to get safe, convenient access to facilities.

10.65 · mark **one** answer

Your vehicle is parked on the road at night. When must you use sidelights?

❑ Where there are continuous white lines in the middle of the road
❑ Where the speed limit exceeds 30 mph
❑ Where you are facing oncoming traffic
❑ Where you are near a bus stop

❑ **Where the speed limit exceeds 30 mph**

You should also park on the left, because the red reflectors fitted to the back of your vehicle (in the light cluster) will be easily picked up by the headlights of traffic using the road.

10.66 · mark **one** answer

You are on a road that is only wide enough for one vehicle. There is a car coming towards you. What should you do?

❑ Pull into a passing place on your right
❑ Force the other driver to reverse
❑ Pull into a passing place if your vehicle is wider
❑ Pull into a passing place on your left

❑ **Pull into a passing place on your left**

They are positioned regularly to allow traffic flow. Stop in one on the left or adjacent to one on the right.

You are driving at night with full beam headlights on. A vehicle is overtaking you. You should dip your lights

❏ some time after the vehicle has passed you
❏ before the vehicle starts to pass you
❏ only if the other driver dips their headlights
❏ as soon as the vehicle passes you

❏ **as soon as the vehicle passes you**

If you dip your lights too early you may reduce your vision; too late and you may dazzle the driver who has overtaken you.

When may you drive a motor car in this bus lane?

❏ Outside its hours of operation
❏ To get to the front of a traffic queue
❏ You may not use it at any time
❏ To overtake slow-moving traffic

❏ **Outside its hours of operation**

The times stated are when the bus lane is in operation.

Signals are normally given by direction indicators and

❏ brake lights
❏ side lights
❏ fog lights
❏ interior lights

❏ **brake lights**

Red is always the colour of danger. The brake lights warn the following drivers that you are slowing down, and therefore they can be used as a signal.

10.70   mark **one** answer

You are parked in a busy high street. What is the safest way to turn your vehicle around so you can go the opposite way?

❏ Find a quiet side road to turn round in
❏ Drive into a side road and reverse into the main road
❏ Get someone to stop the traffic
❏ Do a U-turn

❏ **Find a quiet side road to turn round in**

The key words are busy 'high street'; to turn here would be difficult, inconvenient and potentially dangerous.

10.71   mark **one** answer

To help keep your vehicle secure at night, where should you park?

❏ Near a police station
❏ In a quiet road
❏ On a red route
❏ . In a well-lit area

❏ **In a well-lit area**

This will deter some thieves because the lighting will make observation of them easier.

10.72   mark **one** answer

You are in the right-hand lane of a dual carriageway. You see signs showing that the right-hand lane is closed 800 yards ahead. You should

❏ keep in that lane until you reach the queue
❏ move to the left immediately
❏ wait and see which lane is moving faster
❏ move to the left in good time

❏ **move to the left in good time**

Signs like these are placed to warn you of what is ahead. Deal with the information in good time and it will ease traffic flow and reduce stress.

You are driving on a road that has a cycle lane. The lane is marked by a broken white line. This means that

❏ you should not drive in the lane unless it is unavoidable

❏ you should not park in the lane unless it is unavoidable

❏ cyclists can travel in both directions in that lane

❏ the lane must be used by motorcyclists in heavy traffic

❏ **you should not drive in the lane unless it is unavoidable**

❏ **you should not park in the lane unless it is unavoidable**

The key words are 'broken white line'. Try not to drive or park on them if you can.

What MUST you have to park in a disabled space?

❏ A Blue Badge
❏ A wheelchair
❏ An advanced driver certificate
❏ An adapted vehicle

❏ **A Blue Badge**

The blue badge scheme provides a parking concession for disabled people. This entitlement can be for a driver or a passenger

10.75   mark **three** answers

On which THREE occasions MUST you stop your vehicle?

❏ When in an incident where damage or injury is caused

❏ At a red traffic light

❏ When signalled to do so by a police or traffic officer

❏ At a junction with double broken white lines

❏ At a pelican crossing when the amber light is flashing and no pedestrians are crossing

❏ **When in an incident where damage or injury is caused**

❏ **At a red traffic light**

❏ **When signalled to do so by a police or traffic officer**

The law requires drivers to stop in these circumstances. Penalties are in place for drivers who do not comply with these important requirements.

Section 11
Road and traffic signs

There are 156 questions in this section covering the following subjects:

- ❑ Road signs
- ❑ Speed limits
- ❑ Road markings
- ❑ Regulations

You will need to think about:

- ❑ How to interpret road signs and markings

- ❑ Understanding speed restrictions and general regulations.

Tips

If your heart sank when you saw that there were 156 questions in this section, relax – it's just about to get much easier. Remember this:

 Triangular signs give warnings of dangers ahead

 Rectangular signs give information on where to go, or what to do

 Circular signs give orders; red means you must not (do more than 30 mph for example),

 blue means you must (keep left).

Therefore, a Triangular sign with a pedestrian in it means 'warning pedestrians ahead' (what they are doing will rely on how they appear on the sign); a Rectangular sign with a pedestrian in it might be giving 'directions to pedestrians', and a Circular sign with a pedestrian in it means 'No pedestrians'.

So Triangles warn, Rectangles inform, and Circles give orders.

Road markings are easier than you might imagine too. You can't generally cross a solid line on the road (there are always exceptions to every rule), and as a good rule of thumb, the more paint there is on the road, the more potential danger there is about.

mark one answer

You MUST obey signs giving orders. These signs are mostly in

❏ green rectangles
❏ red triangles
❏ blue rectangles
❏ red circles

❏ **red circles**

Circles give orders (you MUST or MUST NOT); triangles warn (look out for...); rectangles inform (go this way for...).

mark one answer

Traffic signs giving orders are generally which shape?

❏
❏

❏
❏

❏

A red circle gives a prohibitory order meaning 'no'. Circles that give a mandatory order, meaning that you must do something are blue in colour.

mark one answer

Which type of sign tells you NOT to do something?

❏
❏

❏
❏

❏

Circles give orders, red ones mean you MUST NOT do something, blue ones mean you MUST. Rectangles give information.

11.4   mark **one** answer

What does this sign mean?

- ❏ Maximum speed limit with traffic calming
- ❏ Minimum speed limit with traffic calming
- ❏ '20 cars only' parking zone
- ❏ Only 20 cars allowed at any one time

❏ **Maximum speed limit with traffic calming**

Circles give orders, red ones mean you MUST NOT do something, in this case drive at more than 20 mph. The rectangular element gives information.

11.5   mark **one** answer

Which sign means no motor vehicles are allowed?

❏   ❏

❏   ❏

❏

You could see this sign at the entrance to a pedestrian precinct, for example.

11.6   mark **one** answer

Which of these signs means no motor vehicles?

❏   ❏

❏   ❏

❏

You could see this sign at the entrance to a pedestrian precinct, for example.

mark **one** answer

What does this sign mean?

- ❏ New speed limit 20 mph
- ❏ No vehicles over 30 tonnes
- ❏ Minimum speed limit 30 mph
- ❏ End of 20 mph zone

❏ **End of 20 mph zone**

You would see this at the end of a traffic-calmed 20 mph area.

mark **one** answer

What does this sign mean?

- ❏ No overtaking
- ❏ No motor vehicles
- ❏ Clearway (no stopping)
- ❏ Cars and motorcycles only

❏ **No motor vehicles**

If you are driving a motor vehicle or riding a motorbike you must not travel past this sign. The area beyond it has probably been designated as a pedestrian precinct.

mark **one** answer

What does this sign mean?

- ❏ No parking
- ❏ No road markings
- ❏ No through road
- ❏ No entry

❏ **No entry**

Clearly an important sign! You would find these at the end of a one-way street, for example.

11.10   mark **one** answer

What does this sign mean?

❑ Bend to the right
❑ Road on the right closed
❑ No traffic from the right
❑ No right turn

❑ **No right turn**

Circles give orders, red ones mean you
MUST NOT do something, in this case turn
to the right.

11.11   mark **one** answer

Which sign means 'no entry'?

❑   ❑

❑   ❑

❑

'No entry' signs prevent drivers from entering
one-way streets. As well as being unsafe to
wrongly enter a one-way street, it is an
offence that will put three penalty points on
your driving licence along with a fine.

11.12   mark **one** answer

What does this sign mean?

❑ Route for trams only
❑ Route for buses only
❑ Parking for buses only
❑ Parking for trams only

❑ **Route for trams only**

Great care must be taken when dealing with
trams. Do not block their routes because
they are unable to steer around obstacles.

mark **one** answer

Which type of vehicle does this sign apply to?

❑ Wide vehicles
❑ Long vehicles
❑ High vehicles
❑ Heavy vehicles

❑ **High vehicles**

This sign orders the drivers of a high vehicle over 4.4 metres in height, not to proceed beyond that point. There will also probably be warning signs on approach to the hazard.

mark **one** answer

Which sign means NO motor vehicles allowed?

❑   ❑

❑   ❑

❑

You could see one at the entrance to a pedestrian precinct, for example.

mark **one** answer

What does this sign mean?

❑ You have priority
❑ No motor vehicles
❑ Two-way traffic
❑ No overtaking

❑ **No overtaking**

Circles give orders, red ones mean you MUST NOT do something, in this case overtake.

11.16   mark **one** answer

What does this sign mean?

❑ Keep in one lane
❑ Give way to oncoming traffic
❑ Do not overtake
❑ Form two lanes

❑ **Do not overtake**

Circles give orders, red ones mean you MUST NOT do something, in this case overtake.

11.17   mark **one** answer

Which sign means no overtaking?

❑   ❑

❑   ❑

❑

Circles give orders, red ones mean you MUST NOT do something, in this case overtake.

11.18   mark **one** answer

What does this sign mean?

❑ Waiting restrictions apply
❑ Waiting permitted
❑ National speed limit applies
❑ Clearway (no stopping)

❑ **Waiting restrictions apply**

There will also be a plate indicating when the restrictions apply.

mark **one** answer

What does this sign mean?

- End of restricted speed area
- End of restricted parking area
- End of clearway
- End of cycle route

❑ **End of restricted parking area**

Rectangles inform, in this case the end of parking restrictions.

mark **one** answer

Which sign means 'no stopping'?

❑   ❑

❑   ❑

❑

Note the difference between a 'no stopping' sign – a red cross – and a 'no waiting' sign – a red line. This sign would be found on a clearway, for example.

mark **one** answer

What does this sign mean?

- Roundabout
- Crossroads
- No stopping
- No entry

❑ **No stopping**

The object of 'no stopping' signs is to help ensure the free flow of traffic. The 'no stopping' sign prohibits stopping at any time – not even to pick up or set down passengers.

11.22   mark **one** answer

You see this sign ahead. It means

❑ **no stopping**

This clearway sign is in place to ensure a clear route for traffic. You must not stop unless there is an emergency.

❑ national speed limit applies
❑ waiting restrictions apply
❑ no stopping
❑ no entry

11.23   mark **one** answer

What does this sign mean?

❑ **Distance to parking place ahead**

Rectangles inform, in this case the distance to a parking place ahead, should you wish to stop and take a break.

❑ Distance to parking place ahead
❑ Distance to public telephone ahead
❑ Distance to public house ahead
❑ Distance to passing place ahead

mark **one** answer

What does this sign mean?

❏ Vehicles may not park on the verge or footway
❏ Vehicles may park on the left-hand side of the road only
❏ Vehicles may park fully on the verge or footway
❏ Vehicles may park on the right-hand side of the road only

❏ **Vehicles may park fully on the verge or footway**

Rectangles inform, in this case the fact that vehicles may park on the verge or footway.

---

mark **one** answer

What does this traffic sign mean?

❏ No overtaking allowed
❏ Give priority to oncoming traffic
❏ Two-way traffic
❏ One-way traffic only

❏ **Give priority to oncoming traffic**

Circles give orders, red ones mean you must not do something, in this case take priority over oncoming vehicles.

11.26   mark **one** answer

What is the meaning of this traffic sign?

❑ End of two-way road
❑ Give priority to vehicles coming towards you
❑ You have priority over vehicles coming towards you
❑ Bus lane ahead

❑ **You have priority over vehicles coming towards you**

Rectangles inform, in this case the fact that you have priority over oncoming vehicles. However, proceed with caution and be prepared to give way if continuing might cause a collision.

11.27   mark **one** answer

What does this sign mean?

❑ No overtaking
❑ You are entering a one-way street
❑ Two-way traffic ahead
❑ You have priority over vehicles from the opposite direction

❑ **You have priority over vehicles from the opposite direction**

Although this traffic sign gives you a priority, show courtesy and consideration by being prepared to give way if any approaching driver makes a mistake.

11.28   mark **one** answer

What shape is a STOP sign at a junction?

❑   ❑

❑    ❑

❑

A 'stop' sign is shaped differently to all others, so that it is instantly recognisable, no matter what the conditions.

mark **one** answer

At a junction you see this sign partly covered by snow. What does it mean?

❏ Cross roads
❏ Give way
❏ Stop
❏ Turn right

❏ **Stop**

The 'stop' sign is the only octagonal sign, allowing easy identification.

mark **one** answer

What does this sign mean?

❏ Service area 30 miles ahead
❏ Maximum speed 30 mph
❏ Minimum speed 30 mph
❏ Lay-by 30 miles ahead

❏ **Minimum speed 30 mph**

Circles give orders; blue ones mean you must do something, in this case a minimum of 30 mph.

mark **one** answer

What does this sign mean?

❏ Give way to oncoming vehicles
❏ Approaching traffic passes you on both sides
❏ Turn off at the next available junction
❏ Pass either side to get to the same destination

❏ **Pass either side to get to the same destination**

Circles give orders; blue ones mean you must do something, in this case pass either side of the sign.

11.32   mark **one** answer

What does this sign mean?

- ❏ Route for trams
- ❏ Give way to trams
- ❏ Route for buses
- ❏ Give way to buses

❏ **Route for trams**

Great care must be taken when dealing with trams. Do not block their routes as because they are unable to steer round obstacles.

11.33   mark **one** answer

What does a circular traffic sign with a blue background do?

- ❏ Give warning of a motorway ahead
- ❏ Give directions to a car park
- ❏ Give motorway information
- ❏ Give an instruction

❏ **Give an instruction**

Circular signs with blue backgrounds tell you what you must do.

11.34   mark **one** answer

Where would you see a contraflow bus and cycle lane?

- ❏ On a dual carriageway
- ❏ On a roundabout
- ❏ On an urban motorway
- ❏ On a one-way street

❏ **On a one-way street**

Rectangles inform, in this case the presence of a contraflow bus and cycle lane, in an otherwise one-way street. The arrows inform you of the direction of traffic flow.

mark one answer

What does this sign mean?

- ❏ Bus station on the right
- ❏ Contraflow bus lane
- ❏ With-flow bus lane
- ❏ Give way to buses

❏ **Contraflow bus lane**

Rectangles inform, in this case the presence of a contraflow bus lane, in an otherwise one-way street. The arrows inform you of the direction of traffic flow.

mark one answer

What does a sign with a brown background show?

- ❏ Tourist directions
- ❏ Primary roads
- ❏ Motorway routes
- ❏ Minor routes

❏ **Tourist directions**

Rectangles inform and brown signs direct you to a local attraction or place of interest.

mark one answer

This sign means

- ❏ tourist attraction
- ❏ beware of trains
- ❏ level crossing
- ❏ beware of trams

❏ **tourist attraction**

Rectangles inform and brown signs direct you to a local attraction or place of interest.

11.38   mark **one** answer

What are triangular signs for?

❏ To give warnings
❏ To give information
❏ To give orders
❏ To give directions

❏ **To give warnings**

Triangles warn (look out for); circles give orders (you MUST or MUST NOT); rectangles inform (go this way for…).

11.39   mark **one** answer

What does this sign mean?

❏ Turn left ahead
❏ T-junction
❏ No through road
❏ Give way

❏ **T-junction**

Triangles warn of hazards ahead, in this case of a T-junction ahead. The thick line denotes the main road, the thin line the minor one that joins it.

11.40   mark **one** answer

What does this sign mean?

❏ Multi-exit roundabout
❏ Risk of ice
❏ Six roads converge
❏ Place of historical interest

❏ **Risk of ice**

Triangles warn of hazards ahead, in this case of the risk of ice.

mark **one** answer

What does this sign mean?

❏ Crossroads
❏ Level crossing with gate
❏ Level crossing without gate
❏ Ahead only

❏ **Crossroads**

Triangles warn of hazards ahead, in this case of a crossroads where the thick line denotes that you have priority.

mark **one** answer

What does this sign mean?

❏ Ring road
❏ Mini-roundabout
❏ No vehicles
❏ Roundabout

❏ **Roundabout**

Triangles warn of hazards ahead, in this case of a roundabout ahead.

mark **four** answers

Which FOUR of these would be indicated by a triangular road sign?

❏ Road narrows
❏ Ahead only
❏ Low bridge
❏ Minimum speed
❏ Children crossing
❏ T-junction

❏ **Road narrows**

❏ **Low bridge**

❏ **Children crossing**

❏ **T-junction**

Triangles warn of hazards ahead. Both 'Ahead only' and 'Minimum speed' are orders and would be on blue circular signs.

11.44　mark **one** answer

What does this sign mean?

- ❑ Cyclists must dismount
- ❑ Cycles are not allowed
- ❑ Cycle route ahead
- ❑ Cycle in single file

❑ **Cycle route ahead**

Triangles warn of hazards ahead, in this case of a cycle route.

11.45　mark **one** answer

Which sign means that pedestrians may be walking along the road?

❑ 　❑

❑ 　❑

❑

Triangles warn of hazards ahead, in this case a road without a footway may force any pedestrians to walk on the road itself.

11.46　mark **one** answer

Which of these signs means there is a double bend ahead?

❑ 　❑

❑ 　❑

❑

Triangles warn of hazards ahead, in this case of a double bend. The diagram shape tells you that the first bend is to the left.

mark **one** answer

What does this sign mean?

❏ Wait at the barriers
❏ Wait at the crossroads
❏ Give way to trams
❏ Give way to farm vehicles

❏ **Give way to trams**

Triangles warn of hazards ahead. The 'give way' sign is different to all the others, because it is displayed the other way up. This is so that it is instantly recognisable. In this case it is combined with information regarding a tram crossing ahead.

mark **one** answer

What does this sign mean?

❏ Humpback bridge
❏ Humps in the road
❏ Entrance to tunnel
❏ Soft verges

❏ **Humps in the road**

Triangles warn of hazards ahead, in this case of humps in the road. Note the difference between this and the sign for hump back bridge (see question 11.128).

mark **one** answer

Which of these signs means the end of a dual carriageway?

❏   ❏

❏

Triangles warn of hazards ahead, in this case a dual carriageway ends. Note the difference between this and the upper left option which means road narrows ahead.

❏   ❏

11.50   mark **one** answer

What does this sign mean?

❏ End of dual carriageway
❏ Tall bridge
❏ Road narrows
❏ End of narrow bridge

❏ **End of dual carriageway**

Triangles warn of hazards ahead, in this case the end of a dual carriageway. Note the important difference between this sign and the upper left sign in question 11.49 which means road narrows ahead.

11.51   mark **one** answer

What does this sign mean?

❏ Crosswinds
❏ Road noise
❏ Airport
❏ Adverse camber

❏ **Crosswinds**

Triangles warn of hazards ahead, in this case of crosswinds – particularly important to motorcyclists, cyclists, drivers of large or flat-sided vehicles and any driver who has to share the road with one of these vehicles!

11.52   mark **one** answer

What does this traffic sign mean?

❏ Slippery road ahead
❏ Tyres liable to punctures ahead
❏ Danger ahead
❏ Service area ahead

❏ **Danger ahead**

Triangles warn of hazards ahead, usually accompanied by a plate below which specifies the danger.

mark one answer

You are about to overtake when you see this sign. You should

❏ overtake the other driver as quickly as possible
❏ move to the right to get a better view
❏ switch your headlights on before overtaking
❏ hold back until you can see clearly ahead

❏ **hold back until you can see clearly ahead**

It is dangerous to overtake when you see this sign because the dip in the road could be hiding oncoming traffic.

mark one answer

What does this sign mean?

❏ Level crossing with gate or barrier
❏ Gated road ahead
❏ Level crossing without gate or barrier
❏ Cattle grid ahead

❏ **Level crossing with gate or barrier**

Triangles warn of hazards ahead, in this case a gated level crossing. Note the difference between this and a level crossing without gates or barriers.

mark one answer

What does this sign mean?

❏ No trams ahead
❏ Oncoming trams
❏ Trams crossing ahead
❏ Trams only

❏ **Trams crossing ahead**

Triangles warn of hazards ahead, in this case a tram crossing. Great care must be taken when dealing with trams. Do not block their routes because they are unable to steer around obstacles.

11.56   mark **one** answer

What does this sign mean?

❏ Adverse camber
❏ Steep hill downwards
❏ Uneven road
❏ Steep hill upwards

❏ **Steep hill downwards**

Triangles warn of hazards ahead, in this case a steep hill downwards. If the hill was upwards the slope would be reversed.

11.57   mark **one** answer

What does this sign mean?

❏ Uneven road surface
❏ Bridge over the road
❏ Road ahead ends
❏ Water across the road

❏ **Water across the road**

Triangles warn of hazards ahead, in this case of water crossing the carriageway. Remember to check the depth gauges on either side before crossing.

11.58   mark **one** answer

What does this sign mean?

❏ Turn left for parking area
❏ No through road on the left
❏ No entry for traffic turning left
❏ Turn left for ferry terminal

❏ **No through road on the left**

Rectangles inform, in this case of the fact that the road to the left is a dead end.

mark **one** answer

What does this sign mean?

❑ T-junction
❑ No through road
❑ Telephone box ahead
❑ Toilet ahead

❑ **No through road**

Where you see this traffic sign you will not be able to find a through route to another road. This road is a cul de sac so you will only be able to use it for access.

mark **one** answer

Which sign means 'no through road'?

❑   ❑

❑   ❑

❑

Rectangles inform, in this case of the fact that the road ahead is a dead end.

mark **one** answer

Which is the sign for a ring road?

❑   ❑

❑   ❑

❑

Rectangles inform, in this case of the location of a ring road.

11.62   mark **one** answer

What does this sign mean?

- ❑ The right-hand lane ahead is narrow
- ❑ Right-hand lane for buses only
- ❑ Right-hand lane for turning right
- ❑ The right-hand lane is closed

❑ **The right-hand lane is closed**

Rectangles inform, in this case of the fact that the right-hand lane of traffic is closed ahead. Often found at the site of road works, re-position early to ease the general traffic flow.

11.63   mark **one** answer

What does this sign mean?

- ❑ Change to the left lane
- ❑ Leave at the next exit
- ❑ Contraflow system
- ❑ One-way street

❑ **Contraflow system**

Rectangles inform, in this case of the fact that there is a contraflow system ahead with a speed limit.

11.64   mark **one** answer

What does this sign mean?

- ❑ Leave motorway at next exit
- ❑ Lane for heavy and slow vehicles
- ❑ All lorries use the hard shoulder
- ❑ Rest area for lorries

❑ **Lane for heavy and slow vehicles**

Rectangles inform, in this case of a crawler lane for slow-moving vehicles.

mark one answer

A red traffic light means

❑ you should stop unless turning left
❑ stop, if you are able to brake safely
❑ you must stop and wait behind the stop line
❑ proceed with caution

❑ **you must stop and wait behind the stop line**

The decision as to what to do at a red traffic light is easy. You must stop at the line.

mark one answer

At traffic lights, amber on its own means

❑ prepare to go
❑ go if the way is clear
❑ go if no pedestrians are crossing
❑ stop at the stop line

❑ **stop at the stop line**

An amber light on its own means stop. This light comes after green. So if a traffic light has been green for some time you can expect it to change and you need to be ready to stop in time if it does change.

mark one answer

You are at a junction controlled by traffic lights. When should you NOT proceed at green?

❑ When pedestrians are waiting to cross
❑ When your exit from the junction is blocked
❑ When you think the lights may be about to change
❑ When you intend to turn right

❑ **When your exit from the junction is blocked**

If you proceed into the junction and are obliged to stop, and then your lights change to red, your presence on the junction will prevent others from crossing it when their lights change to green.

11.68 mark **one** answer

You are in the left-hand lane at traffic lights. You are waiting to turn left. At which of these traffic lights must you NOT move on?

At some traffic light controlled junctions there are filter lights. The intention is to help traffic flow by allowing traffic to turn in the direction of the filter, provided that the way is clear.

11.69 mark **one** answer

What does this sign mean?

❑ Traffic lights out of order
❑ Amber signal out of order
❑ Temporary traffic lights ahead
❑ New traffic lights ahead

❑ **Traffic lights out of order**

Approach with caution because no one has priority.

11.70 mark **one** answer

When traffic lights are out of order, who has priority?

❑ Traffic going straight on
❑ Traffic turning right
❑ Nobody
❑ Traffic turning left

❑ **Nobody**

Approach with caution because no one has priority.

These flashing red lights mean STOP. In which THREE of the following places could you find them?

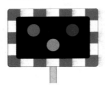

- ❏ Pelican crossings
- ❏ Lifting bridges
- ❏ Zebra crossings
- ❏ Level crossings
- ❏ Motorway exits
- ❏ Fire stations

❏ **Lifting bridges**

❏ **Level crossings**

❏ **Fire stations**

The top two lights are red, stop when they flash even if the way ahead seems clear; the bottom light is amber and warns that the red will flash imminently.

What do these zigzag lines at pedestrian crossings mean?

- ❏ No parking at any time
- ❏ Parking allowed only for a short time
- ❏ Slow down to 20 mph
- ❏ Sounding horns is not allowed

❏ **No parking at any time**

If you park on a zigzag line you will restrict the view of the crossing from other road users as well as the sight of oncoming traffic from the crossing, so causing danger to anyone using the crossing.

11.73   mark **one** answer

When may you cross a double solid white line in the middle of the road?

❏ To pass traffic that is queuing back at a junction
❏ To pass a car signalling to turn left ahead
❏ To pass a road maintenance vehicle travelling at 10 mph or less
❏ To pass a vehicle that is towing a trailer

❏ **To pass a road maintenance vehicle travelling at 10 mph or less**

Where you see a double solid white line in the centre of the road the general message is that you must not cross them. However, like many rules, there are some exceptions such as the one in this answer. Additionally, you may also cross the solid white line to access property or to enter a side road.

11.74   mark **one** answer

What does this road marking mean?

❏ Do not cross the line
❏ No stopping allowed
❏ You are approaching a hazard
❏ No overtaking allowed

❏ **You are approaching a hazard**

The white lines in the centre of the road may be long or short. Where they are short they denote the centre of the road, where they are long markings with short gaps they denote a hazard ahead. You should take particular care not cross hazard warning lines unless you are sure that the road is clear well ahead.

mark one answer

Where would you see this road marking?

❑ At traffic lights
❑ On road humps
❑ Near a level crossing
❑ At a box junction

❑ **On road humps**

Road humps are used to slow traffic down. To ensure that drivers see them, traffic authorities can highlight the change in road level this way.

mark one answer

Which is a hazard warning line?

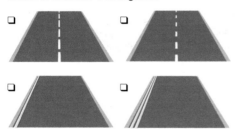

Long lines with short gaps between them in the middle of the road are hazard warning lines. The more paint, the more danger.

mark one answer

At this junction there is a stop sign with a solid white line on the road surface. Why is there a stop sign here?

❑ Speed on the major road is de-restricted
❑ It is a busy junction
❑ Visibility along the major road is restricted
❑ There are hazard warning lines in the centre of the road

❑ **Visibility along the major road is restricted**

Because the major road is on a bend, your vision is restricted to both left and right.

11.78   mark **one** answer

You see this line across the road at the entrance to a roundabout. What does it mean?

- ❏ Give way to traffic from the right
- ❏ Traffic from the left has right of way
- ❏ You have right of way
- ❏ Stop at the line

❏ **Give way to traffic from the right**

This effectively marks the end of your road and the start of another. If you need to stop, stop behind it as you would do at a normal give way line.

11.79   mark **one** answer

How will a police officer in a patrol vehicle normally get you to stop?

- ❏ Flash the headlights, indicate left and point to the left
- ❏ Wait until you stop, then approach you
- ❏ Use the siren, overtake, cut in front and stop
- ❏ Pull alongside you, use the siren and wave you to stop

❏ **Flash the headlights, indicate left and point to the left**

These instructions are not optional. The officer will take into account the prevailing road and traffic conditions before issuing them.

11.80   mark **one** answer

You approach a junction. The traffic lights are not working. A police officer gives this signal. You should

- ❏ turn left only
- ❏ turn right only
- ❏ stop level with the officer's arm
- ❏ stop at the stop line

❏ **stop at the stop line**

When a police officer or traffic warden is directing traffic you must obey any arm signals they give. These are fully explained in the Highway Code.

mark **one** answer

The driver of the car in front is giving this arm signal. What does it mean?

❏ The driver is slowing down
❏ The driver intends to turn right
❏ The driver wishes to overtake
❏ The driver intends to turn left

❏ **The driver intends to turn left**

This signal is often used to inform people in front of the signaller who could not see their brake lights that they intend to slow down.

mark **one** answer

Where would you see these road markings?

❏ At a level crossing
❏ On a motorway slip road
❏ At a pedestrian crossing
❏ On a single-track road

❏ **On a motorway slip road**

Road markings are used to manage traffic flow. Where the area marked with chevrons is bordered by a solid white line, you must not enter the area for any reason, except in an emergency.

mark **one** answer

What does this motorway sign mean?

❏ Change to the lane on your left
❏ Leave the motorway at the next exit
❏ Change to the opposite carriageway
❏ Pull up on the hard shoulder

❏ **Change to the lane on your left**

When you drive on the motorway, overhead gantry signs will show temporary warnings due to traffic or weather conditions. They may be used to indicate a lane closure, a temporary speed limit or a weather warning.

11.84   mark **one** answer

What does this motorway sign mean?

❏ Temporary minimum speed 50 mph
❏ No services for 50 miles
❏ Obstruction 50 metres (164 feet) ahead
❏ Temporary maximum speed 50 mph

❏ **Temporary maximum speed 50 mph**

This is compulsory; generally there will be a hazard ahead.

11.85   mark **one** answer

What does this sign mean?

❏ Through traffic to use left lane
❏ Right-hand lane T-junction only
❏ Right-hand lane closed ahead
❏ 11 tonne weight limit

❏ **Right-hand lane closed ahead**

Always look well ahead and you will have plenty of time to react.

11.86   mark **one** answer

On a motorway this sign means

❏ move over onto the hard shoulder
❏ overtaking on the left only
❏ leave the motorway at the next exit
❏ move to the lane on your left

❏ **move to the lane on your left**

Make sure it is safe to change lane by using the mirrors, particularly your nearside mirror. Notice the difference between this and the sign indicating to leave the motorway at the next exit (see question 11.121).

mark **one** answer

What does '25' mean on this motorway sign?

❏ The distance to the nearest town
❏ The route number of the road
❏ The number of the next junction
❏ The speed limit on the slip road

❏ **The number of the next junction**

All motorway junctions are numbered on a long motorway journey; it can be easier to navigate using junction numbers.

mark **one** answer

The right-hand lane of a three-lane motorway is

❏ for lorries only
❏ an overtaking lane
❏ the right-turn lane
❏ an acceleration lane

❏ **an overtaking lane**

You should use the left-hand lane for driving, and the centre or right-hand lanes for overtaking. Once an overtaking manoeuvre is completed you should move back to the left.

mark **one** answer

Where can you find reflective amber studs on a motorway?

❏ Separating the slip road from the motorway
❏ On the left-hand edge of the road
❏ On the right-hand edge of the road
❏ Separating the lanes

❏ **On the right-hand edge of the road**

Amber studs mark the right-hand edge of the carriageway. Red studs mark the left edge of the carriageway. Green mark the entrance and exit to slip roads (acceleration/deceleration lanes). White studs separate lanes on the carriageway. This is so that in poor visibility you can tell your position on the motorway by the colour of the studs around your vehicle.

11.90　mark **one** answer

Where on a motorway would you find green reflective studs?

- ❏ Separating driving lanes
- ❏ Between the hard shoulder and the carriageway
- ❏ At slip road entrances and exits
- ❏ Between the carriageway and the central reservation

❏ **At slip road entrances and exits**

Amber studs mark the right-hand edge of the carriageway. Red studs mark the left edge of the carriageway. Green mark the entrance and exit to slip roads (acceleration/deceleration lanes). White studs separate lanes on the carriageway. This is so that in poor visibility you can tell your position on the motorway by the colour of the studs around your vehicle.

11.91　mark **one** answer

You are travelling along a motorway. You see this sign. You should

- ❏ leave the motorway at the next exit
- ❏ turn left immediately
- ❏ change lane
- ❏ move onto the hard shoulder

❏ **leave the motorway at the next exit**

Note the difference between this and the sign telling you to move to the left (see questions 11.83 and 11.86).

11.92　mark **one** answer

What does this sign mean?

- ❏ No motor vehicles
- ❏ End of motorway
- ❏ No through road
- ❏ End of bus lane

❏ **End of motorway**

This rectangular sign informs drivers of the end of the motorway. You will need to adjust to different driving conditions. You may be travelling faster than you realise so look out for speed limit signs, and do check your speedometer.

mark **one** answer

Which of these signs means that the national speed limit applies?

☐   ☐

☐   ☐

☐

The actual speed limit will depend on the vehicle you are driving, and the type of road you are driving it on.

mark **one** answer

What is the maximum speed on a single carriageway road?

☐ 50 mph
☐ 60 mph
☐ 40 mph
☐ 70 mph

☐ **60 mph**

This will be marked at the start of the restriction by the national speed limit sign.

mark **one** answer

What does this sign mean?

☐ End of motorway
☐ End of restriction
☐ Lane ends ahead
☐ Free recovery ends

☐ **End of restriction**

You will find this after a hazard, restriction or problem on a motorway.

11.96   mark **one** answer

This sign is advising you to

- ❏ follow the route diversion
- ❏ follow the signs to the picnic area
- ❏ give way to pedestrians
- ❏ give way to cyclists

❏ **follow the route diversion**

At the start of the diversion you will be instructed to follow a symbol, in this case a triangle, for a particular destination (for Brighton follow…). Thereafter you will simply see the symbol accompanied by an arrow giving you the direction to follow.

11.97   mark **one** answer

Why would this temporary speed limit sign be shown?

- ❏ To warn of the end of the motorway
- ❏ To warn you of a low bridge
- ❏ To warn you of a junction ahead
- ❏ To warn of road works ahead

❏ **To warn of road works ahead**

Rectangles inform, in this case of the end of a speed limit at road works ahead. When you get to the restriction the sign will, of course be a circle.

This traffic sign means there is

- ❏ a compulsory maximum speed limit
- ❏ an advisory maximum speed limit
- ❏ a compulsory minimum speed limit
- ❏ an advised separation distance

❏ **a compulsory maximum speed limit**

Rectangles inform, in this case of the end of a speed limit at road works ahead. When you get to the restriction the sign will, of course, be a circle.

You see this sign at a crossroads. You should

- ❏ maintain the same speed
- ❏ carry on with great care
- ❏ find another route
- ❏ telephone the police

❏ **carry on with great care**

Approach with caution because no one has priority.

You are signalling to turn right in busy traffic. How would you confirm your intention safely?

- ❏ Sound the horn
- ❏ Give an arm signal
- ❏ Flash your headlights
- ❏ Position over the centre line

❏ **Give an arm signal**

You might do this if you feel your signal could be hidden to someone directing the traffic for example.

11.101   mark **one** answer

What does this sign mean?

❏ Motorcycles only
❏ No cars
❏ Cars only
❏ No motorcycles

❏ **No motorcycles**

Circles give orders, in this case 'no motorcycles'. Note the difference between this sign and the sign for 'no motor vehicles' (see question 11.5).

11.102   mark **one** answer

You are on a motorway. You see this sign on a lorry that has stopped in the right-hand lane. You should

❏ move into the right-hand lane
❏ stop behind the flashing lights
❏ pass the lorry on the left
❏ leave the motorway at the next exit

❏ **pass the lorry on the left**

Treat this sign as you would the lights on the overhead gantry. Move to the next available lane to the left.

11.103   mark **one** answer

You are on a motorway. Red flashing lights appear above your lane only. What should you do?

❏ Continue in that lane and look for further information
❏ Move into another lane in good time
❏ Pull onto the hard shoulder
❏ Stop and wait for an instruction to proceed

❏ **Move into another lane in good time**

Do not pass a red light, even if you can see no reason for its presence.

mark **one** answer

A red traffic light means

- ❑ you must stop behind the white stop line
- ❑ you may go straight on if there is no other traffic
- ❑ you may turn left if it is safe to do so
- ❑ you must slow down and prepare to stop if traffic has started to cross

❑ **you must stop behind the white stop line**

You should never go through a red light. The white line will be positioned so that pedestrians can cross where appropriate.

mark **one** answer

The driver of this car is giving an arm signal. What are they about to do?

- ❑ Turn to the right
- ❑ Turn to the left
- ❑ Go straight ahead
- ❑ Let pedestrians cross

❑ **Turn to the left**

This signal is often used to reinforce an indicator signal, to someone who may not be able to see the indicators, someone directing traffic for example.

mark **one** answer

When may you sound the horn?

- ❑ To give you right of way
- ❑ To attract a friend's attention
- ❑ To warn others of your presence
- ❑ To make slower drivers move over

❑ **To warn others of your presence**

Sounding your horn has the same meaning as flashing your headlights – to warn of your presence.

11.107   mark **one** answer

You must not use your horn when you are stationary

- ❏ unless a moving vehicle may cause you danger
- ❏ at any time whatsoever
- ❏ unless it is used only briefly
- ❏ except for signalling that you have just arrived

- ❏ **unless a moving vehicle may cause you danger**

The horn is often misused – don't use it as a reprimand, or to say hello. It is used solely to warn or alert others to your presence.

11.108   mark **one** answer

What does this sign mean?

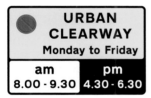

- ❏ You can park on the days and times shown
- ❏ No parking on the days and times shown
- ❏ No parking at all from Monday to Friday
- ❏ End of the urban clearway restrictions

- ❏ **No parking on the days and times shown**

Rectangles inform, in this case of the parking restrictions. Note the circular 'no waiting' sign incorporated with this time plate.

11.109   mark **one** answer

What does this sign mean?

- ❏ Quayside or river bank
- ❏ Steep hill downwards
- ❏ Uneven road surface
- ❏ Road liable to flooding

- ❏ **Quayside or river bank**

Triangles warn, in this case of a possibly unprotected edge of a river bank or dock.

mark **one** answer

Which sign means you have priority over
oncoming vehicles?

Rectangles inform, in this case the fact that
you have priority over oncoming vehicles.
However, proceed with caution and be
prepared to give way if continuing might
cause an accident. Note the difference
between this and the sign on the lower right,
which means the opposite (see also question
11.25).

mark **one** answer

A white line like this along the centre of the
road is a

❏ bus lane marking
❏ hazard warning
❏ give way marking
❏ lane marking

❏ **hazard warning**

Longer lines, and shorter gaps means hazard
ahead.

11.112   mark **one** answer

What is the reason for the yellow criss-cross lines painted on the road here?

- ❏ To mark out an area for trams only
- ❏ To prevent queuing traffic from blocking the junction on the left
- ❏ To mark the entrance lane to a car park
- ❏ To warn you of the tram lines crossing the road

❏ **To prevent queuing traffic from blocking the junction on the left**

If you proceeded onto the junction and stopped, and then the traffic lights changed to red, you would prevent others from using the junction when their lights changed to green, simply by your presence.

11.113   mark **one** answer

What is the reason for the area marked in red and white along the centre of this road?

- ❏ It is to separate traffic flowing in opposite directions
- ❏ It marks an area to be used by overtaking motorcyclists
- ❏ It is a temporary marking to warn of the roadworks
- ❏ It is separating the two sides of the dual carriageway

❏ **It is to separate traffic flowing in opposite directions**

The white lines separate the flow, the red road surface highlights the markings.

mark one answer

Other drivers may sometimes flash their headlights at you. In which situation are they allowed to do this?

❏ To warn of a radar speed trap ahead
❏ To show that they are giving way to you
❏ To warn you of their presence
❏ To let you know there is a fault with your vehicle

❏ **To warn you of their presence**

This answer is correct because that is what flashing your headlights is supposed to mean. Not everyone knows or obeys the rules and they may flash their headlights for other reasons, so always try to make sure what they mean before you decide on any action.

mark one answer

In some narrow residential streets you may find a speed limit of

❏ 20 mph
❏ 25 mph
❏ 35 mph
❏ 40 mph

❏ **20 mph**

This is a traffic-calming measure, it is to protect pedestrians in a particularly busy or hazardous section of a town.

mark one answer

At a junction you see this signal. It means

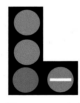

❏ cars must stop
❏ trams must stop
❏ both trams and cars must stop
❏ both trams and cars can continue

❏ **trams must stop**

The green light is for other traffic and they may proceed. The white bar is a unique tram signal.

11.117   mark **one** answer

Where would you find these road markings?

❑ At a railway crossing
❑ At a junction
❑ On a motorway
❑ On a pedestrian crossing

❑ **At a junction**

They outline a mini-roundabout.

11.118   mark **one** answer

There is a police car following you. The police officer flashes the headlights and points to the left. What should you do?

❑ Turn left at the next junction
❑ Pull up on the left
❑ Stop immediately
❑ Move over to the left

❑ **Pull up on the left**

You must stop, but 'Stop immediately' is wrong because it may not be safe to stop immediately.

11.119   mark **one** answer

You see this amber traffic light ahead. Which light or lights, will come on next?

❑ Red alone
❑ Red and amber together
❑ Green and amber together
❑ Green alone

❑ **Red alone**

The sequence of the lights on a traffic light is Red – Red and Amber – Green – Amber – Red. This is so that drivers always know which light comes next in the sequence.

mark **one** answer

This broken white line painted in the centre of the road means

❏ oncoming vehicles have priority over you
❏ you should give priority to oncoming vehicles
❏ there is a hazard ahead of you
❏ the area is a national speed limit zone

❏ **there is a hazard ahead of you**

Longer lines and shorter gaps means there is a hazard ahead.

mark **one** answer

You see this signal overhead on the motorway. What does it mean?

❏ Leave the motorway at the next exit
❏ All vehicles use the hard shoulder
❏ Sharp bend to the left ahead
❏ Stop, all lanes ahead closed

❏ **Leave the motorway at the next exit**

Note the difference between this and the sign that indicates you should move to a lane on the left (see questions 11.83 and 11.86).

11.122   mark **one** answer

What is the purpose of these yellow criss-cross lines on the road?

❏ To make you more aware of the traffic lights

❏ To guide you into position as you turn

❏ To prevent the junction becoming blocked

❏ To show you where to stop when the lights change

❏ **To prevent the junction becoming blocked**

If you proceeded onto the junction and stopped, and then the traffic lights changed to red, you would prevent others from using the junction when their lights changed to green, simply by your presence.

11.123   mark **one** answer

What MUST you do when you see this sign?

❏ Stop, only if traffic is approaching

❏ Stop, even if the road is clear

❏ Stop, only if children are waiting to cross

❏ Stop, only if a red light is showing

❏ **Stop, even if the road is clear**

You must always stop at a stop sign.

11.124   mark **one** answer

Which shape is used for a 'give way' sign?

❏   ❏

❏   ❏

❏

The give way sign is the only triangular sign mounted this way up.

What does this sign mean?

❏ Buses turning
❏ Ring road
❏ Mini-roundabout
❏ Keep right

❏ **Mini-roundabout**

Circles give orders, blue ones give positive instructions, in this case the direction of traffic flow at the site of a mini-roundabout. Note the difference between this sign and the triangular sign warning of a roundabout ahead.

What does this sign mean?

❏ Two-way traffic straight ahead
❏ Two-way traffic crosses a one-way road
❏ Two-way traffic over a bridge
❏ Two-way traffic crosses a two-way road

❏ **Two-way traffic crosses a one-way road**

Triangles warn of hazards ahead, in this case two-way traffic crosses a one-way street. Note the difference between this sign and the sign in question 11.127 which means simply two-way traffic ahead.

What does this sign mean?

❏ Two-way traffic ahead across a one-way road
❏ Traffic approaching you has priority
❏ Two-way traffic straight ahead
❏ Motorway contraflow system ahead

❏ **Two-way traffic straight ahead**

Triangles warn of hazards ahead, in this case two-way traffic ahead. Note the difference between this sign and the sign in question 11.126 which means two-way traffic crosses a one-way street.

11.128   mark **one** answer

What does this sign mean?

☐ Hump-back bridge
☐ Traffic calming hump
☐ Low bridge
☐ Uneven road

☐ **Hump-back bridge**

Triangles warn of hazards ahead, in this case a hump-back bridge. Note the difference between this and the sign for humps in the road (see question 11.48).

11.129   mark **one** answer

Which of the following signs informs you that you are coming to a 'no through road'?

☐   ☐

☐   ☐

☐

Rectangles inform, in this case of the fact that the road ahead is a dead end.

11.130   mark **one** answer

What does this sign mean?

☐ Direction to park-and-ride car park
☐ No parking for buses or coaches
☐ Directions to bus and coach park
☐ Parking area for cars and coaches

☐ **Direction to park-and-ride car park**

This is a directional sign. For the purposes of traffic signs regard this as a rectangle which gives information.

mark one answer

You are approaching traffic lights. Red and amber are showing. This means

❏ pass the lights if the road is clear
❏ there is a fault with the lights – take care
❏ wait for the green light before you cross the stop line
❏ the lights are about to change to red

❏ **wait for the green light before you cross the stop line**

The next light will be green and you must wait for it to appear before driving on.

mark one answer

This marking appears on the road just before a

❏ 'no entry' sign
❏ 'give way' sign
❏ 'stop' sign
❏ 'no through road' sign

❏ **'give way' sign**

This is to reinforce the triangular 'give way' sign which will appear at the junction.

mark one answer

At a railway level crossing the red light signal continues to flash after a train has gone by. What should you do?

❏ Phone the signal operator
❏ Alert drivers behind you
❏ Wait
❏ Proceed with caution

❏ **Wait**

There will be another train along very shortly.

11.134   mark **one** answer

You are in a tunnel and you see this sign. What does it mean?

❏ Direction to emergency pedestrian exit
❏ Beware of pedestrians, no footpath ahead
❏ No access for pedestrians
❏ Beware of pedestrians crossing ahead

❏ **Direction to emergency pedestrian exit**

Rectangles inform, in this case of where the emergency pedestrian exit is. Note this sign is found only in tunnels.

11.135   mark **one** answer

What does this sign mean?

❏ With-flow bus and cycle lane
❏ Contraflow bus and cycle lane
❏ No buses and cycles allowed
❏ No waiting for buses and cycles

❏ **With-flow bus and cycle lane**

Where you see a with-flow bus and cycle lane, during its period of operation, you can expect buses and cycles to pass you on your left.

11.136   mark **one** answer

Which of these signs warns you of a zebra crossing?

❏   ❏

❏   ❏

❏

Seeing this warning sign will give you time to look well ahead for pedestrians on the pavement who intend to cross the road at this point.

mark **one** answer

What does this sign mean?

❏ No footpath
❏ No pedestrians
❏ Zebra crossing
❏ School crossing

❏ **Zebra crossing**

There are a number of traffic signs relating to pedestrians that drivers must be aware of. By acting on these signs you will be better prepared for all possible eventualities.

mark **one** answer

What does this sign mean?

❏ School crossing patrol
❏ No pedestrians allowed
❏ Pedestrian zone – no vehicles
❏ Zebra crossing ahead

❏ **Zebra crossing ahead**

By acting on these signs you will be better prepared for all possible eventualities. Check in your mirrors for following traffic. If you need to slow or stop, your brake lights will inform them of this decision.

mark **one** answer

Which sign means there will be two-way traffic crossing your route ahead?

❏   ❏

❏   ❏

❏

Be ready for traffic approaching from junctions either side of you and avoid needless lane changes just before you reach the junction.

11.140   mark **one** answer

Which arm signal tells you that the car you are following is going to pull up?

❑
❑

❑
❑

❑

While arm signals are seldom used, you do need to know what they mean and how they can be used. When stopping, you could expect a driver to use the 'slowing down' arm signal.

11.141   mark **one** answer

Which of these signs means turn left ahead?

❑
❑

❑
❑

❑

Blue circles tell you what you must do and this sign gives a clear instruction that you must turn left ahead.

11.142   mark **one** answer

Which sign shows that traffic can only travel in one direction on the road you're on?

❑
❑

❑
❑

❑

If traffic can only travel in one direction, you can expect to see this 'one way traffic' sign posted.

mark **one** answer

You have just driven past this sign. You should be aware that

❑ it is a single track road
❑ you cannot stop on this road
❑ there is only one lane in use
❑ all traffic is going one way

❑ **all traffic is going one way**

In a one-way system, you can use either lane and overtake on either side. Use the lane that suits your destination, unless road markings indicate otherwise.

mark **one** answer

You are approaching a red traffic light. What will the signal show next?

❑ Red and amber
❑ Green alone
❑ Amber alone
❑ Green and amber

❑ **Red and amber**

Knowing the sequence of traffic lights will help you to plan your approach correctly. When you see a red and amber signal be aware that other traffic may still be clearing the junction. Do not start to proceed until you have a green light.

mark **one** answer

What does this sign mean?

❑ Low bridge ahead
❑ Tunnel ahead
❑ Ancient monument ahead
❑ Traffic danger spot ahead

❑ **Tunnel ahead**

Where you have a tunnel ahead you will need to prepare. Switch on your dipped headlights, observe any variable message signs and tune your radio to the local frequency where this is indicated.

11.146   mark **one** answer

Which of these signs shows that you are entering a one-way system?

☐   ☐

☐   ☐

☐

When you enter a one-way system, you can expect to be able to use either lane and overtake on either side. Use the lane that suits your destination, unless road markings indicate otherwise.

11.147   mark **one** answer

You are approaching a zebra crossing where pedestrians are waiting. Which arm signal might you give?

☐   ☐

☐   ☐

☐

This signal is used to inform people in front of the signaller who can't see the brake lights, that they intend to slow down.

11.148   mark **one** answer

The white line along the side of the road

☐ shows the edge of the carriageway
☐ shows the approach to a hazard
☐ means no parking
☐ means no overtaking

☐ **shows the edge of the carriageway**

They are particularly helpful when visibility is reduced.

mark **one** answer

You see this white arrow on the road ahead.
It means

❑ entrance on the left
❑ all vehicles turn left
❑ keep left of the hatched markings
❑ road bending to the left

❑ **keep left of the hatched markings**

The hatched markings are there to separate
the flow of traffic.

---

mark **one** answer

How should you give an arm signal to turn
left?

❑

You might use this if you felt that your signal
could be hidden, from someone directing the
traffic for example.

---

mark **one** answer

When may you use hazard warning lights
when driving?

❑ Instead of sounding the horn in a built-up
  area between 11.30 pm and 7 am
❑ On a motorway or unrestricted dual
  carriageway, to warn of a hazard ahead
❑ On rural routes, after a warning sign of
  animals
❑ On the approach to toucan crossings
  where cyclists are waiting to cross

❑ **On a motorway or unrestricted dual
  carriageway, to warn of a hazard ahead**

Note that the question states 'when driving'.
The types of roads in the second answer are
the only places where it is legal to use
hazard warning lights while your car is
moving.

11.152   mark **one** answer

You are waiting at a T-junction. A vehicle is coming from the right with the left signal flashing. What should you do?

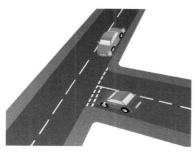

❑ Move out and accelerate hard
❑ Wait until the vehicle starts to turn in
❑ Pull out before the vehicle reaches the junction
❑ Move out slowly

❑ **Wait until the vehicle starts to turn in**

The approaching vehicle might have left the indicator signal on by mistake, or may intend to stop after the junction. Always wait long enough to be sure the vehicle really is turning left.

11.153   mark **one** answer

You are driving on a motorway. There is a slow-moving vehicle ahead. On the back you see this sign. You should

❑ pass on the right
❑ pass on the left
❑ leave at the next exit
❑ drive no further

❑ **pass on the left**

Even though it is attached to a lorry it is still a move to the left sign. The lorry will be a motorway service vehicle at work.

mark **one** answer

You should NOT normally stop on these markings near schools

Ⓐ-SCHOOL KEEP CLEAR-Ⓥ

❏ except when picking up children
❏ under any circumstances
❏ unless there is nowhere else available
❏ except to set down children

❏ **under any circumstances**

They are there to keep the school entrance and exit clear. For safety reasons it is important that both drivers and pedestrians have a clear view of the area.

mark **one** answer

Why should you make sure that your indicators are cancelled after turning?

❏ To avoid flattening the battery
❏ To avoid misleading other road users
❏ To avoid dazzling other road users
❏ To avoid damage to the indicator relay

❏ **To avoid misleading other road users**

Most cars have self-cancelling indicators but they are not foolproof.

mark **one** answer

You are driving in busy traffic. You want to pull up on the left just after a junction on the left. When should you signal?

❏ As you are passing or just after the junction
❏ Just before you reach the junction
❏ Well before you reach the junction
❏ It would be better not to signal at all

❏ **As you are passing or just after the junction**

To signal before the junction would be misleading.

There are 47 questions in this section covering the following subjects:

❑ Licences
❑ Insurance
❑ MOT test certificate
❑ SORN documents
❑ Vehicle registration certificates

You will need to think about:
❑ All the general paperwork related to car ownership and use.

Tips
This section is not large, but it does require memorising facts.

There are only six documents to consider:
❑ MOT
❑ Insurance
❑ SORN
❑ Driving Licence
❑ Vehicle Registration
❑ Road Tax

This section also covers Pass Plus and a few associated laws and regulations. Once you understand each document the questions are generally straightforward.

mark **one** answer

An MOT certificate is normally valid for

❏ three years after the date it was issued
❏ 10,000 miles
❏ one year after the date it was issued
❏ 30,000 miles

❏ **one year after the date it was issued**

All cars over three years old require an MOT certificate. The test is to ensure that your car is safe and its emissions are within the guidelines.

mark **one** answer

A cover note is a document issued before you receive your

❏ driving licence
❏ insurance certificate
❏ registration document
❏ MOT certificate

❏ **insurance certificate**

Most insurance companies issue a 'cover note' to give you insurance cover straight away while the more detailed insurance certificate is being compiled.

mark **two** answers

You have just passed your practical test. You do not hold a full licence in another category. Within two years you get six penalty points on your licence. What will you have to do?

❏ Retake only your theory test
❏ Retake your theory and practical tests
❏ Retake only your practical test
❏ Reapply for your full licence immediately
❏ Reapply for your provisional licence

❏ **Retake your theory and practical tests**

❏ **Reapply for your provisional licence**

These rules are in place to encourage inexperienced drivers to drive carefully.

mark **one** answer

How long will a Statutory Off Road Notification (SORN) last for?

❏ 12 months
❏ 24 months
❏ 3 years
❏ 10 years

❏ **12 months**

A SORN is the document used by the vehicle owner to tell DVLA that a vehicle is not being used on the road. It lasts for 12 months.

12.5   mark **one** answer

What is a Statutory Off Road Notification (SORN) declaration?

❏ A notification to tell VOSA that a vehicle does not have a current MOT
❏ Information kept by the police about the owner of the vehicle
❏ A notification to tell DVLA that a vehicle is not being used on the road
❏ Information held by insurance companies to check the vehicle is insured

❏ **A notification to tell DVLA that a vehicle is not being used on the road**

A Statutory Off Road Notification (SORN) notice allows you to keep a vehicle off road and untaxed for 12 months only.

12.6   mark **one** answer

A Statutory Off Road Notification (SORN) declaration is

❏ to tell DVLA that your vehicle is being used on the road but the MOT has expired
❏ to tell DVLA that you no longer own the vehicle
❏ to tell DVLA that your vehicle is not being used on the road
❏ to tell DVLA that you are buying a personal number plate

❏ **to tell DVLA that your vehicle is not being used on the road**

A SORN declaration tells the DVLA that your vehicle is not being used on the road.

12.7   mark **one** answer

A Statutory Off Road Notification (SORN) is valid

❏ for as long as the vehicle has an MOT
❏ for 12 months only
❏ only if the vehicle is more than 3 years old
❏ provided the vehicle is insured

❏ **for 12 months only**

This declaration is valid for twelve months. If you wish to extend the notification, you must send a further SORN notice.

12.8   mark **one** answer

A Statutory Off Road Notification (SORN) will last

- ❏ for the life of the vehicle
- ❏ for as long as you own the vehicle
- ❏ for 12 months only
- ❏ until the vehicle warranty expires

❏ **for 12 months only**

You are required by law to notify the DVLA if your vehicle is kept off road with a Statutory Off Road Notification. Under a SORN you won't pay road tax until the vehicle is re-registered; remember, it only lasts a year!

12.9   mark **one** answer

What is the maximum specified fine for driving without insurance?

- ❏ £50
- ❏ £500
- ❏ £1000
- ❏ £5000

❏ **£5000**

All cars must be insured for the driver's use on the road. The minimum cover required by law is third party only.

12.10   mark **one** answer

Who is legally responsible for ensuring that a Vehicle Registration Certificate (V5C) is updated?

- ❏ The registered vehicle keeper
- ❏ The vehicle manufacturer
- ❏ Your insurance company
- ❏ The licensing authority

❏ **The registered vehicle keeper**

Your Vehicle Registration Certificate registers your vehicle to you and your home address. You, as the registered vehicle keeper are responsible for keeping the Certificate up to date.

12.11   mark **one** answer

For which of these MUST you show your insurance certificate?

- ❏ When making a SORN declaration
- ❏ When buying or selling a vehicle
- ❏ When a police officer asks you for it
- ❏ When having an MOT inspection

❏ **When a police officer asks you for it**

A police officer can ask to see your insurance certificate. If you don't have it with you, you can be asked to produce it at a police station of your choice within a specified period.

12.12   mark **one** answer

You must have valid insurance before you can

- ❏ make a SORN declaration
- ❏ buy or sell a vehicle
- ❏ apply for a driving licence
- ❏ obtain a tax disc

❏ **obtain a tax disc**

When you renew your road tax disc you will need to produce valid insurance documents.

12.13   mark **one** answer

Your vehicle needs a current MOT certificate. Until you have one you will NOT be able to

- ❏ renew your driving licence
- ❏ change your insurance company
- ❏ renew your road tax disc
- ❏ notify a change of address

❏ **renew your road tax disc**

Where your vehicle is more than three years old, to renew your road tax disc you will need to produce a current MOT certificate.

12.14   mark **three** answers

Which THREE of these do you need before you can use a vehicle on the road legally?

- ❏ A valid driving licence
- ❏ A valid tax disc clearly displayed
- ❏ Proof of your identity
- ❏ Proper insurance cover
- ❏ Breakdown cover
- ❏ A vehicle handbook

❏ **A valid driving licence**

❏ **A valid tax disc clearly displayed**

❏ **Proper insurance cover**

It is a legal requirement that you have a valid driving licence, proper insurance and that you display your tax disc correctly.

12.15   mark **one** answer

When you apply to renew your Vehicle Excise Duty (tax disc) you must have

- ❏ valid insurance
- ❏ the old tax disc
- ❏ the handbook
- ❏ a valid driving licence

❏ **valid insurance**

When you renew your tax disc you will need to have all the necessary documentation, including a valid insurance certificate.

mark **one** answer

A police officer asks to see your documents. You do not have them with you. You may be asked to take them to a police station within

❏ 5 days
❏ 7 days
❏ 14 days
❏ 21 days

❏ **7 days**

While you do not have to carry your vehicle documents with you, if a police officer asks to see them, you will be required to do so within seven days at a police station.

mark **one** answer

When you apply to renew your vehicle excise licence (tax disc) what must you have?

❏ Valid insurance
❏ The old tax disc
❏ The vehicle handbook
❏ A valid driving licence

❏ **Valid insurance**

When you renew your vehicle excise licence you will need to have all the necessary documentation, including a valid insurance certificate.

mark **one** answer

When should you update your Vehicle Registration Certificate?

❏ When you pass your driving test
❏ When you move house
❏ When your vehicle needs an MOT
❏ When you have a collision

❏ **When you move house**

You are the registered vehicle keeper with the DVLA, so you must notify them when you change your address. If you don't, this can lead to problems when you try to sell your vehicle.

mark **one** answer

To drive on the road learners MUST

❏ have NO penalty points on their licence
❏ have taken professional instruction
❏ have a signed, valid provisional licence
❏ apply for a driving test within 12 months

❏ **have a signed, valid provisional licence**

You are not allowed to drive until you have applied for and received your provisional licence and have signed it in ink.

12.20   mark **one** answer

Before driving anyone else's motor vehicle you should make sure that

❑ the vehicle owner has third party insurance cover
❑ your own vehicle has insurance cover
❑ the vehicle is insured for your use
❑ the owner has left the insurance documents in the vehicle

❑ **the vehicle is insured for your use**

Your own vehicle insurance may cover you as a passenger in another person's vehicle but very rarely covers you to drive it.

12.21   mark **one** answer

Your car needs an MOT certificate. If you drive without one this could invalidate your

❑ vehicle service record
❑ insurance
❑ road tax disc
❑ vehicle registration document

❑ **insurance**

If your car is over three years old it requires an MOT certificate, and if you drive without one it will invalidate your insurance policy. The only exception is that you may drive your car to an MOT testing centre to attend a previously booked test.

12.22   mark **one** answer

How old must you be to supervise a learner driver?

❑ 18 years old
❑ 19 years old
❑ 20 years old
❑ 21 years old

❑ **21 years old**

You must also hold a valid driving licence and have a minimum of three years' driving experience after passing your driving test.

12.23   mark **one** answer

A newly qualified driver must

❑ display green 'L' plates
❑ not exceed 40 mph for 12 months
❑ be accompanied on a motorway
❑ have valid motor insurance

❑ **have valid motor insurance**

This is a legal requirement. All motor vehicles (that need a licence to drive them) require a valid insurance certificate.

You have third party insurance. What does this cover?

❏ Damage to your own vehicle
❏ Damage to your vehicle by fire
❏ Injury to another person
❏ Damage to someone's property
❏ Damage to other vehicles
❏ Injury to yourself

❏ **Injury to another person**

❏ **Damage to someone's property**

❏ **Damage to other vehicles**

This is the minimum cover legally allowed.

Vehicle excise duty is often called 'Road Tax' or 'The Tax Disc'. You must

❏ keep it with your registration document
❏ display it clearly on your vehicle
❏ keep it concealed safely in your vehicle
❏ carry it on you at all times

❏ **display it clearly on your vehicle**

The disc should be displayed on the bottom of the windscreen on the nearside (the side closest to the kerb).

Your vehicle needs a current MOT certificate. You do not have one. Until you do have one you will not be able to renew your

❏ driving licence
❏ vehicle insurance
❏ road tax disc
❏ vehicle registration document

❏ **road tax disc**

When you renew your road tax disc you must produce a valid certificate of insurance and also a current MOT certificate if your car is over three years old.

Which THREE pieces of information are found on a vehicle registration document?

❏ Registered keeper
❏ Make of the vehicle
❏ Service history details
❏ Date of the MOT
❏ Type of insurance cover
❏ Engine size

❏ **Registered keeper**

❏ **Make of the vehicle**

❏ **Engine size**

The details recorded are the name of the vehicle's registered keeper, the make of the vehicle and the engine size.

12.28   mark **three** answers

You have a duty to contact the licensing authority when

❑ you go abroad on holiday
❑ you change your vehicle
❑ you change your name
❑ your job status is changed
❑ your permanent address changes
❑ your job involves travelling abroad

❑ **you change your vehicle**

❑ **you change your name**

❑ **your permanent address changes**

As the registered keeper of the vehicle, you are responsible for keeping the registration document up to date.

12.29   mark **three** answers

You must notify the licensing authority when

❑ your health affects your driving
❑ your eyesight does not meet a set standard
❑ you intend lending your vehicle
❑ your vehicle requires an MOT certificate
❑ you change your vehicle

❑ **your health affects your driving**

❑ **your eyesight does not meet a set standard**

❑ **you change your vehicle**

The licensing authority (DVLA) keeps all driver records. You are responsible for informing the DVLA if any of the above change.

12.30   mark **one** answer

The cost of your insurance may reduce if you

❑ are under 25 years old
❑ do not wear glasses
❑ pass the driving test first time
❑ take the Pass Plus scheme

❑ **take the Pass Plus scheme**

Pass Plus is available from ADIs registered with the scheme and can provide an insurance discount.

mark **one** answer

Which of the following may reduce the cost of your insurance?

❑ Having a valid MOT certificate
❑ Taking a Pass Plus course
❑ Driving a powerful car
❑ Having penalty points on your licence

❑ **Taking a Pass Plus course**

It is strongly recommended that all newly-qualified drivers take post-test tuition, to improve on their basic skills and cover gaps in their knowledge or experience, for example motorway driving. The Pass Plus Scheme covers a variety of subjects (including motorways). Ask your instructor for details.

mark **two** answers

To supervise a learner driver you must

❑ have held a full licence for at least 3 years
❑ be at least 21 years old
❑ be an approved driving instructor
❑ hold an advanced driving certificate

❑ **have held a full licence for at least 3 years**

❑ **be at least 21 years old**

This is to ensure learners are accompanied by drivers with some experience.

mark **one** answer

When is it legal to drive a car over three years old without an MOT certificate?

❑ Up to seven days after the old certificate has run out
❑ When driving to an MOT centre to arrange an appointment
❑ Just after buying a second-hand car with no MOT
❑ When driving to an appointment at an MOT centre

❑ **When driving to an appointment at an MOT centre**

If your car is over three years old and has no valid MOT certificate, you must pre-book an appointment at an MOT centre before you drive it there.

12.34   mark **one** answer

Motor cars must first have an MOT test certificate when they are

❏ one year old
❏ three years old
❏ five years old
❏ seven years old

❏ **three years old**

The test is to ensure your car is safe, and its emissions are within the guidelines.

12.35   mark **one** answer

The Pass Plus scheme has been created for new drivers. What is its main purpose?

❏ To allow you to drive faster
❏ To allow you to carry passengers
❏ To improve your basic skills
❏ To let you drive on motorways

❏ **To improve your basic skills**

It is strongly recommended that all newly-qualified drivers take post test tuition, to improve on their basic skills and cover gaps in their knowledge or experience, for example motorway driving. The Pass Plus Scheme covers a variety of subjects (including motorways). Ask your instructor for details.

12.36   mark **two** answers

Your vehicle is insured third party only. This covers

❏ damage to your vehicle
❏ damage to other vehicles
❏ injury to yourself
❏ injury to others
❏ all damage and injury

❏ **damage to other vehicles**

❏ **injury to others**

This is the minimum cover legally allowed.

12.37   mark **one** answer

What is the legal minimum insurance cover you must have to drive on public roads?

❏ Third party, fire and theft
❏ Comprehensive
❏ Third party only
❏ Personal injury cover

❏ **Third party only**

This only covers damage to other people and their property.

mark **one** answer

You claim on your insurance to have your car repaired. Your policy has an excess of £100. What does this mean?

❑ The insurance company will pay the first £100 of any claim
❑ You will be paid £100 if you do not claim within one year
❑ Your vehicle is insured for a value of £100 if it is stolen
❑ You will have to pay the first £100 of the cost of repair to your car

❑ **You will have to pay the first £100 of the cost of repair to your car**

Most insurance companies offer policies with an excess. As a general rule, the higher the excess, the lower the premium.

mark **one** answer

The Pass Plus scheme is designed to

❑ give you a discount on your MOT
❑ improve your basic driving skills
❑ increase your mechanical knowledge
❑ allow you to drive anyone else's vehicle

❑ **improve your basic driving skills**

The Pass Plus Scheme is open to anyone who has passed their driving test. It is designed to help keep you safer on the roads.

mark **one** answer

By taking part in the Pass Plus scheme you will

❑ never get any points on your licence
❑ be able to service your own car
❑ allow you to drive anyone else's vehicle
❑ improve your basic driving skills

❑ **improve your basic driving skills**

It is strongly recommended that all newly-qualified drivers take post test tuition, to improve on their basic skills and cover gaps in their knowledge or experience, for example motorway driving. The Pass Plus Scheme covers a variety of subjects (including motorways). Ask your instructor for details.

12.41   mark **one** answer

The Pass Plus scheme is aimed at all newly qualified drivers. It enables them to

❏ widen their driving experience
❏ supervise a learner driver
❏ increase their insurance premiums
❏ avoid mechanical breakdowns

❏ **widen their driving experience**

The DSA strongly recommends that all new drivers complete some post-test tuition. Discuss your requirements with your driving instructor.

12.42   mark **two** answers

New drivers can take further training after passing the practical test. A Pass Plus course will help to

❏ improve your basic skills
❏ widen your experience
❏ increase your insurance premiums
❏ get cheaper road tax

❏ **improve your basic skills**

❏ **widen your experience**

Improve your basic skills and cover gaps in your knowledge or experience with post-test tuition, such as motorway driving lessons.

12.43   mark **one** answer

The Pass Plus Scheme is operated by DSA for newly qualified drivers. It is intended to

❏ improve your basic skills
❏ reduce the cost of your driving licence
❏ prevent you from paying congestion charges
❏ allow you to supervise a learner driver

❏ **improve your basic skills**

The DSA strongly recommends that all new drivers complete some post-test tuition. The Pass Plus scheme covers a variety of subjects including motorway driving. Ask your instructor for more details.

12.44   mark **one** answer

For which of these must you show your motor insurance certificate?

❏ When you are taking your driving test
❏ When buying or selling a vehicle
❏ When a police officer asks you for it
❏ When having an MOT inspection

❏ **When a police officer asks you for it**

You do not have to carry vehicle documents such as your motor insurance certificate with you. If you are stopped by a police officer who asks to see this, you can produce it at a police station of your choice within seven days.

12.45 — mark **three** answers

Which THREE of these do you need before you can drive legally?

- ❏ A valid driving licence
- ❏ A valid tax disc displayed on your vehicle
- ❏ A vehicle service record
- ❏ Proper insurance cover
- ❏ Breakdown cover
- ❏ A vehicle handbook

❏ **A valid driving licence**

❏ **A valid tax disc displayed on your vehicle**

❏ **Proper insurance cover**

Do be sure that you have a valid driving licence and sufficient insurance cover before driving, as well as displaying your tax disc in the front window correctly

12.46 — mark **one** answer

A friend wants to help you learn to drive. They must be

- ❏ at least 21 and have held a full licence for at least one year
- ❏ over 18 and hold an advanced driver's certificate
- ❏ over 18 and have fully comprehensive insurance
- ❏ at least 21 and have held a full licence for at least three years

❏ **at least 21 and have held a full licence for at least three years**

The law requires that any supervising driver be at least 21 years old and must have held a full licence for at least three years. The reason for this to ensure that the person accompanying you is a responsible adult who also is an experienced driver.

12.47 — mark **one** answer

Your motor insurance policy has an excess of £100. What does this mean?

- ❏ The insurance company will pay the first £100 of any claim
- ❏ You will be paid £100 if you do not have a crash
- ❏ Your vehicle is insured for a value of £100 if it is stolen
- ❏ You will have to pay the first £100 of any claim

❏ **You will have to pay the first £100 of any claim**

While having such an excess will help to keep the cost of your policy down, if you do have to make a claim you will have to pay the excess yourself.

Section 13
Accidents

There are 79 questions in this section covering the following subjects:

- ❑ First aid
- ❑ Warning devices
- ❑ Reporting procedures
- ❑ Safety regulations

You will need to think about:
- ❑ The scene of an accident

- ❑ Prioritising first aid

- ❑ What you have to do if you are involved in an accident

- ❑ The rules and regulations regarding breakdowns and accidents.

Tips

Treating the injured is best left to people with the correct training. However, most of the first aid questions in this section are of a basic nature and you should be able to work out a lot of the answers. Likewise some of the rules and regulations questions are logical and straightforward. Some will need memorising, like how long you have to report an accident (24 hours).

If you are having trouble memorising facts, try writing them down or making notes as you study. It can stimulate and help the memorising process.

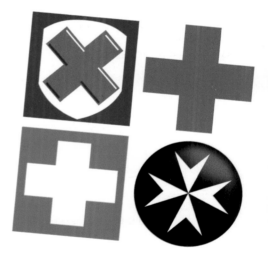

mark **one** answer

You see a car on the hard shoulder of a motorway with a HELP pennant displayed. This means the driver is most likely to be

❏ a disabled person
❏ first aid trained
❏ a foreign visitor
❏ a rescue patrol person

❏ **a disabled person**

If a disabled person is unable to walk to the nearest emergency phone, they will stay in the vehicle with the hazard warning lights on and display the help pennant.

mark **two** answers

For which TWO should you use hazard warning lights?

❏ When you slow down quickly on a motorway because of a hazard ahead
❏ When you have broken down
❏ When you wish to stop on double yellow lines
❏ When you need to park on the pavement

❏ **When you slow down quickly on a motorway because of a hazard ahead**

❏ **When you have broken down**

Hazard warning lights must not be used to justify illegal parking. The Highway Code is clear about the situations when their use is permitted.

mark **one** answer

When are you allowed to use hazard warning lights?

❏ When stopped and temporarily obstructing traffic
❏ When travelling during darkness without headlights
❏ When parked for shopping on double yellow lines
❏ When travelling slowly because you are lost

❏ **When stopped and temporarily obstructing traffic**

You must not use your hazard warning lights as an excuse to stop or park where you are not supposed to, or when moving, except in specific circumstances.

13.4 — mark **one** answer

You are going through a congested tunnel and have to stop. What should you do?

- ❑ Pull up very close to the vehicle in front to save space
- ❑ Ignore any message signs as they are never up to date
- ❑ Keep a safe distance from the vehicle in front
- ❑ Make a U-turn and find another route

❑ **Keep a safe distance from the vehicle in front**

The Highway Code provides advice on separation distances in traffic, so, put this into practice by leaving sufficient space with the vehicle in front. This will help you to pass it if you need to.

13.5 — mark **one** answer

On the motorway, the hard shoulder should be used

- ❑ to answer a mobile phone
- ❑ when an emergency arises
- ❑ for a short rest when tired
- ❑ to check a road atlas

❑ **when an emergency arises**

If you need to do any of the others leave the motorway either at the next exit or service area first.

13.6 — mark **one** answer

You arrive at the scene of a crash. Someone is bleeding badly from an arm wound. There is nothing embedded in it. What should you do?

- ❑ Apply pressure over the wound and keep the arm down
- ❑ Dab the wound
- ❑ Get them a drink
- ❑ Apply pressure over the wound and raise the arm

❑ **Apply pressure over the wound and raise the arm**

Both actions will help reduce blood loss.

13.7
mark **one** answer

You are at an incident where a casualty is unconscious. Their breathing should be checked. This should be done for at least

☐ 2 seconds
☐ 10 seconds
☐ 1 minute
☐ 2 minutes

☑ **10 seconds**

Two seconds won't tell you anything; 10 seconds should, and one or two minutes is wasting valuable time.

13.8
mark **one** answer

Following a collision someone has suffered a burn. The burn needs to be cooled. What is the shortest time it should be cooled for?

☐ 5 minutes
☐ 10 minutes
☐ 15 minutes
☐ 20 minutes

☑ **10 minutes**

The burn should be cooled using a cold, clean and non-toxic liquid. Ten minutes should be enough time to reduce the pain by removing the heat from the burn.

13.9
mark **one** answer

After a collision someone has suffered a burn. The burn needs to be cooled. What is the shortest time it should be cooled for?

☐ 30 seconds
☐ 60 seconds
☐ 5 minutes
☐ 10 minutes

☑ **10 minutes**

It is important to cool a burn for at least 10 minutes. Use a clean, cold non-toxic liquid preferably water. Keep in mind that the person may be in shock.

13.10
mark **one** answer

A casualty is not breathing normally. Chest compressions should be given. At what rate?

☐ 50 per minute
☐ 100 per minute
☐ 200 per minute
☐ 250 per minute

☑ **100 per minute**

This is the correct medical advice.

13.11   mark **one** answer

A person has been injured. They may be suffering from shock. What are the warning signs to look for?

❏ Flushed complexion
❏ Warm dry skin
❏ Slow pulse
❏ Pale grey skin

❏ **Pale grey skin**

This is medically correct, and a generally accepted key symptom of someone suffering from shock.

13.12   mark **one** answer

You suspect that an injured person may be suffering from shock. What are the warning signs to look for?

❏ Warm dry skin
❏ Sweating
❏ Slow pulse
❏ Skin rash

❏ **Sweating**

The signs of shock are sweating, a rapid pulse, pale grey skin and rapid shallow breathing.

13.13   mark **one** answer

An injured person has been placed in the recovery position. They are unconscious but breathing normally. What else should be done?

❏ Press firmly between the shoulders
❏ Place their arms by their side
❏ Give them a hot sweet drink
❏ Check the airway is clear

❏ **Check the airway is clear**

Injuries should be dealt with in the order ABC – Airway, Breathing, then Circulation and bleeding.

13.14   mark **one** answer

An injured motorcyclist is lying unconscious in the road. You should always

❏ remove the safety helmet
❏ seek medical assistance
❏ move the person off the road
❏ remove the leather jacket

❏ **seek medical assistance**

Ring for the ambulance service, or make sure someone else does. Paramedics will administer medical assistance.

13.15 mark **one** answer

You are on a motorway. A large box falls onto the road from a lorry. The lorry does not stop. You should

❏ go to the next emergency telephone and report the hazard
❏ catch up with the lorry and try to get the driver's attention
❏ stop close to the box until the police arrive
❏ pull over to the hard shoulder, then remove the box

❏ **go to the next emergency telephone and report the hazard**

The operator who answers your call will know your location and will be able to quickly summons the appropriate emergency services.

13.16 mark **one** answer

You are going through a long tunnel. What will warn you of congestion or an incident ahead?

❏ Hazard warning lines
❏ Other drivers flashing their lights
❏ Variable message signs
❏ Areas marked with hatch markings

❏ **Variable message signs**

As soon as the Highways Agency are aware of congestion or an incident they will alert drivers using this type of information matrix.

13.17 mark **one** answer

An adult casualty is not breathing. To maintain circulation, compressions should be given. What is the correct depth to press?

❏ 1 to 2 centimetres
❏ 4 to 5 centimetres
❏ 10 to 15 centimetres
❏ 15 to 20 centimetres

❏ **4 to 5 centimetres**

First aid advice is to place two hands in the centre of the chest and press down 4 to 5 centimetres at a rate of 100 times per minute. Give 30 chest compressions.

13.18 mark **two** answers

You are the first to arrive at the scene of a crash. Which TWO of these should you do?

❏ Leave as soon as another motorist arrives
❏ Make sure engines are switched off
❏ Drag all casualties away from the vehicles
❏ Call the emergency services promptly

❏ **Make sure engines are switched off**

❏ **Call the emergency services promptly**

To make the scene safe, ensure all engines are switched off and the emergency services have been called.

13.19   mark **one** answer

At the scene of a traffic incident you should

- ❏ not put yourself at risk
- ❏ go to those casualties who are screaming
- ❏ pull everybody out of their vehicles
- ❏ leave vehicle engines switched on

❏ **not put yourself at risk**

At the scene of a traffic incident you must not create any further risks to others or yourself.

13.20   mark **three** answers

You are the first person to arrive at an incident where people are badly injured. Which THREE should you do?

- ❏ Switch on your own hazard warning lights
- ❏ Make sure that someone telephones for an ambulance
- ❏ Try and get people who are injured to drink something
- ❏ Move the people who are injured clear of their vehicles
- ❏ Get people who are not injured clear of the scene

❏ **Switch on your own hazard warning lights**

❏ **Make sure that someone telephones for an ambulance**

❏ **Get people who are not injured clear of the scene**

At an accident scene you can help in practical ways – switching on your hazard lights helps to make the scene safe; phoning for help and getting uninjured people out the way will help save lives and reduce risk.

13.21   mark **one** answer

You arrive at the scene of a motorcycle crash. The rider is injured. When should the helmet be removed?

- ❏ Only when it is essential
- ❏ Always straight away
- ❏ Only when the motorcyclist asks
- ❏ Always, unless they are in shock

❏ **Only when it is essential**

Where a rider has been injured do not remove their helmet unless this is necessary to keep them alive.

You arrive at a serious motorcycle crash.
The motorcyclist is unconscious and bleeding.
Your THREE main priorities should be to
- ❏ try to stop the bleeding
- ❏ make a list of witnesses
- ❏ check their breathing
- ❏ take the numbers of other vehicles
- ❏ sweep up any loose debris
- ❏ check their airways

❏ **try to stop the bleeding**

❏ **check their breathing**

❏ **check their airways**

Where there are injuries at a crash scene,
think ABC – Airways, Breathing and
Circulation.

You arrive at an incident. A motorcyclist is
unconscious. Your FIRST priority is the
casualty's

- ❏ breathing
- ❏ bleeding
- ❏ broken bones
- ❏ bruising

❏ **breathing**

Your first priority when dealing with an
unconscious person is to make sure that
they can breathe. This could include clearing
their airway from obstruction.

At an incident a casualty is unconscious.
Which THREE of these should you check
urgently?

- ❏ Circulation
- ❏ Airway
- ❏ Shock
- ❏ Breathing
- ❏ Broken bones

❏ **Circulation**

❏ **Airway**

❏ **Breathing**

Think ABC – Airways, Breathing and
Circulation. An unconscious casualty may
have difficulty breathing, so check that their
airway is clear by tilting the head back gently
and unblock if this is necessary. Make sure
that they are breathing. Where there is any
bleeding, stem the flow by placing clean
material over any wounds, taking care not to
press on any objects in the wound.

13.25   mark **three** answers

You arrive at the scene of an incident. It has just happened and someone is unconscious. Which THREE of these should be given urgent priority to help them?

❏ Clear the airway and keep it open
❏ Try to get them to drink water
❏ Check that they are breathing
❏ Look for any witnesses
❏ Stop any heavy bleeding
❏ Take the numbers of vehicles involved

❏ **Clear the airway and keep it open**

❏ **Check that they are breathing**

❏ **Stop any heavy bleeding**

Think Airways, Breathing and Circulation (ABC). Once first aid has been administered, stay with the casualty and make sure that the ambulance service has been called.

13.26   mark **three** answers

At an incident someone is unconscious. Your THREE main priorities should be to

❏ sweep up the broken glass
❏ take the names of witnesses
❏ count the number of vehicles involved
❏ check the airway is clear
❏ make sure they are breathing
❏ stop any heavy bleeding

❏ **check the airway is clear**

❏ **make sure they are breathing**

❏ **stop any heavy bleeding**

An unconscious casualty might well experience difficulty breathing. Do ensure that their airway is clear by tilting the head back gently and unblock if necessary, then make sure that they are breathing. Where there is bleeding, stem the flow by placing clean material over any wounds without pressing on any objects that might be in the wound.

13.27   mark **three** answers

You have stopped at an incident to give help. Which THREE things should you do?

- ❏ Keep injured people warm and comfortable
- ❏ Keep injured people calm by talking to them reassuringly
- ❏ Keep injured people on the move by walking them around
- ❏ Give injured people a warm drink
- ❏ Make sure that injured people are not left alone

- ❏ **Keep injured people warm and comfortable**
- ❏ **Keep injured people calm by talking to them reassuringly**
- ❏ **Make sure that injured people are not left alone**

Where you stopped at a crash scene, do not move injured people unless there is a real risk of further danger. Ensure that no one gives the casualties anything to drink or eat

13.28   mark **three** answers

You arrive at an incident. It has just happened and someone is injured. Which THREE should be given urgent priority?

- ❏ Stop any severe bleeding
- ❏ Give them a warm drink
- ❏ Check they are breathing
- ❏ Take numbers of vehicles involved
- ❏ Look for witnesses
- ❏ Clear their airway and keep it open

- ❏ **Stop any severe bleeding**
- ❏ **Check they are breathing**
- ❏ **Clear their airway and keep it open**

We must minimise the risk of any further dangers at the crash scene and then check that the injured person's airway is clear so that they are able to breathe and also take steps to stem any bleeding

13.29   mark **one** answer

Which of the following should you NOT do at the scene of a collision?

- ❏ Warn other traffic by switching on your hazard warning lights
- ❏ Call the emergency services immediately
- ❏ Offer someone a cigarette to calm them down
- ❏ Ask drivers to switch off their engines

- ❏ **Offer someone a cigarette to calm them down**

We do want to keep casualties or witnesses calm. Offering someone a cigarette at a crash scene increases the risk of fire. Do not do this.

13.30   mark **two** answers

There has been a collision. A driver is suffering from shock. What TWO of these should you do?

❑ Give them a drink
❑ Reassure them
❑ Not leave them alone
❑ Offer them a cigarette
❑ Ask who caused the incident

❑ **Reassure them**

❑ **Not leave them alone**

Someone's injuries may not be obvious, so stay with the casualties and talk to them to give them reassurance.

13.31   mark **one** answer

You have to treat someone for shock at the scene of an incident. You should

❑ reassure them constantly
❑ walk them around to calm them down
❑ give them something cold to drink
❑ cool them down as soon as possible

❑ **reassure them constantly**

Stay with the casualty and talk with them quietly and firmly to calm and reassure them. Also, keep them warm, but do not give them anything to drink or eat. Do not move them, in case they are injured.

13.32   mark **one** answer

You arrive at the scene of a motorcycle crash. No other vehicle is involved. The rider is unconscious and lying in the middle of the road. The FIRST thing you should do is

❑ move the rider out of the road
❑ warn other traffic
❑ clear the road of debris
❑ give the rider reassurance

❑ **warn other traffic**

Other approaching vehicles put the rider in a very vulnerable position, so warn them of the danger by using your hazard warning lights.

13.33   mark **one** answer

At an incident a small child is not breathing. To restore normal breathing you should breathe into their mouth

❑ sharply
❑ gently
❑ heavily
❑ rapidly

❑ **gently**

If a child has stopped breathing, check that the airway is clear, then begin mouth-to-mouth resuscitation. Breathe very gently and continue the procedure until the child can breathe without help.

At an incident a casualty is not breathing. To start the process to restore normal breathing you should

❏ tilt their head forward
❏ clear the airway
❏ turn them on their side
❏ tilt their head back gently
❏ pinch the nostrils together
❏ put their arms across their chest

❏ **clear the airway**

❏ **tilt their head back gently**

❏ **pinch the nostrils together**

Unblocking the airway and gently tilting the head back will help the casualty to breathe. Mouth to mouth resuscitation can then be administered if required

You arrive at an incident. There has been an engine fire and someone's hands and arms have been burnt. You should NOT

❏ douse the burn thoroughly with clean cool non-toxic liquid
❏ lay the casualty down on the ground
❏ remove anything sticking to the burn
❏ reassure them confidently and repeatedly

❏ **remove anything sticking to the burn**

Removing anything sticking to the burn could cause further damage and infection to the wound. You must first cool the burn and check the casualty for shock.

You arrive at an incident where someone is suffering from severe burns. You should

❏ apply lotions to the injury
❏ burst any blisters
❏ remove anything stuck to the burns
❏ douse the burns with clean cool non-toxic liquid

❏ **douse the burns with clean cool non-toxic liquid**

Use a clean, cold and non toxic fluid. Its coolness will help to take the heat out of the burn and relieve the pain.

13.37   mark **two** answers

You arrive at an incident. A pedestrian has a severe bleeding leg wound. It is not broken and there is nothing in the wound. What TWO of these should you do?

- ❑ Dab the wound to stop bleeding
- ❑ Keep both legs flat on the ground
- ❑ Apply firm pressure to the wound
- ❑ Raise the leg to lessen bleeding
- ❑ Fetch them a warm drink

❑ **Apply firm pressure to the wound**

❑ **Raise the leg to lessen bleeding**

Apply a pad of clean material to the wound with a clean piece of cloth. Raising the leg will reduce the flow of blood

13.38   mark **one** answer

At an incident a casualty is unconscious but still breathing. You should only move them if

- ❑ an ambulance is on its way
- ❑ bystanders advise you to
- ❑ there is further danger
- ❑ bystanders will help you to

❑ **there is further danger**

A casualty must only be moved if they are likely to be in danger where they are. Unnecessary movement could cause further injury.

13.39   mark **one** answer

At a collision you suspect a casualty has back injuries. The area is safe. You should

- ❑ offer them a drink
- ❑ not move them
- ❑ raise their legs
- ❑ not call an ambulance

❑ **not move them**

Keep the casualty calm by talking to them. Do not attempt to move them as this might cause further injury. Do ring for the ambulance service as soon as possible.

13.40   mark **one** answer

At an incident it is important to look after any casualties. When the area is safe, you should

- ❑ get them out of the vehicle
- ❑ give them a drink
- ❑ give them something to eat
- ❑ keep them in the vehicle

❑ **keep them in the vehicle**

Provided that that there is no danger, do not move casualties who are trapped in their vehicle.

mark **one** answer

A tanker is involved in a collision. Which sign shows that it is carrying dangerous goods?

There will be an orange label on the rear or the side of the lorry. Report what this says when you ring the emergency services.

mark **three** answers

You are involved in a collision. Because of this which THREE of these documents may the police ask you to produce?

- ❑ Vehicle registration document
- ❑ Driving licence
- ❑ Theory test certificate
- ❑ Insurance certificate
- ❑ MOT test certificate
- ❑ Vehicle service record

❑ **Driving licence**

❑ **Insurance certificate**

❑ **MOT test certificate**

Where you are involved in a collision that results in damage or injury you must stop. The police can ask you to produce your driving licence, insurance and MOT test certificates.

mark **one** answer

After a collision someone is unconscious in their vehicle. When should you call the emergency services?

- ❑ Only as a last resort
- ❑ As soon as possible
- ❑ After you have woken them up
- ❑ After checking for broken bones

❑ **As soon as possible**

Where a person is unconscious, they could have serious injuries that are not obvious at the time. It is therefore important to ensure that the emergency services arrive as soon as possible.

13.44   mark **one** answer

A casualty has an injured arm. They can move it freely but it is bleeding. Why should you get them to keep it in a raised position?

❑ Because it will ease the pain
❑ It will help them to be seen more easily
❑ To stop them touching other people
❑ It will help to reduce the blood flow

❑ **It will help to reduce the blood flow**

Where a casualty is bleeding heavily, raising the limb to a higher position will help to reduce the blood flow.

13.45   mark **one** answer

You are going through a tunnel. What systems are provided to warn of any incidents, collisions or congestion?

❑ Double white centre lines
❑ Variable message signs
❑ Chevron 'distance markers'
❑ Rumble strips

❑ **Variable message signs**

Do take notice of the instructions given on variable message signs. The information will tell you about any incidents or congestion ahead and give advice what to do.

13.46   mark **one** answer

A collision has just happened. An injured person is lying in a busy road. What is the FIRST thing you should do to help?

❑ Treat the person for shock
❑ Warn other traffic
❑ Place them in the recovery position
❑ Make sure the injured person is kept warm

❑ **Warn other traffic**

You can warn other traffic, for instance, by switching on hazard warning lights or displaying an advance warning triangle (not to be used on a motorway anymore).

mark two answers

At an incident a casualty has stopped breathing. You should

- ❏ remove anything that is blocking the mouth
- ❏ keep the head tilted forwards as far as possible
- ❏ raise the legs to help with circulation
- ❏ try to give the casualty something to drink
- ❏ tilt the head back gently to clear the airway

❏ **remove anything that is blocking the mouth**

❏ **tilt the head back gently to clear the airway**

Unblocking the airway and gently tilting the head back will help the casualty to breathe. They will then also be in the correct position to be given mouth-to-mouth resuscitation if this is necessary.

mark four answers

You are at the scene of an incident. Someone is suffering from shock. You should

- ❏ reassure them constantly
- ❏ offer them a cigarette
- ❏ keep them warm
- ❏ avoid moving them if possible
- ❏ avoid leaving them alone
- ❏ give them a warm drink

❏ **reassure them constantly**

❏ **keep them warm**

❏ **avoid moving them if possible**

❏ **avoid leaving them alone**

The effects of trauma might not be obvious. Immediate treatment will help to minimise the effects of shock.

mark one answer

There has been a collision. A motorcyclist is lying injured and unconscious. Unless it's essential, why should you usually NOT attempt to remove their helmet?

- ❏ Because they may not want you to
- ❏ This could result in more serious injury
- ❏ They will get too cold if you do this
- ❏ Because you could scratch the helmet

❏ **This could result in more serious injury**

Where some is injured, avoid them making unnecessary movements as these may aggravate the injuries. It is best to leave the motorcyclists helmet in place.

13.50   mark **one** answer

You have broken down on a two-way road. You have a warning triangle. You should place the warning triangle at least how far from your vehicle?

- ❏ 5 metres (16 feet)
- ❏ 25 metres (82 feet)
- ❏ 45 metres (147 feet)
- ❏ 100 metres (328 feet)

- ❏ **45 metres (147 feet)**

45 metres is recommended on two-way roads and 150 metres on a dual carriageway. You should not use a warning triangle on a motorway; it is too dangerous.

13.51   mark **three** answers

You break down on a level crossing. The lights have not yet begun to flash. Which THREE things should you do?

- ❏ Telephone the signal operator
- ❏ Leave your vehicle and get everyone clear
- ❏ Walk down the track and signal the next train
- ❏ Move the vehicle if a signal operator tells you to
- ❏ Tell drivers behind what has happened

- ❏ **Telephone the signal operator**

- ❏ **Leave your vehicle and get everyone clear**

- ❏ **Move the vehicle if a signal operator tells you to**

If faced with this situation, you should leave and clear the vehicle before phoning the signal operator. Only return to move the car if instructed to do so.

13.52   mark **two** answers

Your tyre bursts while you are driving. Which TWO things should you do?

- ❏ Pull on the handbrake
- ❏ Brake as quickly as possible
- ❏ Pull up slowly at the side of the road
- ❏ Hold the steering wheel firmly to keep control
- ❏ Continue on at a normal speed

- ❏ **Pull up slowly at the side of the road**

- ❏ **Hold the steering wheel firmly to keep control**

You will need both hands firmly on the wheel in order to control the car, and using the gears or brakes is likely to make your car swerve. When possible, it is safest just to let your car roll to a halt at the side of the road.

13.53   mark **two** answers

Which TWO things should you do when a front tyre bursts?

❑ Apply the handbrake to stop the vehicle
❑ Brake firmly and quickly
❑ Let the vehicle roll to a stop
❑ Hold the steering wheel lightly
❑ Grip the steering wheel firmly

❑ **Let the vehicle roll to a stop**

❑ **Grip the steering wheel firmly**

Grip the wheel to keep control, but avoid braking which could cause you to lose control of the vehicle.

13.54   mark **one** answer

Your vehicle has a puncture on a motorway. What should you do?
❑ Drive slowly to the next service area to get assistance
❑ Pull up on the hard shoulder. Change the wheel as quickly as possible
❑ Pull up on the hard shoulder. Use the emergency phone to get assistance
❑ Switch on your hazard lights. Stop in your lane

❑ **Pull up on the hard shoulder. Use the emergency phone to get assistance**

The hard shoulder of a motorway is a dangerous place and the third answer is the safest course of action. It can be particularly dangerous to try to change an offside wheel since this may put you very close to fast-moving traffic in the left-hand lane.

13.55   mark **one** answer

You have stalled in the middle of a level crossing and cannot restart the engine. The warning bell starts to ring. You should

❑ get out and clear of the crossing
❑ run down the track to warn the signal operator
❑ carry on trying to restart the engine
❑ push the vehicle clear of the crossing

❑ **get out and clear of the crossing**

A train may arrive within seconds so this answer is the only safe possibility.

13.56   mark **two** answers

You are on a motorway. When can you use hazard warning lights?

- ❏ When a vehicle is following too closely
- ❏ When you slow down quickly because of danger ahead
- ❏ When you are towing another vehicle
- ❏ When driving on the hard shoulder
- ❏ When you have broken down on the hard shoulder

- ❏ **When you slow down quickly because of danger ahead**

- ❏ **When you have broken down on the hard shoulder**

These are the only permissible uses for hazard warning lights on a motorway.

13.57   mark **three** answers

You have broken down on a motorway. When you use the emergency telephone you will be asked

- ❏ for the number on the telephone that you are using
- ❏ for your driving licence details
- ❏ for the name of your vehicle insurance company
- ❏ for details of yourself and your vehicle
- ❏ whether you belong to a motoring organisation

- ❏ **for the number on the telephone that you are using**

- ❏ **for details of yourself and your vehicle**

- ❏ **whether you belong to a motoring organisation**

It is important to provide all these details so that your problem can be dealt with as speedily as possible.

13.58   mark **one** answer

Before driving through a tunnel what should you do?

- ❏ Switch your radio off
- ❏ Remove any sunglasses
- ❏ Close your sunroof
- ❏ Switch on windscreen wipers

- ❏ **Remove any sunglasses**

They will seriously impair your vision if you wear them in the artificial light condition of the tunnel.

13.59   mark **one** answer

You are driving through a tunnel and the traffic is flowing normally. What should you do?

- ❑ Use parking lights
- ❑ Use front spot lights
- ❑ Use dipped headlights
- ❑ Use rear fog lights

❑ **Use dipped headlights**

Remember – see and be seen.

13.60   mark **one** answer

You are driving through a tunnel. Your vehicle breaks down. What should you do?

- ❑ Switch on hazard warning lights
- ❑ Remain in your vehicle
- ❑ Wait for the police to find you
- ❑ Rely on CCTV cameras seeing you

❑ **Switch on hazard warning lights**

When stationary, the hazard warning lights are to be used when your vehicle creates an unavoidable hazard, for example when you have broken down.

13.61   mark **one** answer

When driving through a tunnel you should

- ❑ Look out for variable message signs
- ❑ Use your air conditioning system
- ❑ Switch on your rear fog lights
- ❑ Always use your windscreen wipers

❑ **Look out for variable message signs**

You will not only be warned of problems ahead, but also in some cases advised of the best actions to take, in response to the problem.

13.62   mark **two** answers

What TWO safeguards could you take against fire risk to your vehicle?

- ❑ Keep water levels above maximum
- ❑ Carry a fire extinguisher
- ❑ Avoid driving with a full tank of petrol
- ❑ Use unleaded petrol
- ❑ Check out any strong smell of petrol
- ❑ Use low octane fuel

❑ **Carry a fire extinguisher**

❑ **Check out any strong smell of petrol**

To reduce the risk of a fire starting in the engine, you do need to check out any strong smell of fuel. Carrying a fire extinguisher means that you will be prepared to put a fire out, minimising the danger.

13.63   mark **one** answer

You are on the motorway. Luggage falls from your vehicle. What should you do?

❏ Stop at the next emergency telephone and contact the police
❏ Stop on the motorway and put on hazard lights while you pick it up
❏ Walk back up the motorway to pick it up
❏ Pull up on the hard shoulder and wave traffic down

❏ **Stop at the next emergency telephone and contact the police**

Do not try to retrieve items from the carriageway that have fallen from any vehicle as it would be dangerous.

13.64   mark **one** answer

While driving, a warning light on your vehicle's instrument panel comes on. You should

❏ continue if the engine sounds all right
❏ hope that it is just a temporary electrical fault
❏ deal with the problem when there is more time
❏ check out the problem quickly and safely

❏ **check out the problem quickly and safely**

Never ignore warning lights. Familiarise yourself with the manufacturer's handbook and follow its advice.

13.65   mark **one** answer

You have broken down on a two-way road. You have a warning triangle. It should be displayed

❏ on the roof of your vehicle
❏ at least 150 metres (492 feet) behind your vehicle
❏ at least 45 metres (147 feet) behind your vehicle
❏ just behind your vehicle

❏ **at least 45 metres (147 feet) behind your vehicle**

45 metres is recommended on a two-way road and 150 metres on a dual carriageway. Note you should not use a warning triangle on a motorway because it is too dangerous.

13.66   mark **one** answer

Your engine catches fire. What should you do first?

❏ Lift the bonnet and disconnect the battery
❏ Lift the bonnet and warn other traffic
❏ Call a breakdown service
❏ Call the fire brigade

❏ **Call the fire brigade**

Lifting the bonnet may well feed the fire by giving it more oxygen. Calling a breakdown service is not appropriate in an emergency such as this.

13.67   mark **one** answer

Your vehicle breaks down in a tunnel. What should you do?

❏ Stay in your vehicle and wait for the police
❏ Stand in the lane behind your vehicle to warn others
❏ Stand in front of your vehicle to warn oncoming drivers
❏ Switch on hazard lights then go and call for help immediately

❏ **Switch on hazard lights then go and call for help immediately**

When stationary, the hazard warning lights are to be used when your vehicle creates an unavoidable hazard, for example when you have broken down. Use one of the emergency phones provided to call for help.

13.68   mark **one** answer

Your vehicle catches fire while driving through a tunnel. It is still driveable. What should you do?

❏ Leave it where it is with the engine running
❏ Pull up, then walk to an emergency telephone point
❏ Park it away from the carriageway
❏ Drive it out of the tunnel if you can do so

❏ **Drive it out of the tunnel if you can do so**

The main dangers in a tunnel fire are suffocation and smoke. If possible, drive the burning vehicle out of the tunnel, otherwise pull over, switch of the engine, use the hazard warning lights and phone for help.

13.69   mark **one** answer

You are driving through a tunnel. Your vehicle catches fire. What should you do?

❏ Continue through the tunnel if you can
❏ Turn your vehicle around immediately
❏ Reverse out of the tunnel
❏ Carry out an emergency stop

❏ **Continue through the tunnel if you can**

Doing this will reduce the chances of a major incident and will also reduce the risk of harm to others.

13.70   mark **two** answers

You are in a tunnel. Your vehicle is on fire and you CANNOT drive it. What should you do?

❏ Stay in the vehicle and close the windows
❏ Switch on hazard warning lights
❏ Leave the engine running
❏ Try and put out the fire
❏ Switch off all of your lights
❏ Wait for other people to phone for help

❏ **Switch on hazard warning lights**

❏ **Try and put out the fire**

Switching on your hazard lights alerts others to your position. The risk of fire in a tunnel is high and it should be dealt with for the safety of all.

13.71   mark **one** answer

When approaching a tunnel it is good advice to

❏ put on your sunglasses and use the sun visor
❏ check your tyre pressures
❏ change down to a lower gear
❏ make sure your radio is tuned to the frequency shown

❏ **make sure your radio is tuned to the frequency shown**

On approach to many tunnels, signs will give inform drivers of a radio frequency to tune into for information such as congestion or incidents.

13.72   mark **one** answer

Your vehicle has broken down on an automatic railway level crossing. What should you do FIRST?

❏ Get everyone out of the vehicle and clear of the crossing
❏ Telephone your vehicle recovery service to move it
❏ Walk along the track to give warning to any approaching trains
❏ Try to push the vehicle clear of the crossing as soon as possible

❏ **Get everyone out of the vehicle and clear of the crossing**

Lives may be at risk, so, the first action to take is to get everyone out of the vehicle and clear of the crossing.

13.73   mark **three** answers

Which THREE of these items should you carry for use in the event of a collision?

- ❏ Road map
- ❏ Can of petrol
- ❏ Jump leads
- ❏ Fire extinguisher
- ❏ First aid kit
- ❏ Warning triangle

❏ **Fire extinguisher**

❏ **First aid kit**

❏ **Warning triangle**

It is good advice to keep this equipment in your car. In the event of an incident it can provide invaluable help. It might even save a life.

13.74   mark **one** answer

You have a collision while your car is moving. What is the FIRST thing you must do?

- ❏ Stop only if someone waves at you
- ❏ Call the emergency services
- ❏ Stop at the scene of the incident
- ❏ Call your insurance company

❏ **Stop at the scene of the incident**

It is a legal requirement that you if you are involved in a collision that you must first stop. You will then be able to assess the situation and take necessary actions.

13.75   mark **four** answers

You are in collision with another moving vehicle. Someone is injured and your vehicle is damaged. Which FOUR of the following should you find out?

- ❏ Whether the driver owns the other vehicle involved
- ❏ The other driver's name, address and telephone number
- ❏ The make and registration number of the other vehicle
- ❏ The occupation of the other driver
- ❏ The details of the other driver's vehicle insurance
- ❏ Whether the other driver is licensed to drive

❏ **Whether the driver owns the other vehicle involved**

❏ **The other driver's name, address and telephone number**

❏ **The make and registration number of the other vehicle**

❏ **The details of the other driver's vehicle insurance**

Do try to stay calm and do not rush. Before you leave the scene, make sure that you have all the details needed.

13.76   mark **one** answer

You lose control of your car and damage a garden wall. No one is around. What must you do?

❑ Report the incident to the police within 24 hours
❑ Go back to tell the house owner the next day
❑ Report the incident to your insurance company when you get home
❑ Find someone in the area to tell them about it immediately

❑ **Report the incident to the police within 24 hours**

Should the property owner not be available at the time, you must report the incident to the police as soon as you can, or in any case, within 24 hours.

13.77   mark **one** answer

You are in a collision on a two-way road. You have a warning triangle with you. At what distance before the obstruction should you place the warning triangle?

❑ 25 metres (82 feet)
❑ 45 metres (147 feet)
❑ 100 metres (328 feet)
❑ 150 metres (492 feet)

❑ **45 metres (147 feet)**

45 metres is the recommended distance that will normally be sufficient to give other drivers time to respond to the warning. Use your hazard warning lights as well and don't forget to collect your warning triangle before you leave the scene.

13.78   mark **one** answer

You have a collision while driving through a tunnel. You are not injured but your vehicle cannot be driven. What should you do FIRST?

❑ Rely on other drivers phoning for the police
❑ Switch off the engine and switch on hazard lights
❑ Take the names of witnesses and other drivers
❑ Sweep up any debris that is in the road

❑ **Switch off the engine and switch on hazard lights**

Think of other traffic. To reduce the risks, switch on your hazard warning lights straight away, then turn your engine off. You should then ring for help from an emergency telephone point.

You are driving through a tunnel. There has been a collision and the car in front is on fire and blocking the road. What should you do?

❑ Overtake and continue as quickly as you can
❑ Lock all the doors and windows
❑ Switch on hazard warning lights
❑ Stop, then reverse out of the tunnel

❑ **Switch on hazard warning lights**

Having pulled over to the side and stopped, you need to switch on your warning lights. If you can locate a fire extinguisher use it to put out the fire, taking care. Do not open the bonnet. You should then ring for help from an emergency telephone point and administer first aid to anyone who is injured.

Vehicle loading

There are 15 questions in this section covering the following subjects:

- ❏ Stability
- ❏ Towing regulations

You will need to think about:

- ❏ How loading will affect your vehicle

- ❏ The rules and regulations regarding child and baby seats

- ❏ The rules and regulations regarding loading and towing.

Tips

Some of this may be outside your experience, but it is only a small section, and once you have learnt the rules, and applied some sound judgement (are passengers allowed to ride in a caravan being towed?) you are almost finished.

When you are studying give yourself a reward when you have reached a goal. Of course if this is the first time you have reached the end of the final section, the chances are you will have to study a bit more before you can be confident of retaining all the information with relevant post-test tuition.

mark two answers

You are towing a small trailer on a busy three-lane motorway. All the lanes are open. You must

❑ not exceed 60 mph
❑ not overtake
❑ have a stabiliser fitted
❑ use only the left and centre lanes

❑ **not exceed 60 mph**

❑ **use only the left and centre lanes**

Vehicles towing are subject to extra regulations, such as these. With a reduced speed limit in place, using the right-hand lane in normal traffic conditions is not appropriate.

mark one answer

If a trailer swerves or snakes when you are towing it you should

❑ ease off the accelerator and reduce your speed
❑ let go of the steering wheel and let it correct itself
❑ brake hard and hold the pedal down
❑ increase your speed as quickly as possible

❑ **ease off the accelerator and reduce your speed**

All three of the other options would be likely to make the problem worse.

mark one answer

How can you stop a caravan snaking from side to side?

❑ Turn the steering wheel slowly to each side
❑ Accelerate to increase your speed
❑ Stop as quickly as you can
❑ Slow down very gradually

❑ **Slow down very gradually**

Ease off the accelerator and allow the combination to settle and steady itself, avoiding harsh movements or use of any control.

14.4   mark **two** answers

On which TWO occasions might you inflate your tyres to more than the recommended normal pressure?

❑ When the roads are slippery
❑ When driving fast for a long distance
❑ When the tyre tread is worn below 2mm
❑ When carrying a heavy load
❑ When the weather is cold
❑ When the vehicle is fitted with anti-lock brakes

❑ **When driving fast for a long distance**

❑ **When carrying a heavy load**

Use the manufacturer's handbook to check for correct pressures for these circumstances.

14.5   mark **one** answer

A heavy load on your roof rack will

❑ improve the road holding
❑ reduce the stopping distance
❑ make the steering lighter
❑ reduce stability

❑ **reduce stability**

A heavy load on the roof will shift the centre of gravity of your vehicle and could make you more likely to skid or roll over.

14.6   mark **one** answer

You are towing a caravan along a motorway. The caravan begins to swerve from side to side. What should you do?

❑ Ease off the accelerator slowly
❑ Steer sharply from side to side
❑ Do an emergency stop
❑ Speed up very quickly

❑ **Ease off the accelerator slowly**

Ease off the accelerator and allow the combination to settle and steady itself, avoiding harsh movements or use of any control.

mark **two** answers

Overloading your vehicle can seriously affect the

❏ gearbox
❏ steering
❏ handling
❏ battery life
❏ journey time

❏ **steering**

❏ **handling**

If you overload your vehicle you will make both of the above harder and more unpredictable. It is your responsibility as the driver to ensure the vehicle is loaded safely.

mark **one** answer

Who is responsible for making sure that a vehicle is not overloaded?

❏ The driver of the vehicle
❏ The owner of the items being carried
❏ The person who loaded the vehicle
❏ The licensing authority

❏ **The driver of the vehicle**

If you overload your vehicle you will make the steering and handling unpredictable. It is your responsibility as the driver to ensure the vehicle is loaded safely.

mark **one** answer

You are planning to tow a caravan. Which of these will mostly help to aid the vehicle handling?

❏ A jockey wheel fitted to the towbar
❏ Power steering fitted to the towing vehicle
❏ Anti-lock brakes fitted to the towing vehicle
❏ A stabiliser fitted to the towbar

❏ **A stabiliser fitted to the towbar**

This does exactly what its name suggests and helps to stabilise the combination of trailer or caravan being towed and the towing vehicle. But remember, even with a good stabiliser fitted the handling characteristics will still be vastly different.

mark **one** answer

Are passengers allowed to ride in a caravan that is being towed?

❏ Yes, if they are over fourteen
❏ No, not at any time
❏ Only if all the seats in the towing vehicle are full
❏ Only if a stabiliser is fitted

❏ **No, not at any time**

Passengers moving about inside the caravan could make it unstable and cause loss of control.

14.11   mark **one** answer

A trailer must stay securely hitched up to the towing vehicle. What additional safety device can be fitted to the trailer braking system?

- ❑ Stabiliser
- ❑ Jockey wheel
- ❑ Corner steadies
- ❑ Breakaway cable

❑ **Breakaway cable**

This system means that if the tow-bar failed for some reason, the trailer or caravan's brakes would be applied – forcing the unit to stop while the 'breakaway cables' would brake, allowing the towing vehicle to drive clear.

14.12   mark **one** answer

Why would you fit a stabiliser before towing a caravan?

- ❑ It will help with stability when driving in crosswinds
- ❑ It will allow heavy items to be loaded behind the axle
- ❑ It will help you to raise and lower the jockey wheel
- ❑ It will allow you to tow without the breakaway cable

❑ **It will help with stability when driving in crosswinds**

A good stabiliser can make the combination easier to handle.

14.13   mark **one** answer

You wish to tow a trailer. Where would you find the maximum noseweight of your vehicle's tow ball?

- ❑ In the vehicle handbook
- ❑ In The Highway Code
- ❑ In your vehicle registration certificate
- ❑ In your licence documents

❑ **In the vehicle handbook**

The noseweight can be measured by using a gauge available from caravan accessory stockists.

mark one answer

Any load that is carried on a roof rack should be

❑ securely fastened when driving
❑ loaded towards the rear of the vehicle
❑ visible in your exterior mirror
❑ covered with plastic sheeting

❑ **securely fastened when driving**

It is your responsibility as the driver to ensure the vehicle is loaded safely. Remember, putting any items on a roof rack will raise the centre of gravity and consequently affect the handling characteristics of the vehicle.

mark one answer

You are carrying a child in your car. They are under three years of age. Which of these is a suitable restraint?

❑ A child seat
❑ An adult holding a child
❑ An adult seat belt
❑ An adult lap belt

❑ **A child seat**

As the driver you are responsible for the safety of any passengers under the age of 14. Make sure you know the law relating to carrying children in your car.

Notes

Practical Test
for car drivers

Once you've passed your Theory Test, you then have to show the DSA examiner you're ready to take to the road alone – in your Practical Test.

Using all of our experience and know-how in helping people pass, we've put together a comprehensive guide to it. Packed full of expert advice and answers, this book will help you make the most of your driving lessons and progress faster.

Your Practical Test book includes:

– The 45 driving skills on which you'll be tested

– Insider tips from instructors and examiners

– A guide to safe driving habits

– Eco-friendly driving tips

– How to overcome any test-day nerves.

It also contains a structured programme of extra practice sessions you can do with a qualified driver beside you – with advice for them from the professionals on how best to help you.

Only £5.99

Available:
- online at www.bsm.co.uk
- from your local BSM Centre
- by calling us on 08457 276 276
- from all good bookshops